Becoming a Family

BANGLES
BINDIS
AND
BABIES

A Memoir

Elizabeth Chennamchetty

EC PRESS

Copyright © 2017 Elizabeth Chennamchetty

All rights reserved.
No part of this book may be reproduced, stored in a retrieval system, or transmitted by any means, electronic, mechanical, photocopying, recording, or otherwise, without written permission from the author.

Some names and identifying details have been changed to protect the privacy of individuals.

Published by ECPress

Cover and Interior Book Design by Monkey C Media, MonkeyCMedia.com
Author photograph by Ania Rzepko

Printed in the United States of America

Publisher's Cataloging in Publication Data

Names:	Chennamchetty, Elizabeth, author.
Title:	Bangles, bindis and babies : becoming a family a memoir / Elizabeth Chennamchetty.
Description:	San Diego : EC Press, [2017]	At head of title: Becoming a family.
Identifiers:	ISBN: 978-0-9983615-0-5 (paperback)	978-0-9983615-3-6 (hardcover)	978-0-9983615-1-2 (ebook)	978-0-9983615-2-9 (ePub)	LCCN: 2017900491
Subjects:	LCSH: Intermarriage--United States.	Intermarriage--India.	Interethnic marriage--United States.	Interethnic marriage--India.	Intergroup relations.	Personality and culture.	Multiculturalism.	Cultural fusion.	Married people--Biography.	LCGFT: Autobiographies.	BISAC: BIOGRAPHY & AUTOBIOGRAPHY / Personal Memoirs.
Classification:	LCC: HQ1031 .C44 2017	DDC: 306.84/50973--dc23

To my partner and my children.
I am forever grateful for the adventure of you.
There are so many ways to make a family,
whether temporary or forever, you all have
filled my heart.

And to time. 10pm–2am, thank you.
Without you, seven years of writing
would never have happened.

CONTENTS

Chapter 1:   Really, Son? A White Girl? 7
Chapter 2:   Namaste 40
Chapter 3:   The Taj 64
Chapter 4:   Converting Rupees to Dollars............ 77
Chapter 5:   We Do. Yes, We Do!................... 89
Chapter 6:   DINKs 108
Chapter 7:   Serving the Underserved 122
Chapter 8:   Wife of an Immigrant 136
Chapter 9:   The Bollywood Effect.................. 149
Chapter 10: Unexpected Company 172
Chapter 11: A South Indian Bride.................. 183
Chapter 12: Calling All Eggs and Sperm............. 194
Chapter 13: Halfway There........................ 206
Chapter 14: Swimming in the Dregs 224
Chapter 15: Temporary Love 248

Chapter 16: And Then There Were Two 264

Chapter 17: Who Needs a Time-Out?................ 286

Chapter 18: Recalculating Route 301

Chapter 19: Déjà Vu 319

Chapter 20: Global Citizens 329

Chapter 21: One-Hit Wonder 341

Chapter 22: Om................................... 365

Acknowledgements................................. 391

CHAPTER 1

Really, Son? A White Girl?

I slip out of bed and dart to the bathroom. The linoleum floor is cold on my bare feet. *I'm glad Vijay spent the night last night*, I think as I finish quietly and rush back, slipping under the covers.

"Good morning," Vijay whispers anxiously, as if he's committed a sin by staying over. It feels like we're kids and he snuck through the window last night without our parents knowing. But we're not kids. We're in graduate school, he's pushing thirty, and his parents are back in India actively looking for a suitable wife.

He's hypervigilant about mattress movement since he's never shared a bed with anyone. My feet are still cold from the bathroom floor. Wanting to snuggle, I scoot closer to him.

"Hey!" His eyes widen.

I cock my head, uncertain. "What?"

"What are you doing?" His uncomfortable tone surprises me.

"I don't know? What am I doing?"

His body recoils. "You're rubbing my feet!"

"Huh?"

"Feet should not touch," he states.

"My feet are cold!" I playfully scoot closer. "What do you mean feet *should not touch*? Have we never cuddled feet?"

"No. We haven't. Not on purpose." Vijay keeps his distance. "In India I would show respect to a superior by touching my hands to their feet; you don't *rub* them."

"A superior?"

"Yes. Someone superior in age and position." He continues. "The elder then places their hands on the head of the person who is touching their feet and gives a blessing."

"A blessing?" I raise an eyebrow.

"It's usually a blessing for prosperity or a long life or something."

No one has ever touched his feet. He has never cuddled anyone's feet before and the thought is clearly overwhelming to him.

"Okay," I say, slowly moving my lonely feet to *my* corner of the bed.

It feels like a bit of an overreaction, but also makes me realize how little I know about his culture. Pulling the covers up a little farther, I wonder, *What do I know about India really? What am I getting myself into? I only met him a few months ago. I'm sleeping with an Indian man who is about to be arranged in marriage.*

This is almost as shocking to me as receiving an acceptance

Really, Son? A White Girl?

letter from UMass in the first place. I am not sure I would have so enthusiastically accepted it had I known that coming to UMass would lead me to sharing my bed, and eventually my life, with a man who resists foot cuddling.

Six months earlier, I was just a twenty-one-year-old SoCal girl with a plan.

The U-Haul is full of clothes and discarded furniture from the retirement community in Maryland where I just completed an internship. Passing Puffer's Pond, I turn into the parking lot of the Puffton Village apartment complex, pulling an eighties-something Saturn my uncle gave me. I have everything I need. Everything but a job. It's 2002, a month before my first semester.

Unpacked boxes crowd my small apartment. If I want to stay long, I'd better find a way to pay for it. The school will provide benefits, including in-state tuition, if I work for my program. So I begin scouring job bulletins and filling out applications.

The week classes begin, my phone rings. "Hello, Elizabeth?" It's a man's voice.

"Yes."

"This is Professor Sine. Are you interested in the teaching assistant position?"

Thrilled about the opportunity, I accept without hesitation. "Yes! I am. Thank you!"

"Come by tomorrow for orientation," he tells me. "Arnold House, room 312."

I fold my phone and place it in my pocket, sighing in relief. This offer just saved me thousands of dollars.

The half-mile walk to campus is easy. Arriving typically early, I climb the steps of the old brick building, looking for room 312. Wearing my best sandals, slightly wrinkled khakis, a collared sleeveless top and hair pulled into a bun, I wonder if I'm over- or under-dressed. A nervous twinge excites me as I make my way down the hall, surprised I'm actually here. My little brother has always been *the smart one*. I had written my admission essay on emotional intelligence, crossed my fingers and submitted it along with my totally average GRE scores. This might be difficult, but I'm determined to graduate. The chance of a good career and decent salary when I'm done is motivating me. The ability to take care of myself is absolutely necessary.

The door to 312 is unlocked. A large conference table takes up most of the space in the trapezoidal room. As I sit at attention quietly with a pen and notepad, seven women and two men trickle in. Most of them are returning for their second year. They begin to make small talk. Judging from accents I may be the only Californian, and I'm definitely the tallest of the lot. I observe my new colleagues in the School of Public Health silently as we wait for our professor to arrive.

My fellow teaching assistants quickly become study partners, friends and a convenient social outlet. We explore the quaint Amherst community of Emily Dickinson and Robert Frost together, meeting for happy hour, taking hikes and attending school plays.

An Indian doctor named Vijay intrigues me most. A clean-shaven guy with thick, wavy black hair, he is quiet, polite and mild-mannered. His charming British Indian accent captivates me. We discover we live in the same apartment complex and begin walking home after teaching sessions.

"Hey Vijay." Picking up my pace, I wave in his direction.

Really, Son? A White Girl?

We meet in front of Arnold House. "Oh, hello, Ellisabetth," he answers stiffly.

"You can call me Liz." My name sounds like a tongue-full in his mouth. "Shall we?" I gesture home.

Day after day we walk.

"Are you from Massachusetts?" he asks.

"No, California. You?"

"I moved a lot as a kid. My father worked his way up the ranks of the Indian army and Indian air force, so we moved every two or three years."

"Do you like it here? Is it what you thought it'd be?" I'm curious.

"Oh yes. This is a beautiful place."

"You think your folks will come out for a visit while you're here?" I ask.

"I don't think so. No one in my family has ever left India."

"Never? Really? Well, are they excited for you?"

"I think they miss me. My mom is mostly concerned. The lack of family structure, prevalent divorce rate, and the fact I could get shot at any moment are all scary to her. We've seen the movies." He glances my way.

Chuckling at first, I realize I've never *really* thought about the negative aspects of my country. Uncomfortable with the criticism, I try to reflect fairly. For the first time I consider the double-edged sword the United States is for the world. My pride is quickly renewed as he shares his opportunity in coming to the States.

For him, the goal is clear and simple: he has come to further his education with a graduate degree, complete a residency and make money. Once achieved, he'll move back to India using the experience he's gained to work in his country, enter an arranged marriage to a suitable Indian girl, have babies and care for his parents in their old age.

His future is planned and decided. He tells me these things without the slightest bit of emotion. He knows this is what he will do. This is what he has grown up knowing and there is no need or reason to change it. Attending medical school was not his decision. His parents expected him to become a doctor, and so, he went to medical school and became a doctor. They expect him to marry well, so he will. He is a good son.

His clear direction captivates me. His willingness to live this plotted-out life. His contentment with it. I've never met someone who was told what he would become, who he would marry and how he should lead his life, and accepts it so easily. Is he content? Does he realize he has options? Does he care?

Of all the things he shares, the most fascinating aspect of his life is his upcoming arranged marriage possibilities. Why would he want to marry a complete stranger?

"You mean you're going to marry someone you don't know?" I probe, as we walk home after class.

"Why not?" he asks. "It's a good way to find a mate. Your parents investigate options so you are sure to find a good match," he says confidently, scanning the road before we cross.

"What if your parents make a mistake? Or, what if she's mean or a terrible housewife? Are you looking for a housewife? What if you don't have anything in common?" I rattle off, still alarmed. "What if you aren't like-minded?" My eyes glance his way; he doesn't seem concerned.

He unlocks the door to his apartment and we enter. "Those things aren't important. If you put two reasonable people together in a partnership, they can learn to love each other. If not love, then at least respect each other," he explains.

Really, Son? A White Girl?

My mother is a strong, hardworking woman who enjoys her independence. As a kid, I doubted she would ever date *or* marry again. And what about *my* past relationships? What would my life be like if I was stuck married to any of my past lovers? "So, do you have a choice?" I ask, studying his face, certain he isn't pulling my chain. He believes this is a good option. Not just good. The only one. "I can't imagine starting off a relationship like that and knowing you can't do anything to get out of it," I say.

He doesn't respond. I'm not sure if I've insulted him, but he doesn't show any sign of dissatisfaction with my curiosity.

So I ask, "What kind of girl can you get? Are you *worth* a lot?" It feels wrong to ask this. Putting a value on him and an innocent unmarried woman, ranking their marketability.

"I can fetch a nice girl," he confirms assuredly. "I'm continuing my education here so when I go home I'll be even more marketable."

"So, you're sure you want to go home once you've finished?"

His entire life is decided. I used to think I was driven. People call me a planner all the time. I have binders and organizers ready to go, categorizing my goals. My plans are goals according to what I want and think I need. Vijay, however—his life is *planned*. He will get a graduate degree from the States, get married to someone he will or will not love, have kids, work his whole life and be . . . happy?

"After my residency, yes," he says without hesitation. "I'll be able to do a lot with a degree from the States. Besides, my family is there. I don't think the U.S. is a good fit in the long term."

"So, what's on your profile?" I continue. "Do you have a profile or something?"

"Something like that. My parents are asking families about girls who may be a match," he says. He pulls pictures out of a photo album. "I sent these to my family. They'll show them to a potential bride's family."

I tease him about whether the floral grandma couch in one of the pictures is part of the marital package. He just looks back at me, unresponsive. He doesn't understand sarcasm.

"No. We got really lucky! Someone left that next to the dumpster last semester and we collected it." He's confident, calm, composed.

My mind is racing. He's a proud dumpster diver? I feel a twinge of sadness. He is so nice and seems so optimistic. A secondhand sofa is part of college life. But he feels lucky for his dumpster find.

What if he marries badly? *He* should choose his wife, marry for love. He's a composed, soft-spoken catch. His parents should have no problem finding him a bride. Am I really processing this . . . find him a bride? How will his future bride feel about him? He seems perfectly content with this plan. As my mind zigzags around his marriage possibilities, some pictures fall out of the back of his photo album. He's shirtless, in red sweats, flexing his muscles.

Really, Son? A White Girl?

"What are these?" I pick them up off the floor.

"Oh!" Chuckling uncomfortably, he grins. "I work out. Free weights. I have this Arnold Schwarzenegger book. It's quite nice." He gestures toward his bookshelf.

"Oh no, that's okay. I'm not interested in reading a Schwarzenegger book," I giggle.

He smiles sheepishly. I glance at the pictures before handing them back. They're surprising. You'd never know by the clothes he wears, but this guy is quite defined. Our fingers touch as I hand him the photos.

"How old are you?" I ask.

"I'm twenty-eight," he tells me, placing the pictures back in the album.

As the weeks pass, his curiosity in me grows too. "What's it's like to grow up in America? Is it really like the movies?"

"Sort of . . . I guess . . . I grew up in Southern California. My mom raised me and my little brother. We didn't have any family around. It was just the three of us. I went to public schools and lived in the same house from kindergarten through high school," I tell him. "Everyone in the United States gets a free education and the opportunity to participate in athletics. I swam. It's always been a big part of my life."

"How about dating? Have you had boyfriends?" he asks.

"Yes, I've had boyfriends. My parents didn't arrange them and sometimes didn't even approve. I was raised to be independent and make my own decisions." I say this feeling awkward for the first time, as if divulging a secret. He seems open-minded but may have a hard time relating.

Having Vijay as a friend, I now know more Indian people than I have ever known before, not that that's saying much.

Learning about India's geography, traditions and foods is a new favorite activity that we spend our downtime discussing. Vijay emphasizes India's diversity. His Indian friends at UMass also begin to teach me about these differences.

On Vijay's assigned cooking night in his apartment, he makes vegetarian meals and brings me samples. My house starts to smell of strong curries and rice, as we share chana masala, palak paneer, curds and pickle. He teaches me to eat with my hands, South Indian style. I mix the food on my plate with my fingers and scoop the curry onto my hand. Then, push it into my mouth with my thumb as instructed.

"Something looks wrong." He scrunches his eyebrows.

"Okay." My hands wait.

"What *is* it?" He pauses, thinking. "OH!" He straightens up. "You need to switch hands!"

"What?"

"Switch hands," he says. "That hand is for wiping."

"Wiping what?"

"For the toilet," he clarifies.

"Why would you need to . . . oh? You mean there isn't any toilet paper in India?" I ask. "*Really?*" But can see from his expression that he is quite serious.

"Sure . . . There is toilet paper in big cities, but most people don't use it. I had to learn how to use toilet paper when I got here. It's kind of weird."

On Vijay's off nights from cooking duty, I teach him how to make American dishes, like quiche and salad. He eats it with a napkin on his lap and a fork and knife in his hands. He doesn't need any direction. He's learned this long ago.

Really, Son? A White Girl?

Vijay continually emphasizes Indian diversity and how much the culture and language change from state to state.

"So it's like speaking French in Texas, German in New Mexico and Spanish in Florida?" I'm confused but interested, so settle in, crossing my legs on the couch. "It isn't a dialect?"

"Not quite." He turns his body toward me, realizing he needs to explain further. "The script is different too." His arm stretches across the back of the couch. "It's more like Chinese, Japanese and Korean."

"The alphabet is different? Wow! So how many languages do you understand?"

"I moved around a lot, so I can understand quite a few," he explains. "Every three years I moved from one state to another because we are a military family, and so I was able to learn many of the states' languages." I catch myself watching his lips move as he speaks and wonder if he noticed.

I can't believe one country has so many different languages. "I feel like I barely know English. My high school German teacher was great, but the poor guy never had a chance with me." I think about how reluctant we are to have multiple languages in the States and wonder how we'd manage if each of our states spoke a different language, with a different alphabet.

As time goes on, Vijay and I start to venture away from our apartment complex, going to movies and out to eat. He continues to be sweet, kind and thoughtful. His ability to compromise is unbelievable. His willingness to accept American culture is incredible considering the one he describes growing up in. It is almost as if he wanted to drop one lifestyle off on the jetway and pick up this one at baggage claim. He's not interested in bridging the gap nor does he encourage me to participate in Indian culture. But I look for opportunities anyhow.

"Let's do something with the Indian Association," I suggest one evening over dinner.

"Okay, we have a festival coming up. I can try to borrow clothes from someone, if you want to dress traditionally," Vijay offers. "The festival is called Doom. I've drawn some art for it. You'll see it there." His eyes light up. He seems proud.

"That would be great!" I'm interested in seeing what he's created and excited to try Indian foods I haven't had before.

A Nepali friend, Saraswati, lets me borrow clothes for the night. The hall is filled with Indian students. They dance and sing in the traditional styles of their states back home. They wear colorful traditional clothing, all embroidered with intricate designs. I learn all the women are wearing outfits that are either called saris or salwar kameez suits. They dance with elaborate squats and poses reminding me of a rhythmic, bell-filled kind of tai chi—only loud. The men wear clothing called kurta pajama suits that are embroidered and colorful as well. They, too, seem to universally enjoy dancing. I try new Indian dishes and desserts that makes me wonder how many flavors of food I've been missing. Indian or otherwise, I need to try unfamiliar things more often.

As the second semester picks up steam, the earth warms and plants begin to bloom. We start walking to and from campus together more regularly. We also take breaks between study sessions, walking around Puffer's Pond, very close to the Puffton Village apartment complex. The tree-lined walk is pleasant and gives us more quiet time alone. We're forming a bond that I'm unsure about. It's somewhere in between a friendship and a courtship. I don't think I've ever been courted and he's never dated. Neither of us know what we're doing.

I swim laps regularly at the UMass pool and talk to Vijay about how much I miss the beach and being on a competitive swim team.

"Do you wear a bathing suit like on *Baywatch* when you swim?" He smiles, imagining a female lifeguard bouncing down the beach.

"Yeah . . . sort of. Minus the boobs," I say, trying to bring him back down to reality.

"Women don't show that much skin in India." He sounds protective.

"No bathing suits?" I ask. "Why? What do they swim in?"

"Clothes," he says, meeting my eyes. I feel a ping in my gut. I imagine how heavy clothes become in the water and think it's terrible.

"So there aren't any swim teams?" I ask.

"Have you ever watched the Olympics?" He pauses and looks up at me. "We don't have a lot of swimmers. Education is the focus in India. Not athletics. That's why I signed up for figure skating last winter," I look in his eyes, thinking maybe I heard him wrong. "My first winter was fun! I got to have my first snowball fight and sculpted my first snow babe!" he says as if a high school boy molding his first girlfriend. He adds with a sigh, "I woke up the next morning and partiers had knocked her head off during the night."

"Figure skating?" I smile, envisioning Vijay spinning on ice skates and sculpting a snow babe. "You're joking!" Then realize who I'm asking. He's not much of a joker.

"No. I had never been around snow and ice before. I wanted to experience it and learn a sport, so I signed up," he tells me. "I was the only guy in the class."

I smile as he talks, processing all this information. *Figure skating? Really?*

"So, what'd you get in figure skating? Were you good at it?" I ask.

"I took it pass/fail. All my housemates told me if I got a bad grade it would mess up my GPA," he says practically.

Adorable, I think, imagining this twenty-eight-year-old Indian man figure skating, spinning and balancing on one leg as a bunch of undergraduate East Coast college girls practice beside him. "I can ice-skate, but I've never taken figure skating before. I'm more of a water girl." I remind him, "I want to move back once I graduate. The New England experience is new and different, but I belong near the ocean, in California!"

He tells me he loves Massachusetts and can't imagine living anywhere else during his stay in the U.S.

The spring semester flies. We spend more time together than apart. We begin flirting about silly things like how kind we find each other and over-complimenting the other's food preparations. Clearly toying with a relationship, I secretly wonder if this is turning into something bigger. I'm hesitant to say anything to him about my own feelings and concerned about his family's expectations. I've never met someone like Vijay. He has a kind heart. He's generous. He's a reasonable guy, not rash or macho. He doesn't seem to judge anyone. He always listens and considers what he's hearing before responding. He likes to try new things. I mean, figure skating? But, he is also doing everything he is supposed to be doing. Everything his parents want him to be doing, seemingly content with what's expected of him.

I mull over *whatever this is* for a few weeks and finally decide to say something. What do I have to lose, right? "What do you think your family would say if we were to date?" I ask after class as we walk from Arnold House to our apartment complex.

Vijay keeps walking silently. Then he says, "Well . . ." He pauses briefly. "Let's not put all our eggs in one basket."

That's kind of a weird response, I think to myself. I glance at his anxious face as we walk, then put my head down when he doesn't make eye contact. I assume this means he isn't ready to tell anyone how much time we're spending together. For whatever reason, I just keep talking. Not really sure how to respond, I try to clarify. "Do you think if you dated someone, it would mess up your arranged marriage possibilities?" I ask. "Would it cause trouble with your family or status or something?"

"I like you," he confirms, in his pragmatic *I'm thinking* way. "This isn't anything I thought could happen for me. I never considered dating a non-Indian before. Sure, I've thought about what it would be like to date someone. I never thought I'd date a white girl." His voice trails.

Not sure how to read him, now I'm the quiet one. He has laid out the issue. But does that mean he wants to date or not? He leaves me at the bus stop that separates our apartments and heads for his. I walk home thinking about what just happened. I'm not really sure, but I think I may be starting a relationship with someone who is about to get arranged to be married.

The next morning, I dive into the pool at school and start a swim. I swam competitively through childhood, so if I have access to a pool, I'll use it to think things through. I have no idea how he feels about our conversation. I swim my warm-up mulling over what I may have done. Then I start my set, copying a workout written on a board from the team practice that morning. I count my laps, *one, three, five, seven,* getting lost in thought. *Maybe I shouldn't have said anything. This is totally going to mess everything up. What is the goal? He is actively looking for a wife. What if dating doesn't work out? We make good friends. What am I doing?*

Back in my apartment that evening, Vijay comes over with fresh dhal and rice. "I miss the beach and being on a swim team," I tell him, trying to find a way to bring up my inner thoughts during my morning swim. We revisit the *Baywatch* conversation we had a few days before instead.

In the coming weeks, we give dating a try. Vijay acts as though we're committed, I guess because the two relationship categories that exist in his world are single and married. We go through the stages of a high school romance at the rate of a high-speed train. He begins spending more nights in my apartment than his own, and his belongings gradually make their way to my place and stay.

"Are you planning on taking that back to your apartment?" I call out to him as I look at a shaving kit on my bathroom counter.

"Why?" Vijay responds, from the bedroom.

"I just got out of a relationship. I don't really want a housemate," I suggest, flushing the toilet, then climbing back in bed and pulling up the comforter.

Really, Son? A White Girl?

"It's just easier if some stuff is here," he tells me sweetly. Every weekend Vijay dutifully calls his parents to fill them in on his American adventure. His mom begins most conversations by following up on news about a shooting, somewhere in the States. She asks if he was close, if he was hurt and if he feels safe, regardless of how far away it occurred.

"No, Ma," he explains. "Detroit isn't anywhere near Amherst."

I sit and listen to him talk about his course work, whether he has caught a cold, if he is getting enough to eat and if he feels safe after September 11. She worries about how much money he has, if it's enough, if he needs more, and reminds him how much his family misses him. He always tells them he is eating well, feels very safe, has a job and misses them too.

Eventually, these conversations include me.

I sit at the table, sipping tea, when his expression suggests his mother has posed an uncomfortable question. "Son, I am using your snaps to look for a match," he hears trough the receiver. I feel like I shouldn't be present for this conversation. I'm not sure I want to know how he is responding to a potential bride scenario.

He hesitates, takes a breath and begins. "Ma, I found a girl I want to date." He shifts in his seat and makes eye contact with me. A pause follows and he looks nervous. I continue to watch, trying to imagine what his mother must be saying on the other end. I really don't know a lot about her, but Vijay assures me his parents are quite liberal and open-minded.

"Oh son! You have found a nice girl?! Where are her parents from?" I envision what she's saying based on his responses.

"California," he states. He looks over at me and I crinkle my nose, knowing what is going to come next.

"No, son, I am asking where in India is her family from?" I can hear chatter from the receiver as his mother speaks excitedly. "Are they a nice, good family? What do her parents do? Is she a doctor?" An anxious pause follows.

"They are not from India," he responds. I watch him to gauge the import of this statement. He looks totally calm. My stomach turns and I doubt his decision to tell them. What if this is too much? What if we don't stay together?

"What?!" Silence follows. I imagine what she's thinking . . . *But I don't understand. Where else is there?*

"California," he says. "They are from California. It's a big state on the west side of the United States."

"Where?" she asks.

"I'm on the East Coast right now, Ma. It's on the other side of the country," he explains.

He listens to her.

"They are white people, Ma," he states.

Every week, from then on, he provides more information. I sit on the sofa, at the desk or at the kitchen table and watch the conversations play out. Sometimes he speaks in English for my benefit; sometimes he gives me the play-by-play after he hangs up. I understand the arrangement. I know he has never been with anyone else before and I feel like I am corrupting him. I'm a bad influence on this not-so-young, innocent Indian man, and now he's telling his parents about me like we're in high school.

"Hi, Ma. How are you?" He pauses. "Ma . . . Ma . . . I think you should stop searching for brides," he says, glancing at me.

Really, Son? A White Girl?

I sit cross-legged on my sofa watching, trying to read his face and listen to his end of the conversation.

"Yes, I know you already have the pictures." He listens some more. "Don't talk to any more families. I am going to try dating. I would like to try this before I agree to a marriage," he says, while pacing back and forth around the kitchen table.

"Yes. They are nice snaps," he says in response to what he's hearing. "Yeah, Ma, I think they are nice," he repeats and glances my way. "I'm sure I could fetch a good bride," he agrees, but redirects quickly.

"No, Ma. I won't fly back to meet girls right now." His mouth slants. My heart sinks a little as my emotional pendulum swings from totally confident to the far warning-culture-clash side. He says good-bye and hangs up the phone.

"You have to understand where she is coming from." He walks to the couch and sits next to me.

"Okay. Where is she coming from?" I ask without budging.

"They had a plan for me. I am to be arranged. It never occurred to any of us that this was a choice. It's just not part of their reality," he continues. "Or mine, before you."

I say I understand, but do I? I feel bad for them. I don't know what it's like, but can imagine the heartache they face as they realize their dreams are being squashed by this outsider.

I ask him to describe his family to me. He shares a family photo album that was made for his trip to the U.S. He tells me he has an older brother who is also a doctor. His father is a doctor and colonel in the Indian air force, and his mother is a nurse. When Vijay and his brother were born, his mother quit working so she could care for them and be a devoted daughter-in-law.

I look at the pictures of him as a child.

"Oh, you wanted to be a doctor since you were little?" I ask.

"What?" Vijay looks confused.

"This picture?" I say.

"Oh no," he says emphatically. "My father was a doctor and my mother was a nurse. It was expected that I would go to medical school," he explains.

"Oh yeah, I remember you telling me that. But, I don't get it," I say. "You don't want to be a doctor now?" I ask.

"Not really," he admits.

"What do you want to be?" I ask, shocked.

"Well, I probably would have studied computer engineering."

"Why don't you go back to school and do that?" I ask.

He looks at me like I'm crazy. "Why would I do that?"

"So that you're *happy*?" I say. It's clear by the look on his face that his own happiness isn't really part of his professional equation, so I don't press the issue.

REALLY, SON? A WHITE GIRL?

Little by little our life stories unravel, mostly focusing on the differences in our two upbringings. I explain what it's like to be the product of divorce and several remarriages. He asks why people can't solve their differences through talking and suggests parental involvement.

"What do you mean 'parental involvement'?" I ask.

"Well, in India if two married people have an argument that cannot be rectified, the parents are consulted," he explains.

"Consulted for what?" I ask.

"Well, if the two married people can't get along, the family intervenes and tries to fix it. Then that's the end of it."

"Oh my God!" I say. "Ummm . . . if we ever have a problem are we going to do that?" I can't imagine it.

"Why not?" he says. "It's a good system."

"I don't think I like that system. We need to communicate and solve our own problems," I tell him.

"So how did you grow up? Did you live in any other states?"

"No. I lived in California my entire childhood. My mom raised my brother and me, worked full time as an office manager and tried to balance our needs." I realize the contrast.

"All by herself?"

"All the rest of my family is either in Texas or Maryland. We didn't have anyone else around. As a result, I think my brother and I grew up to be two pretty independent people. She worked hard and took care of us. I got my work ethic from her. She's a really good mom." I stop for a moment.

"So did she tell you what you should study?" He's curious.

"Of course she wanted me to go to college, but she never told me what I should become, and even though she loves me, she certainly doesn't want me to move back in with her after

I graduate. My independence from my parents doesn't mean I don't love them or respect their opinions, though."

He is as interested in my cultural view as I am of his.

Week after week, conversations continue with his family.

"Ma, she is taller than me." He pauses.

"I don't know, two inches I guess." His mouth curls empathetically. The conversation is sidetracked as they discuss whether or not he's been getting enough to eat. Then, right back to the bigger issue.

"Yes, Ma, she was dating another guy before me."

After she responds, he says, "No, they just broke up." There's another pause, and I can only imagine what he's hearing.

"Yes, they probably had sex." His eyes flutter my way.

"No, he was not her first boyfriend." He looks at the receiver. The call is over.

"I think that was a hard pill to swallow." Vijay holds the phone in his hand. He looks at me. "They just don't understand this. I am so far away. I know if they meet you, if they can see what I see, it will be fine. They will like you. How could they not like you?"

"I don't know if they'll see what you see," I say, a little worried, slowly realizing that being tall and white is probably going to be the least of my problems.

He shrugs. "Shall we go to lunch?"

He stays the course and continues to include me in his weekly conversations with his parents. He both provides new information and recaps previous conversations that are still not understood or accepted.

"No, she is not a doctor."

Really, Son? A White Girl?

"No, she's not an engineer either."

"She is getting a master's degree. Yes . . . I know she won't be a doctor. It's going to be okay." He looks over at me. I stare back, thinking how proud I used to feel about this accomplishment.

We begin to care about one another on a deeper level. He began grad school a year before I did, so there are only a few more months left before he graduates and moves on to a residency. Even though he was already a doctor in India, he'll have to complete a residency before practicing medicine in the United States. He's been accepted into a program in Chicago. So he'll move after graduation and we'll have to start a long distance relationship. We start to wonder if it's a good idea to devote this much energy to our relationship. Our conclusion is always yes.

Each Saturday morning, he dutifully calls his mother and the cultural education continues.

"Ma, her parents are divorced." An awkward pause follows.

"No, they aren't going to get back together." He listens for a while.

"Yes, they live in two different states, one thousand kilometers apart," he says.

"No, they are remarried to other people," he explains and pauses. "I'm pretty sure it isn't a break. They aren't going to get back together."

"No, they aren't married to other white people. They are married to Mexican people. Mexican people from America . . . Mexican Americans." With a smile, he adds, "It's like she has two moms and two dads."

They've heard enough. His parents finally throw in the towel. They realize their weekly calls are not going to occur without discussing this new topic. Giving in, they listen with silent disapproval.

The following week comes. It is time.

"Ma. Talk to Liz," Vijay says. I look up, surprised, as he passes the phone to me.

"Will you talk to my parents?" he asks, waving the phone in front of my face.

I look at him, forehead creased, wishing I had more warning. "Uhhh . . ." I say anxiously, putting it to my ear. "Hello? How are you?" is the only thing I can think of.

"Oh. Uuuhh . . . hi . . . Lisss? How are you??" a long pause follows. "Vijju?! Vijju?!" They're frantic, worried words. With that, the phone is passed back to Vijay.

They are definitely not ready to meet me.

Vijay's family is disappointed and saddened. Their bright son with so much potential, who could find a good Indian bride, is squandering his life away on a too-tall, white American girl, with significant familial baggage and low social status. Each family member tries to convey his or her fears, disappointment and cultural expectations. They call, e-mail and send letters. What will happen to their son? Why did he have to go to America, a country with a high divorce rate, crime and a poor family support structure? He is doomed. Why did he have to leave his India? Why break tradition and cultural expectations? Why is he doing this to the family? They try to validate the significance of his circumstances and convince him of his inevitable demise.

His grandfather talks of patriotism and how sending Vijay to America will be his greatest blunder. He was, after all, a freedom fighter. His grandfather sacrificed everything for his family and country. Now Vijay has turned his back on them. This, the ultimate insult from his favorite grandson.

His mother cries and worries. What is to become of her successful son whom she raised with such hope for a good life? She wonders what she must have done wrong in her past life, why she is so unlucky, and most of all, what will everyone say. Her ideal bride is a girl who understands, follows and respects their culture, a girl who has graduated medical or engineering school, someone who will take care of them in their old age and most importantly, someone who will act like an Indian daughter-in-law should. How can such a misguided decision have taken place? How can so much sacrifice lead to such a devastating gaffe?

"It's okay, son! Date her, then come back and marry a nice Indian girl!" is the final solution offered. "We don't have to tell anyone."

Back in his apartment, his Indian housemates warn him too.

"Dude, what you are thinking?" his roommate, Kishore, asks.

"I like her." Vijay's stubborn.

"I don't think it's a good idea, dude. You aren't ready for this. It's not going to work out with a white girl. There are too many cultural differences. Don't you think you're rushing things?" another housemate asks in a concerned voice over chicken masala.

"It'll be fine," he sits, confidently eating.

Later, he shares these conversations with me.

"My housemates are worried about us too." We sit and talk over breakfast in our pj's.

"What is there to worry about?" I place my hand on his knee.

"Well, what if this doesn't work out? It will make everything a lot more complicated for me," he explains, as if he is just starting to consider this problem.

"I don't think anything bad will come of this. If we decide not to stay together, what will happen? Do you think you'd get arranged anyway?" I ask.

"I don't know . . ." He considers my questions, then shrugs. "Yes, probably."

"So, that's the same plan you had to begin with." Trying to reassure him, I smile.

Undeterred by his friends and family, he keeps dating me, insisting I am different from their stereotypes. We have a connection that won't waver. He is unlike anyone I have ever dated. He tells me I am an unusual American.

I spend a significant amount of time trying to excuse his so-called insight into self-indulgent Americans, and assure him that most do love their families even though they don't want to live with their in-laws. I suggest personal independence can be a good thing. He continues to give me examples of typical dysfunctional American families, mostly citing TV.

I tell my family about him. They are glad I'm happy but worried we are rushing into a more serious commitment. Vijay is nervous about what my family thinks. He suggests they won't like him because he's from India.

"My mom and dad both recently remarried and are both in biracial relationships now. My brother is dating a girl from El Salvador. Race and culture isn't really part of the equation," I assure him.

Really, Son? A White Girl?

He stares skeptically at me. He doesn't believe they won't care about his ethnicity.

"As long as you're a nice person with some direction in life, it's all good," I assure him.

"Is that sarcasm?" He's trying to learn.

"No!" I say, rolling my eyes. "You are never going to get sarcasm, are you?" I tease. "You'll just have to meet them. You'll see."

The last few weeks of the semester go by. Vijay starts to prepare for graduation and his move to Chicago. I still have a year of school left to sort all of this out. I'm not sure how I feel about a future move to Chicago. A residency takes four years. I really had my heart set on moving back to SoCal. But, I don't really have a hometown to go back to. My mom has moved to Orange County with her new husband, who I call Papi. Chicago sounds like an amazing city and a new experience. The factor that may sway my ultimate decision, however: I think I'm falling in love with Vijay.

"We should go away for the weekend before you graduate and leave for Chicago," I suggest.

Vijay has been listening to my American mix of music for the entire semester, which includes my obsession with musicals. Today, I'm listening to *Les Misérables*. It's by far my favorite score. I've memorized it without ever having seen the production.

"We could take the train to New York," I suggest. "I just found out the last Broadway performance of *Les Misérables* is coming up. I'd love to see it."

Vijay agrees.

I tell him to pack his suit and a pair of walking shoes so we can make the most of the weekend.

In Manhattan we play typical tourist, going to the Statue of Liberty, taking the subway through the city, visiting museums and finally heading back to the hotel to get ready for our big night.

"You packed a suit and tie, right?" I ask.

Vijay has a guilty expression. "I forgot my tie," he admits.

"It's okay. We'll stop at a street vendor and buy one!" I say optimistically.

"Do I really need one?" he asks.

"Yes!" I tell him. "Yes, you do."

Approaching the entrance to the theater, we can see patrons gathered, mostly wearing jeans or shorts and T-shirts. They mull about, waiting for the doors to open.

"A suit, Liz?" Vijay looks at me. "I guess we didn't really have to buy this tie."

"I've always dressed up. I thought for sure people would dress up for the last weekend *ever*!" I'm disappointed people aren't taking this as seriously as I am. I'm also a little embarrassed I made such a big deal about the tie. We enter the theater, find our terrible seats behind a post and settle in for the show. It's even better than I imagined.

On the Amtrak back to Amherst, I rest my head on Vijay's shoulder and ask him to teach me some Telugu words. "Vijay, how do you say 'I love you' in Telugu?"

There's a noticeable pause.

"That isn't really a thing people say," he tells me. "Shall I teach you the literal translation?" he asks.

Really, Son? A White Girl?

I pick my head up to look at him. "Okay." I guess I still want to know. My mental dialogue starts asking questions. No one ever says "I love you"? That isn't something he heard regularly growing up?

"Okay, well, let's see. You'd say, '*Nenu mimalni premistunnanu.*' But, that isn't something a parent would say to a child. It's more what a lover would say. It's literally 'I am loving you,'" he tells me.

"So, did your parents say something else to tell you they loved you?" I ask.

"No."

I don't press further and return my head to his shoulder. "*Nenu mimalni premistunnanu,*" I say softly.

Back from the weekend, Vijay and I walk down the Arnold House staircase for afternoon classes. "Why don't we just get married?" Vijay says, mid-step.

"What?!" I say with a chuckle. I look at his serious face and pause. "Are you crazy? We barely know each other."

"I'm committed," he tells me. "Besides, it'll be easier to convert to a green card from a student visa. I won't have to get a J-1 waiver to stay in the States if we get married," he explains.

"Um . . . no," I tell him. "Too bad about the visa. We can't get married yet. Let's have a conversation about whether or not I'll follow you to Chicago instead." I smile.

He's willing to play Russian roulette with his marriage by getting arranged to a complete stranger. *What is he thinking?! He knows I'm not completely bonkers. I guess that's better than the alternative. Is it?* I'm not so sure this new perspective makes me feel very good. I want to marry someone who loves me because I am the best possible person for him, not because the alternative is unknown or because it's a practical decision to make the immigration process easier. Then again, to him this love is something he may not have ever had in his life . . . something that you have to *maybe* grow into. Some people may question motives. I certainly didn't call up my friends and family to share our proposal story. Even so, I still care about him and understand his uber-practical point of view.

I didn't grow up in a two-parent household. After her divorce, my mom didn't date anyone until my junior year of high school. I never saw her wear a ring or saw anyone dote on her. But I still want a romantic proposal with a ring. What about *rock her world* and *diamonds are a girl's best friend*? Aren't those phrases universal the world over? My idea of a perfect proposal does not take place pragmatically in a stairwell. I may never be able to brand Vijay a romantic, but I'm confident, if the time comes, he can do better than this.

Vijay graduates a few months later and heads to Chicago to begin his residency in psychiatry. So begins the long-distance relationship.

I replace Vijay's presence in my apartment with a new housemate, Saraswati, the Nepali friend who'd lent me clothes

Really, Son? A White Girl?

for the Doom festival. She is in the same program and began the same semester I did. With my new roomie I get a new cultural viewpoint. She has lived in both Nepal and the United States for extended periods of time and understands each of our cultures. Since we all studied and worked together, she also knows us both well. She begins to tease me with stories of rural India and the expectations I am sure to inherit if I become the daughter-in-law of a traditional Hindu family.

"Run," she tells me. "Run away and don't look back."

"What?!" I ask, shocked by her advice.

"I love you both, but let me paint the picture for you," she teases me.

She dramatically tells me if we marry and Vijay dies, I should be leery of going back to India because the wife is expected to sacrifice herself, or worse, is thrown on a fire to burn with her husband. She adds, if I'm lucky, his family is progressive and will let me live, dress me in white clothing, sell my jewelry and smash my bangles into a thousand pieces. I shall then live with his family, serving and caring for his parents in their old age.

Before my nightly call to Vijay, I do some research on Indian wife-burning to see how much of a lie she just told me. The most shocking thing I learn is that it is actually a real thing *and* it was made illegal in 1987. In the eighties! *The eighties!*

After I compose myself, I call Vijay for our evening chat, fixated on uncovering exactly how he feels about this custom. I'm also curious how liberal he thinks his family is about welcoming *any* potential daughter-in-law to their family. I inform him, "In America, when a woman's husband dies, the wife's jewelry accompanies her to the next husband."

He takes this news in stride and says, "The last reported case of wife-burning was at least ten years ago."

Reported, I think. Like that means anything. Who reports something like that? "Ten years?!" I say. "I was alive ten years ago! That is not very long ago."

"It mostly happens in villages," he assures me.

I ask Saraswati about love and marriage.

"I told you, girl. Run," she says.

"Really?" I ask. "Don't you want us to work out?"

"Sure. I just don't think you understand what you're getting into," she explains. "Do you really want to marry someone who might not understand love the way you do?"

"I don't know," I answer. This gives me pause. The concern seems valid and honestly, is the one that scares me the most.

Vijay and I talk regularly over the phone the rest of the summer as we try to figure out our next move. He flies in from Chicago to visit for a few days. I plan a trip for us to SoCal. We go to the community lake, lounge in the pool and relax at my mom's house. He leaves pleasantly surprised, believing now that he will be accepted.

Saraswati, my cultural advisor, provides guidance and counsel every time something pops up. I feel lucky to have her viewpoint and the support of a friend who knows us both. We talk about culture over dinner and on our way to class, allowing the dialogue Vijay and I shared to continue.

Sitting next to Saraswati in our community health education class, I stretch my arm forward across my desk, bumping my textbook. It falls to the ground, touching Saraswati's foot.

Really, Son? A White Girl?

She immediately recoils, quickly touching the book with her hands, then bringing her hands to her eyes and touching them, murmuring a chant or something.

"What are you doing?" I whisper to her.

"Oh Liz! A book is knowledge," she whispers back. "You should never allow a book to touch the lowest part of your body. Knowledge is to be respected. It's bad karma for your foot to touch such an important thing as knowledge."

This is the second foot encounter I've had in less than six months. I make a mental note to totally avoid feet. Apparently, South Asians really do take the foot thing seriously.

CHAPTER 2

Namaste

I fly through the next semester with much more than a full load and three jobs, completing the graduation requirements by December. Wasting no time, I head west with a full moving van and tow dolly pulling my trusty old Saturn. Chicago, here I come. Education complete, I'm once again jobless.

Vijay continues his weekly phone calls to his mother.

"Ma, I want to bring Liz to India to meet you." He pauses as his mother talks excitedly on the other end of the line.

"Yes. We can come for two weeks at the most." This pause is longer.

"No, work won't give me a month or two. Two weeks is

what I get for the year. No one gets that much time in the United States," he explains.

"Tell them I'm a vegetarian," I interject in his ear while he's talking. Genius, thinking I've finally thought of something we have in common.

Vijay holds the receiver over his head and whispers, "They aren't vegetarians."

"Damn it!" I groan.

Settling into Vijay's studio apartment is easy. We decide to go to India before I begin a new job, so the trip is fast approaching. I begin to pepper Vijay's Indian friends with questions.

"What is it like? What will I see? What should I do?"

Everyone has a different answer, but the most intriguing advice is, "Whatever you do, don't go with any expectations."

No expectations? Really? I'm a planner. I can't handle *no expectations*. I have a binder full of tourism ideas and Lonely Planet must-see destinations marked and categorized. I've been told we'll be staying in northern India, at an air force base in Kanpur. How can I go without expectations?

Vijay agrees. "What you expect to see, hear and do will be very different from what you will actually see, hear and do."

I continually ask Vijay about his childhood and family, and to describe his relationships with these people. I make him draw a family tree so I have a basic understanding of who's who. He either lacks the desire or doesn't have a good memory because he doesn't share much, but I am undeterred.

He shifts my focus on the trip to requests he's received from friends and family in India. They begin to pour in as people learn we are coming. We're asked to bring a camcorder, laptop, candy and a few books. I've never been given a gift list before when going to visit someone.

"The dollar is strong, Liz," he explains with a shrug.

"It just seems like these are pretty extravagant requests," I suggest, glancing over his shoulder as he reads his e-mail.

"We should buy these things and give them away in India. It takes a lot longer to make rupees. It's how it's done."

"The dollar may be strong, but we have to live using dollars here," I add, realizing I shouldn't butt in. We aren't married. I don't have a job yet. We're about to take what I consider to be an expensive trip. I should keep my mouth shut. But, the fact that we're surviving on $45,000 a year, in Chicago, is nagging at me. I need to find a job!

"I do have one request for you before we go," Vijay tells me.

"You do? Okay." A little surprised, I turn toward him.

"You really need to get rid of your piercing before you meet my parents," he insists.

"Really?" I ask.

"Yes. I can't introduce you to my parents with a tongue ring," he says.

"Okay. I'll take it out." He hasn't ever asked me to change anything about myself. He verbally paraded my cultural deficiencies in front of his parents without shame or apology for months. If this is what's going to send them over the edge, I'll take it out.

"I could explain a nose ring, but I can't explain that," he tells me.

"It's gone," I say, knowing I've outgrown this rebellious teenage choice.

Several weeks pass and we board the plane to India with tickets that required a renewed passport, a visa and knowledge that our relationship will be changed forever. Incredibly naïve, I travel to India to meet the folks and see what Vijay calls home.

Staring out the little plane window, I tell myself to stay open-minded. I'm incredibly eager to learn, observe and most importantly, go with the flow. My gut pings with excitement as I reflect on how lucky I am to have such an amazing opportunity. What a great experience to see another part of our world! I feel empowered to take the best of each of our cultures and create a super-culture of our own, romanticizing they will meld beautifully into a perfect utopia.

I daydream as the flight takes us from Chicago to Amsterdam and then to Delhi. What will I learn from this trip? To understand sacrifice, hard work, failure and success in more than one way, to see what it's like to live in a developed and developing country—what a gift.

One transfer left: a commuter flight from Delhi to Lucknow. Quickly after we take off, we're descending. I load my camera with a fresh roll of film, ready to capture the smaller Lucknow airport as soon as the cabin door opens. Walking down the stairway and onto the tarmac it is evident India and the United States are not comparable. For starters, I'm a good foot taller than everyone around me. Also, my jeans suddenly feel too tight, inappropriate. I instantly start to sweat. It drips down my face onto my shirt and accentuates my self-consciousness.

I hoist my carry-on over my shoulder and walk into baggage claim without another white person in sight. Dozens of eyes stare at me, then to my companion, and eventually search for who might be receiving us. I suddenly recall Vijay mentioning that his grandfather, who trained in the British military during occupation, was the only one in his family to ever meet a white person before. That information didn't sink in until now. I have never been stared at before for looking different. I have never been the minority. I reach for Vijay's hand, but he does not give it to me. I quickly occupy my fingers with the hem of my shirt, wondering what's made him unresponsive.

People begin to murmur nonchalantly. I watch as they swivel their heads from side to side as if participating in some sort of head-shaking dance that I can't understand. I freeze for a moment and scan the brightly dressed crowd. I can smell the distinct lack of deodorant and hear the noisy commotion of people, animals and cars honking on the sun-drenched street outside the airport walls. I now feel the full gravity of Dorothy's statement, "We're not in Kansas anymore." This is a different world. India feels extreme.

Vijay's father finds us in baggage claim. His salt-and-pepper hair and business attire make him look distinguished. He nods and says something to Vijay. He stares at me, deer-in-headlights style. After looking me over, he offers a quick smile and an awkward, "Hi." Vijay quickly translates, "Follow them." I look in the direction he's pointing and realize we have help.

The soldier in uniform who is our driver and a sewadar (low-ranking military orderly) confirm his father's rank as they load the bags into the sky-blue 1960s Ambassador and rush around us, making sure all of our needs are met. They stand at attention and listen to their senior officer's direction carefully. The British Raj welcome offers a glimpse into what kind of trip we are about to have.

Namaste

I slide onto the springy bench seat of the Ambassador and reach for a seat belt that isn't there. After a brief search, I realize I'm not going to find one. We drive on the left side of the road, playing chicken with other cars, bikes, cows, horses, children and rickshaws on our way to the military base in Kanpur.

Vijay's father watches me and laughs as he observes my anxiety elevate from the sensory overload. I sit at attention, fixated on the view from my window. I can't get myself to look away or have any sort of conversation with anyone. There are all sorts of smells, sounds and sights that are new to me: heavier smog than I'm used to, food odors, honking, yelling, barking, animals of all kinds, slums, shoeless half-naked children in the street. The barrage of images smacks me in the face. I find myself in a state of confused anticipation. Our driver leans on the horn continually for the hour it takes to get to Kanpur. Occasionally I let out a gasp at the scenes unfolding before me, and I repeatedly reach for a seat belt that doesn't exist. The death-defying drive is intense, and although I'm sure today will be my last day on earth, the rush is fantastic.

I'm told we're close to the base. Before entering the compound where Vijay's father is stationed, we stop for chai at a tea stall. This, I'm informed, is a frequent drink of choice. I'm not sure hot chai is a great option, since I'm dripping in sweat, but I sit on the bench and wait as instructed. The tiniest cup of tea I've ever seen is passed to me in a clay pot. As I sip from the small worn pot, wondering if I am going to get hepatitis A the film of warm milk coats my lip and the cool clay feels oddly comforting.

Finishing quickly, I realize my counterparts are still sipping. The outside world is chaotic, but these moments don't need to be rushed. I need to slow down and absorb all of this.

It takes only ten more minutes to get home. The car stops in front of a gated compound and the sewadar hops out, opens the metal driveway gate and closes it as soon as the car passes the entrance. He shuffles his feet, creating dust as he goes. Another staff member appears and opens the door to the car, and I step onto the dirt driveway. I look at Vijay for my next move, feeling somewhat royal with all this unanticipated special attention.

We approach the house together. A petite man reaches for our baggage, which surely weighs as much as he does. Vijay's mother opens the front door with a big smile and a mother's love in her eyes. She's a small lady, about five feet tall, with long, wavy black hair clipped neatly back behind her ears.

Wearing a beautiful salwar kameez and holding a round metal tray of what looks like spices, she says something in Telugu, the language of their home state, Andhra Pradesh. Then without delay, she smears tilak, a red mark made with vermilion powder paste, on our foreheads. She follows with rice, which sticks on the paste. I bend down to meet her hand as I receive my paste. After this she begins to throw extra rice at us from the tray she holds. We are told to enter the house with our right foot first, which causes me to stumble since my left foot is already crossing the threshold. Luckily, I am able to switch in time to prevent lifelong misfortune.

The sun sets for the day, as we visit with Vijay's family: his grandfather, called Thatha, his cousin and his parents. We sit on chairs in the middle of the lawn, surrounded by lush mango trees, perfectly manicured by their gardener. Photo albums sit on a side table. I pick one up and look through the pages of Vijay and his older brother, Sanjay, when they were small.

"Sanjay and his friend will join us tomorrow," Vijay tells me.

Thatha sits across from me and smiles. He's in his late seventies, with a shaved head and glasses. He's wearing a sheet around his waist, like a relaxed maxi skirt. I've never seen a man wear this before, but am sure I will see a lot more of this type of clothing. I have to remember to ask Vijay what it's called. Thatha begins to recite Telugu words and asks me to repeat them. We do this exercise repeatedly, for a good hour, until my accent is understandable.

"*Rundee*," he says with a rolled "r."

"*Run dee*," I say.

"No, no, no. Again. *Rundee*," he repeats.

By the end of the hour, I have learned: "Please come here" (*Rundee*), "Please sit down" (*Koorch-o-ndee*), and "Please take" (*Teesk-o-ndee*). Having accomplished his goal, Thatha swivels his head side to side and reflects silently for a few minutes. Then, sitting up a little straighter, he asks me what color I think he is. Not sure where we're going with this, I respond, "Brown?"

I instantly wish I knew more about the British occupation and current race relations in the country.

"No, no, no." He shakes his head in disagreement.

I sit back tentatively.

"You see, here in India we have many different colors," he explains.

"Oh, okay." I watch him, waiting.

"That chap. Over there." He points at Vijay's cousin standing across the yard. "See him, do you?"

"Yes," I respond, looking in the direction he is pointing.

"Well, you see, he is black." He pauses and scans the group. "And you see Vijay over there?" He points again.

"Yes." I look back at him.

"Well, you see, he is brown." He smiles at me, nodding his head side to side.

"Uhh, okay," I say.

"And I . . . I am white," he explains proudly.

"Okay, umm . . ." I'm not sure what to say.

"And you!" His eyes widen, then squint excitedly.

Here it comes, I think, wincing in anxious anticipation at what I'm about to hear.

"You are pink!" he says with the biggest grin of all.

"Okay." I laugh a little. "I don't think I've been called pink before."

"Yes, yes, yes. You see?" He swivels his head from side to side. With great happiness, he heads for the door to the house. I take his lead and find our room. Still jet-lagged, I need sleep. It's been only six hours since I stepped off the plane and I already know this is going to be some trip.

The following morning, loud thuds on the roof wake me. "What on earth?" I tap Vijay to wake him.

"They're beating the roof," Vijay says groggily. "They beat the roof to make the monkeys scatter when the sun comes up."

"They beat them off?" I mutter to myself as I get out of bed and head for the bathroom.

"No . . . the roof," he clarifies. "It scares them and they scurry."

Running my fingers through my hair, I look in the bathroom mirror and take out my toothbrush. Once presentable, I leave our room and walk down the hall toward the dining room table. As soon as I leave, a man begins sweeping the floor behind us.

"How many servants do you guys have?" I ask, looking back at the man squatting and sweeping as we go. Vijay doesn't respond right away. I've never had anyone cook my meals or clean my house, other than my mother. "Geez, Vijay! You have a driver, cooks, cleaners, monkey roof-beaters, gardeners, dog groomers . . ." I look at him in amazement.

"Yes," Vijay says without elaborating. He isn't being arrogant and he isn't embarrassed, either. He just says yes. I had no idea how important his father is. He told me his father ran the hospital base, but it just didn't sink in until right now.

I'm greeted at the table by Sanjay. He arrived late in the night while we were sleeping. He giggles and smiles as I share my interest in the monkeys in the yard.

"They are destructive pests," Vijay's mom explains as we sit and eat the spicy, saucy chickpea food called chana masala, my new favorite breakfast.

"I want to see one!" I exclaim. I walk to the door followed by exclamations of "No!"

"They bite," Sanjay explains.

I stand at the screen and watch my first group of monkeys in their mango-tree-filled yard. I watch them from a distance and envy the babies hanging on their moms without a care in the world, swinging from the branches eating mangos.

Vijay's father takes note of my monkey interest and spends a significant amount of time trying to find exciting monkey scenarios. He has stories of monkeys who ride the backs of dogs around the compound, monkeys who can juggle mangos and monkeys who will fetch things.

With my dreams of befriending a monkey fading, I draw my attention to grazing cows, wandering street pigs, cats and dogs. Cows are everywhere—on the side of the road, in front of cars, working, sitting and grazing. Two emaciated-looking cows near the house meander down the road, completely uninterested in my presence until one realizes I am standing on prime grass, then head-butts me in the thigh.

Giving up on animals, I decide to take a shower before our first trip into the city. The bathroom is all tile—no curtain or tub. There is a bucket below a faucet with a plastic cup that resembles a measuring pitcher. Vijay filled the bucket with water earlier that morning. He then gave me the bucket-bath crash course. I lather my body and pour the water cup over my head. I take a squirt of the shikakai shampoo, which looks like black tar in my hand. I wonder if I am dyeing my hair as I lather.

After a successful bucket shower, I open my suitcase to ponder my clothing choices. I saw many men wearing Western clothing when we drove from the airport to the house, but was hard pressed to see a woman wearing any. They all seemed to be wearing saris, burkas or salwar kameez suits. I don't have any of these. I packed shorts and tank tops, anticipating heat. But now I feel rather naked. I put my skin-hugging jeans back on with a fresh T-shirt, feeling conspicuous.

We leave the house with the caveat that I am to stay close and tell someone where I am going at all times. Although an independent traveler in the Western world, I understand that here, I may need to be chaperoned.

The driver drops us off at a bustling market in town. Stalls and shops line the streets. The crowded corridors between stores are loud and thrilling. Women with flowing saris walk in and out of shops. None of them seem to be with partners. I don't see any women holding hands with men. The absence of affection is striking. Men, on the other hand, stand hand in hand or arm in arm, talking, laughing and walking.

"There are a lot of gay couples in this town," I say to Vijay.

"What?" He looks at me. "It's illegal to be gay in India."

"What?" I say. "It's illegal?"

"There are no openly gay people here," he clarifies.

"All these men. They have their arms around each other; some are holding hands, walking together. They are affectionate," I say.

"That's because sex and dating are not allowed here," he continues. "No one will hold hands with a lover here. It's a sexually repressed society. That's why so many men are affectionate with each other."

"Is that why you wouldn't hold my hand earlier?" I ask. "At the airport?"

"Yes. It isn't appropriate, Liz," he tells me.

"My hand is lonely," I tell him with a smile. "Anytime you want to test a social norm, you are welcome to!"

He doesn't respond, and I know I've culturally gone too far. My hand will stay lonely in India. Married or not.

As we walk along the street, we pass many food carts. The urge to try something new overpowers the concern for hygiene. Jalebi, orange flour-dough coils deep-fried, then dipped in sugar syrup, is my new favorite sweet. They are crunchy and gooey, sweet and hot. I'm pretty sure I could eat them all day.

Meandering from store to store, I lick my fingers thinking about what I'm going to try next. As I look around I notice people staring and the child rag pickers, as they are referred to, following me. It will take another trip to India before I understand what they are thinking. *Baap rey?! That is one big white girl! What do they feed people where she is from?*

I'm told I need to buy some saris and salwar kameez suits if I'm going to be comfortable while traveling here. I agree to the suggestion but wonder if finding enough material to make an outfit big enough is possible. It seems a lot of the material comes at a standard width. I'm easily a foot taller than the tallest Indian girl in eyeshot. But, I'm more than willing and excited to give this new fashion a try.

I'm also interested in purchasing handicrafts. Apparently

purchasing things has a protocol that I fear I will never get used to. I'm told I'm a walking American dollar sign and there is no way I'll ever get a fair price. After a few barters gone bad, I'm placed in a corner while someone else is assigned to get a *reasonable* price. I'm asked to list items I may want, even though I have no idea what is available. On the occasion that I do go into a shop, I witness the inevitable argument that has to happen with the shopkeeper in order to purchase anything.

I love looking at all the handicrafts and textiles. Once I identify something I want, I tell Vijay. He asks the seller the price. We are supposed to look at him with complete disgust, which I have a hard time doing because I'm busy smiling at him. Vijay then gives an extremely low counteroffer. The seller acts as if we have insulted him and then we act as if we will leave immediately without purchasing the item. That's when, miraculously, everyone decides to settle. In the end, everyone swivels their head side to side in agreement. All are satisfied.

Who am I to say I think all the prices are or are not fair? Vijay doesn't seem fazed either way. Should I voice my desire to purchase an item for full asking price? My longing to go with the flow, do as they do, leaves me feeling a little awkward and cheap. Another dollar could make someone's day. But, I don't have to live here. They do. They have to pay these prices in rupees.

Friends and family begin to visit the house. They start making comments. Openly. Honestly. Within earshot.

"You are really tall," I am told.

"Yes," I say.

"You are taller than Vijay."

"I know," I agree, thinking that's pretty obvious.

"That's not normal," I'm told. "He can't be married to someone taller than him." *Married?* I think to myself. They look me over, concerned about my height.

"Well, I don't have any expendable body parts. So I'll probably stay this height." I smile.

A disapproving stare follows.

Back in our room I ask Vijay about the marriage comment.

"Oh yeah," he tells me. "My mom just told everyone we are already married."

"She *what*?" I gasp.

"Well, she doesn't have any other way of explaining this scandal. Why would we be sleeping in the same room?" He looks at me.

"Those jeans make you look plumpy, Liss," Vijay's mom tells me.

Now I really feel bad about my jeans. Clearly a cultural truth, I'm not sure how to respond to this comment either. Do I say okay? Thank you for letting me know?

"Put on a nice salwar kameez," I'm offered. "It will look better, Liss."

I'm going to need to grow thicker skin.

We spend our days exploring the temples, tombs, churches and marketplaces of Kanpur. I learn about Indian history, the British invasion and more about Vijay's family and his grandfather's role as a British V.C.O. (Viceroy Commissioned Officer), freedom fighter, and finally an Indian police officer. They are rightfully proud of their family history.

The majority of people we encounter are poorer than Vijay's family. There is much talk about giving back to the community. Vijay's father is an example of this generosity. Vijay tells me he has helped a family that lives on the river Ganga. I'm unclear about what assistance was provided, but I'm told we've been invited to dinner in appreciation at their watermelon field. I get in the car without asking many questions and make many assumptions, foremost, that dinner will be held in someone's home.

We drive for some time through the city of Kanpur. I'm told we are approaching our destination. I start to think a little bit about the family as I soak in the scene—rickshaws, food carts, kids, animals, fields—from the car window. Perhaps this family has many children to feed or a lack of furniture or clothing. I make assumptions about their needs and what *poor* in India means. As we drive off the paved road onto the dirt and start bouncing around the farmland, I realize what we are about to face is so far beyond my fleeting judgment. This experience will redefine me, and if our axle breaks the visit may last all night.

When it becomes too difficult for the car to navigate the potholes, we get out and walk. A swarm of people, all men, approach us. It looks like they are carrying something. As they get closer I can see a wooden chair held high by four people, one at each leg. The group climbs up a sand dune to meet us. A frenzied conversation and hand gestures ensue, then more of that head-swiveling dance, which by now I've learned means yes. Vijay's mother is hoisted onto the chair and carried down an embankment. I look across the field. A blanket lies on the ground about thirty yards from where we stand. I watch, glancing over at Vijay, who is already following the mob, and quickly catch up.

As we gather in the open field, I slowly realize this is where we are going to have dinner. I look at the people assembled. They stare right back at me. I begin to wish I'd brought some American trinkets to hand out to the crowd of about twenty men and boys. I could kill Vijay for not explaining the situation before we got here. I try to show my gratitude but know they have no idea what I'm saying. As I rely on my boyfriend for translation, I slowly realize that he has not recognized the importance of thorough interpretations. I would really prefer to have every word translated from now on.

Neighbors from all over came to see the spectacle that is me. They are dressed in their finest clothes and are warm and welcoming. They put out their best blanket, probably their only one, and invite us to sit. I don't know what to do. Sit on their blanket? Sit in the dirt? If I refuse, do I run the risk of insulting the host? I'm completely conflicted and rely on my translator to make my decision, sitting on the blanket.

After a few moments of silently sitting, I can feel the stares from the group. I don't understand anything anyone is saying. I look to Vijay's family for guidance. They all sit and talk amongst themselves. I look around the large field and the watermelon crop. I lean in to Vijay, asking, "Is it all right for me to explore?"

"Sure. Let's take a walk," Vijay agrees.

We walk around the sand dunes, looking at all the watermelon patches. A young man with two clay pots walks to a freshly dug water hole. He scoops water out of it and goes from plant to plant, watering each individually. Then he returns to the hole to fill the pot again. This is his job. He maintains the watermelon fields. He does this all day, every day.

A woman in a green sari appears and greets us excitedly. She squats by a small fire and begins to prepare a meal. She is the only woman in the group and her purpose is obvious: to feed us.

"Is that cow dung?" I ask, looking at our dinner cooking over the flame.

"Yep," Vijay says.

I watch her squat over the fire next to a thatched fence to protect against the wind. She begins to make our dinner using the cow dung cakes as fuel.

"Wow!" I continue to watch as she prepares a metal plate for each of her guests.

I'm given a plate and the visitors gather around and watch. The chapati, a flat tortilla-like bread, is folded neatly next to my curry. I break a piece off with my finger and scoop some curry onto the chapati. I look up at our audience.

"Are they not eating?" I ask Vijay.

"No," Vijay says.

I put my plate down and try to decide what to do. I feel guilty eating in front of these people. They feel honored to have us here. Do I insult the woman's cooking by not eating or eat in front of everyone? I didn't bring anything with me to give them. I didn't know all these people would be here. I am conflicted on so many levels I'm not sure what to do.

I turn my attention to some of the younger residents. "What grade are you in school?" I ask a child through Vijay.

"They aren't in school," Vijay translates. "They need to work in the fields."

"Oh . . ." My heart hurts. "Why am I this ignorant?" I rhetorically say to him.

"They told me they plan to send their little brother if they can. They are all saving up," Vijay explains.

I spend the rest of the evening reflecting on this experience. I want to give these new people in my life enough money to send all the children to school and hire help for their fields. I want to help all the people I've seen that haven't had the same opportunities I have had in life. There are more than a billion people here. What is the solution? I have a lot to think about.

The next morning, Sanjay is eager to show me around. He enthusiastically tells me he's taking me out. The driver takes Sanjay, Vijay's cousin and me back to the sacred river, Ganga, to explore. I'm told it is cleanup day. People are bathing in the polluted water and a crew from Eco Friends is rowing a boat around, scooping up dead bodies. As I watch, my tour guides explain that many people can't afford to have the bodies cremated and sometimes, to save wood, the crematory puts a burning body out before it has completely burned. They throw the partially charred body into the sacred river.

Bodies are being pulled from water where people are bathing. I can sense the strong devotion to this holy river and see mourners' flowers floating by peacefully, yet it is also overwhelmingly polluted by the practices that hold so much meaning to people. We stand and watch. I try to wrap my mind around what I am seeing. So many feelings strike at once: respect for the devotion, anger that the river is so polluted, sorrow for the poor who bathe here and confusion by the contradictions.

Picture Translation:

Water is life! Clean Ganga, Clean Water, Clean Life

Please cooperate to make efforts of Eco Friends successful,
Please do not pollute Ganga and do not let anyone pollute it,
Please do not afloat dead bodies in Ganga
Please do not dump polythene [bags] in Ganga

I was supposed to be prepared; I bought and read books on traveling to India. But I slowly begin to realize the Western world's travel books oversimplify the country. They categorize by weekend escapes and breathtaking views. They don't talk of the poverty, the despair, the heartbreaking choices. They don't dump you in the middle of a town with all its extremes; they assume you'll be taking a day trip to the Taj Mahal from your resort, skipping life. The travel books gloss over India's extremes in a romantic fashion that left me wanting to embrace yoga and greet everyone using *Namaste*. One could easily read the charming reality written and be left feeling spiritual. Definitely not in a half-charred-dead-body-floating-down-the-Ganga way.

Sometime later we get back into the car and head for town. Walking through the city, we see a street artist sitting on the curb with a packet of henna supplies.

"Oh! I want to get henna!" I exclaim. "It looks amazing. I've never done it before."

"Sure, Liz," says Vijay's brother as he and his cousin take on this special project. They start a heated argument with the vendor and hands start flying.

"What's going on?" I ask.

"It's just ridiculous! We aren't paying one hundred-fifty rupees for you to get henna! Who does he think we are?" Sanjay starts walking away in disgust. "Come on, Liz," he says, encouraging me to follow suit.

"Wait! One hundred-fifty rupees? That's fine with me. That's only three U.S. dollars, right?" I pick up my pace to keep up.

"We aren't paying more than fifty rupees," they agree, committed in their decision. "He knows you have money. You are an American dollar sign."

The street artist runs up behind us, agreeing to their deal. I sit down on the curb and feel bad for the vendor as I try to figure out how to give a tip. All of my money is with my tour guides for *protection*. Once he's finished, I look at my hands. They are gorgeous peacocks.

My protectors instruct me on proper hand placement as we make our way through the crowd to the car. "Okay, Liz! You have to hold your hands up until the henna dries. Don't touch anything or it will be ruined. Understand?"

"I understand." I stare at my hands as we walk.

The henna was applied like frosting piped on a cake. The lines are thin and intricate. I'm told the paste will flake away once dry and reveal a tattoo of sorts. It should last days.

We find our driver, get back in the car and drive home. I hold my hands in the air, hoping they will dry properly. Once inside the compound gate, the sevadar opens my car door and escorts me into the house. Dinner is laid out on the dining room table. Vijay's mom welcomes us and then looks immediately at my hands.

"OH Liss . . . What you have done?!" she asks with urgency in her voice.

"Do you like it?" I ask.

"How will you eat your dinner?" A little disappointment in her voice, she continues. "OH Liss . . . it's okay. I know! Mama will feed you," she says, grabbing a plate and piling it high with food.

"Oh, no thank you. That's okay. I don't need to eat right now," I say.

"Oh you must eat. You don't eat enough. No food in you. You sit. Sit. Sit. Sit, Liss," she insists.

"Okay." I sit, reminding myself: *Go with the flow*. I'm uncomfortable, but refusing may be insulting.

Sanjay watches this transaction from across the table. "Oh son, don't you worry," she says, looking up at her oldest child.

"I see on your face you are worried. Mommy will feed your wife too when you get one. I love you both."

And so I sit on the end of my chair, hands in the air, as food is fed to me. I don't mean fed with a fork and spoon. I mean full-on South Indian-style, bare-hand eating. The scoop-and-shovel method. Vijay's mother carefully mixes the curry, rice and curds between her fingers and pushes the food into my mouth gently. I'd say I feel like a little bird being fed by its mother, but I'm twice this woman's size. So, I feel more like an elephant with a keeper who drew the short straw.

When visiting a South Indian family, even if you're stationed in the north, eating with your hands is proper etiquette. This is probably the most intimate moment I'll ever share with Vijay's mother. As I sit chewing a curry I've never had before, I think, *this has been one hell of a day.*

The next morning, I am presented in the sitting room with tea and finger foods as onlookers arrive in the traditional way. I sit on a red velvety sofa made for people five feet tall. Five feet, I am not.

As the small talk lingers and the conversation turns back into something I can't understand, I begin to realize just how much of a storyteller Vijay's father is. Having been told various facts about me, he feels he has an understanding of who I am.

A humorous, good-natured man, he has made a point of seeing to my happiness while here. He is also a commanding officer in the air force. He directs the base hospital and has a serious side that makes clear he is in charge, a man to be respected. He certainly feels he can speak on my behalf.

Through his stories, my athletic abilities become more and more impressive with each new officer who comes to visit. It's true I swam on high school and college teams, and there's no doubt I enjoy competition and a good swim. But, let's be real: I will never set the world on fire with my swimming ability. By the end of the week, however, I was a five-to-ten-mile daily, open-water swimmer.

When introduced to people for the first time, I want to be accurate and truthful, but I'm not sure that correcting Vijay's father, on his turf, in front of his subordinates, is the best course of action.

"Oh wow! Five miles is a little long for a daily ocean swim. I actually swam on a team." I pause. "In a pool." I pause longer this time, observing the dissatisfaction in his face. "I still do laps. But I'm not on a team anymore," I add.

He looks at me a little disappointed, crosses his arms and chuckles.

"That's not to say the occasional jetty swim is out of the question," I add as I notice the corners of his mouth drop slightly.

"Oh, she is being modest, so shy you know." The topic is dropped and another begins.

CHAPTER 3

The Taj

Each morning I lie in bed frantically jotting notes. Lately, my thoughts flow faster than my pen. I pause briefly, thinking about all the things I'd like to include. My daydream ends as I become aware of a dispute across the hall. I'm pretty sure one of the voices is Vijay's. I've never heard him raise his voice or argue with anyone. He is always so mellow. I'm surprised and find myself clinging to every sound of his mother tongue. I can't understand any of it and am glad I'm not present.

"Well, we can't do anything about it," I hear Vijay say in English as he stomps through the door of our room.

"What was that about?" I ask. I see he's agitated. He is calm with me, but uncomfortable. I'm witnessing this personality trait for the first time.

"You," he says, still annoyed.

"Me?! What about me?" I ask, worried I've done something inappropriate.

"You are too tall." Vijay shoots me a look.

"Huh?!" I try not to laugh.

"My mom isn't angry," Vijay explains. "She would just prefer that you not be as tall as you are."

Since I don't know what was said, only the volume of the conversation, I know it was an actual disagreement. I've noticed Indians do tend to speak quickly and loudly, but I know the difference between a conversation and an argument. I guess I can consider myself lucky. Of all the things they could fight about, she has picked my height, which I can't change.

"I have to fly to Chennai to get my passport stamped," Vijay says. "It's a long flight and short stay, so I think I should go alone. You can stay with my family."

"Okay. When do you leave?"

"Tomorrow," he says.

I wouldn't have been nervous about Vijay's trip before the argument, but I've become aware of the simple differences. How many unspoken problems will arise? His family knows English, but it's a choice to speak it, not a norm. How much will I miss in translation?

Vijay leaves the following morning before the sun comes up. He'll be gone a few days, as everything in India takes time. As soon as I wake up and see the vacant pillow I feel nervous. I know I will be cared for, but my security blanket and primary translator in all cultural interactions has just left me. I take my time getting dressed, and head to the dining room table to figure out what the day holds.

A trip to Agra has been arranged. We are going to see the Taj Mahal. From the part of the conversation I can understand, it sounds like a straightforward trip. We will rent a car and drive 286 kilometers (about 178 miles), bringing a servant and a driver for assistance. Vijay's father has to work, but all the other men, including Vijay's cousin, Thatha, Sanjay and a friend, will accompany me.

I'm told to pack an overnight bag and the car is loaded. We will leave first thing in the morning. Vijay calls to tell me he has reached Chennai. He is staying with an aunt he had lived with during his final years of high school.

"I'll see you soon," I tell him before saying good-bye, trying to sound upbeat.

"Oh yeah! I forgot to ask. Is it okay if I buy my aunt a washing machine?" he asks. "They don't have one. It would help them out."

I think about his question for a minute. I'm not sure why he's asking me what he can and cannot do with his own money, but it sounds fine to me. "Go ahead," I tell him. "Well, wait. How much is a washing machine?" I'm curious. "A few hundred dollars," he tells me. We say good night and I tell him I'll see him when we are back from Agra.

I wake up early and take my place in between the guys in the back of the car. We start with small talk about the States. Thatha quickly takes over, deciding this is an excellent time to teach me a Hare Krishna chant. An excited Thatha claps his hands in time and encourages me to imitate: "Come on, Liz . . . Hare Krishna. Hare Rama . . . Hare Krishna . . . Hare Rama . . ."

The Taj

I do the best I can, repeating the monotonous chant over and over until he's satisfied I feel it.

The younger guys interrupt our religious revival by sharing candid stories about various family members and asking questions about America.

"Are you afraid to walk in the street?" I'm asked.

"No. Why?" I say, wincing as I look out the window to see uniformed schoolchildren walking amid unorganized traffic.

"You could be shot at any moment, right?" I'm asked.

"Well, not exactly." My focus shifts from people-watching back to my intrigued travel companions.

"You can just walk into a store and buy a gun, can't you?" Everyone waits for my answer.

"I don't know how it works, actually." Purchasing a gun isn't something I've ever considered doing myself.

Disappointed, they change the topic. "Families don't have respect for each other in America," Vijay's cousin tells me. "People don't take marriage seriously, do they? We've seen all the movies in the cinema. We know all about America. Go on. Name a movie. We'll tell you if we've seen it," he continues. "Name a star. I know all the stars."

Time passes. I see more uniformed schoolchildren sitting on the ground of their outdoor classrooms with slate boards in their hands. I watch a milkman riding his bike on his door-to-door route, emaciated animals working with overloaded goods on their backs and women in saris with babies strapped to their bodies laying bricks on the very road we are traveling. I look across the street and see a bus on the side of the road with a motorcycle lying under it. The passengers have gotten off and are standing alongside it. They are watching as someone tries to retrieve the bike or investigate; it's hard to say which. Great beauty aside total devastation. Extreme poverty aside shining luxury car dealerships.

I tighten my seat belt and Sanjay, his friend and cousin all laugh at my insecurity. I tell them I don't want to die, and if we get in an accident, the seat belt is my only chance at life. They continue to tease.

"It's not like there is a nine-one-one system," I exclaim.

"Nine-one-one?" they ask.

"You know, if someone gets into an accident . . ." I'm getting blank stares. I explain the United States emergency response system.

"We have one hundred. It's our emergency number. But, sometimes no one comes," they tell me, giggling.

"So what happens to someone if they get hit by a car or something?" I ask.

"Someone will scoop them up and take them to the hospital," they explain.

I check my seat belt again.

The farther we go, the more I wonder where we are. At times it seems as if our driver isn't sure how to get to Agra. We pull over to ask a random gentleman in the street for directions. He points toward a building and says, "Go that way for a while and then turn right and ask the next guy at the house with a thatched roof." I don't see any street signs or signals until we get to the heart of the city and even then, they are clear as mud. The closer we get to a larger population, the more people I see begging in the streets, shoeless, burned or legless, making their way between the cars, pleading for rupees.

Seven hours after our journey began, we finish the 170-mile

drive and arrive at the Delhi hotel we've booked. I'm not sure how we made it.

"We have two rooms at the hotel," Sanjay tells me as the car enters the hotel parking lot. "There is one room for the boys and one for you and Thatha." He smiles as he gets out of the car.

I look over at the man who has made me recite religious songs in Hindi and wonder what our night together entails, quickly realizing it doesn't matter. One hundred and seventy miles in India can really take it out of a person. It isn't exactly like driving on the freeway in SoCal.

I'm asleep as soon as my head hits the pillow. I don't wake up until the drapes are pulled with the sunrise and a Hare Krishna chant and yoga session begins.

"I wrote a book on yoga, Liz," I hear Thatha say, as I rub my eyes.

"Yes. Vijay told me about your book," I reply in agreement.

"Ah yes, so let's get started. Go on. Sit like this," he says as he places his feet on his knees in Padmasana, the Lotus pose.

"Okay. Let me brush my teeth. I'll be right back."

I brush quickly and get into position, knowing full well this eighty-year-old man has absolutely no problem standing on his head.

As soon as we start, Sanjay walks in. "What are you doing, old man?" he asks. "Don't make her do this."

"I don't mind," I say, even though I am slightly uncomfortable with my yoga ability. I dislike his condescending tone.

"No, no. The Taj awaits," Sanjay continues, waving his arms. "Let's go." The other boys pour into the room behind him.

We gather our things and check out. I'm grateful to get going and looking forward to sightseeing. Most of all, the Taj Mahal. We walk to the car and wake the servant and driver. I hadn't thought about where they'd sleep, but would never have thought it would be the car. Another tidbit to digest.

We don't drive long before I see the Taj Mahal from the window and feel excited. We drive up and down streets, looking for parking. Eventually, we're dropped in front of the ticket booth at the outer gate of the monument. Two segregated lines, one for men and another for women, are at the entrance. The first thing Sanjay notices is my admission rate.

"But she is an Indian now," he insists, arguing with the ticket taker.

She looks at me with an unapologetic smile. "The full rate," she confirms.

"This is an outrage," Sanjay continues." We don't want to pay a Western rate. She is a part of this family. She should get the Indian rate."

I watch the conversation bounce back and forth. I'm slightly embarrassed this discussion is taking place, but no one else in my group seems to be.

They pay the Western rate for my admission, and I'm ushered into a line for female visitors, leaving the rest of my group in the male line. My line goes quickly and I'm inside the gate far ahead of the men. All the women sit together, waiting for their male companions. I look from left to right. On my left are Indian women sitting with their children, waiting. On the right, mostly white travelers on a guided tour.

I walk to the left. I'm in India. I'll experience India. The women and children look at me as I walk over and take a seat next to them on the step. Muffled murmurs and then excited chatter begin. They start to smile and make eye contact. A bold lady walks over, puts her baby in my arms, smiles and takes a picture. I smile back, offering a better pose.

The Taj

They all swivel their heads in agreement that this was in fact a good choice and continue to speak with each other and gesture toward me. I point to my camera and to them, pantomiming, "Can I take your picture too?" They swivel their heads in excitement and gather. I check my camera for film and take their picture.

I don't have to wait long before I reunite with my party. The women all look at each other with excitement as they realize all the people I'm traveling with are also Indian. They speak softly to one another as if plotting some secret plan. From that moment on, I have a following. They take pictures with me, have me hold their children, touch me and point at me as we tour the Taj Mahal. I wonder what is going on. Here we are at this glorious monument and this puzzling focus on me seems misguided.

We make our way past the outer gate to the front of the Taj. It is the most incredible display of workmanship I've ever seen. Intricate detail and seamless slabs of carved marble and jeweled inlay surround me. I am awestruck. We take our shoes off and climb the hot marble steps into the tomb. I don't know how to feel. It's so hard to reconcile this incredible beauty with its tortured story.

Bangles, Bindis and Babies

We eventually make our way back to the car and start driving to another temple. I sit staring out the window at the peacocks in trees as we drive. I think about the intricately cut marble slabs I just witnessed. A tremendous gesture of one man's love for his wife that cost other men countless hours. An incredibly romantic gesture for a woman he loved, plagued by a greedy son in search of the throne imprisoning his father, and in death, placing him next to his mother, albeit off center.

My daydream is interrupted when I hear Vijay's brother say, "Oh look, there's a bear. Stop the car!"

"A *what*?!" I look out the window in alarm, thinking for a brief moment I'm going to see a bear roaming freely in a field.

Instead a gigantic bear is right outside my window. About a foot outside my window. But this bear isn't meandering down some random field looking for food. No, this bear stands at attention. It is in chains, muzzled and declawed. Everyone in the car turns to look at me in excitement.

"Keep going! Don't stop!" I say hysterically. "We can't give money to support that guy." I don't even know where to begin. I can't believe my eyes. I look down in shock, paralyzed. I replay what I just saw. *A bear? A real bear? Is that what I really saw? Declawed? Chained? Muzzled? Oh my God.* I can feel my

The Taj

heart pounding and I don't know what else to say. I feel the car lurch back into traffic and accelerate. Maybe I should have paid to take a picture. PETA needs to get on this.

They can't understand why I'm appalled at such a lucky find and wonderful photo opportunity. They look at me for a moment. The car goes silent for a while. No one ever brings up the bear again.

We arrive at the Fatehpur Sikri royal palace and barter with a tour guide, but only after having me hide behind a stone wall while the guide's price is negotiated. Let's just say when I pop out from behind the wall, the man feels a bit ripped off.

Finally, the inevitable happens. I need to use the restroom. To my relief, I see a sign that says *Toilet*. I walk confidently up to the door and open it, assuming that means there will be an actual toilet. But I quickly discover the term is used loosely. It is actually a hole in the ground behind a wall.

I am wearing the traditional salwar kameez, which consists of a knee-length dress-like top with slits up the sides and a very baggy pant, similar to the harem pants of the eighties. With all the extra material hanging, the last thing I want to do is get it dirty and walk around smelling like a sewer the rest of the day. So I take them off completely, squat over the hole and successfully poop. My legs are dry and the extra material is dry. Excited that my experience is clean, I skip out of the bathroom, pants back on.

"Guess what?! I did it! It was a hole, not a toilet, and I totally took care of business. Yes!" I excitedly recount my adventure to Vijay's brother, hoping he can understand the extreme satisfaction I feel.

"That's nice, Liz. Congratulations." Sanjay's smile widens.

"Maybe you should talk to Vijay about your excitement. I don't think I should hear about it."

I don't think I would have been as proud to successfully poop in a hole had I not brought baby wipes with me. Cheating, I suppose, but I'm not quite ready for the alternative—my finger. This also reminds me of when Vijay taught me to eat with my hands. There is a reason people eat and shake with the right. I think about the potential problems I could have in the future if I forget to bring wipes and decide I'll trim my nails when I get back to the house.

A young rag picker finds me as soon as I exit the toilet. She follows me, offering a small metal trinket. I'm not interested in buying it from her, and I know whatever money she gets for it will go to whoever sent her out here. I wave good-bye to her but she continues to follow, persistent in her request. I ask Vijay's brother for translation. He confirms that she wants me to buy the trinket. The guys walk ahead and I follow. The tour guide educates us as we go.

The little girl is tenacious. She's a tiny thing, with a ripped dress, a dirty face, big brown eyes and black matted hair that's been pulled behind her ears. She trots along behind me energetically. I decide to give her candy instead of money, some little treat she can enjoy immediately. She chews happily, scampering next to me.

After an hour we round the compound toward the car. I've never wanted to bring a child home with me more badly than I do right now. Our servant opens the door and the little girl tries to climb into the car. Vijay's brother shoves her away. She is crying. I am watching. We drive away as she stands defeated, crying and watching the car. I wave through the back window.

"What are you doing?" I hear, with slight urgency.

I try to explain myself. "Oh, I feel so bad! Poor thing, I'm just waving goodbye. This is heartbreaking."

"No. What are you doing?" I'm asked again.

"What?" I ask. "I don't understand." I look at Sanjay, confused.

"That wave you are doing. That wave means 'come with me,'" he says.

"What?! What do you mean?" I'm desperate now.

"When you wave that way, you are telling someone to follow you. No wonder she wanted to get in the car," I'm told.

"Are you kidding me? How are you supposed to wave?" He shows me as I plead.

"We need to go back and explain. This is terrible," I say franticly.

"That's her life," he tells me. "They'll probably beat her for not successfully getting any money from you!"

I can't decide if he's teasing, but no matter what, I am horrified. I guess I'll call it Indian sarcasm, but whatever it is, it's hard core. This is our last stop before heading home. I try to sleep most of the way, totally distraught over what I've done to a poor helpless child with absolutely no hope of a better existence. To me, she represents all of the children who have no hope in India. I know she will haunt me.

I don't think I've ever been more excited to see anyone as I am when Vijay walks through the door, back from his trip to Chennai. His family has been hospitable and kind, but unfamiliar. Vijay feels safe, like home, love. I am glad he's back in my grasp.

The following day it's time to say good-bye. It's tearful for everyone, and the boys giggle and take pictures as I hug each of them.

"What's so funny?" I ask.

"Girls don't hug boys in public," they explain, clicking away on their cameras in the driveway. I look around. It's just us in the driveway. "What's public about it?" I feel silly now too, but I'll play along.

"Do it again—I'm going to record it on video," I'm told.

I comply with the request as they giggle.

CHAPTER 4

Converting Rupees to Dollars

W alking hand in hand, once again, it's just us. We reach our gate and sit, waiting to board. I squeeze Vijay's hand.

"Please tell me more of your story!" I tell Vijay.

"What do you mean?" he asks.

"Tell me about coming to America. I can't imagine what it must have been like. You came all alone. No one in your family had ever left India before you. I can't picture what it must have been like. Were you nervous? You never seem nervous. Did you research where to go? How did you pick UMass?" I start listing all my questions. "Can you remember flying into Boston for the first time?" A small smile appears as he thinks back.

He squeezes my hand and begins as our flight is announced

and we make our way down the jetway. "Of course I remember," he tells me. "I was the first to leave India. No one has ever left."

"Were you scared?" I interrupt.

"No! I was excited." He smiles. "I was always kind of the black sheep of the family. Everyone always told me that growing up. I didn't know what to expect when I got to the U.S. I applied for several top-ten schools and heard back from UMass first, so I accepted that. I didn't know anything about Massachusetts when I accepted the admission," he continues. "My port of entry, Boston, was my first slice of the American dream. It was August twenty-third, 2001, right before September eleventh happened. I was quite literally, as my friends later referred to me, FOB—fresh off the boat. I had no idea how I was going to get from Boston to Amherst. But I was fairly sure I would be mugged, probably at gunpoint, thanks to the Indian I sat next to on the flight over. He had lived in Detroit for some time. I made my way through a friendly, pre-9/11 customs and immigration, wondering if America would be anything like the one I knew from TV."

His story is interrupted as the flight attendants do their preflight cabin check and safety presentation. The flight takes off as scheduled. I cuddle up next to him and close my eyes, listening to his words, trying to envision the story he tells . . .

It's August 2001. Vijay just arrived at Logan International Airport, about to begin graduate school. Carrying a burgundy hard-shell briefcase, he follows the signs to baggage claim and looks for his flight posted on the monitors. Standing in front of the turnstile, he inches his way up to other FOBs.

"Hi," he greets them. "Are you studying at university?" he asks in his British English.

"Yes." They avoid eye contact.

"So am I! Which one?" He's eager to know; they may be his ride. They all scan for luggage.

"UMass, Amherst," an Indian man replies.

"Oh great! Can I have a ride?" He inches closer. "I'm also going to UMass, Amherst. I am meeting Amit from AP. I have his address. He is my contact upon arrival."

"Oh yeah! We know Amit," one of the men says. "I'm not sure we'll have room for you in the car. How were you planning on getting there?"

"Bus, I think. I have these coins and was told I could make a call from a phone in a booth. But, if you're going there I can sit in the back with the bags! It's not a problem," he suggests.

"I'm not sure we'll all fit with all these bags . . . The phones in the booth are called pay phones, but most don't work. Do you have a cell?" the friendliest guy in the bunch asks.

"No." Vijay inches closer, discouraged but determined. The others recognize his disappointment and glance at one another.

As the last of the bags are lugged off the baggage carousel, they sympathetically agree, "Come with us, we can squeeze you in."

He feels lucky to have this new knowledgeable connection and gladly sits in the back of the sedan, legs on top of luggage, with the other passengers. The Oldsmobile is stuffed with the worldly possessions of these new immigrants. Hopes and dreams high, they drive on the lush tree-lined New England highway toward graduate studies, each with his own expectations.

The three bags Vijay packed contain the many items that his family imagined could not be purchased in the United States: a pressure cooker, a pot and pan, a good kurta pajama to wear during fancy occasions and spices: turmeric, chili powder, garam masala. Three suitcases and three lists accompany him, items checked and ready for use when he settles.

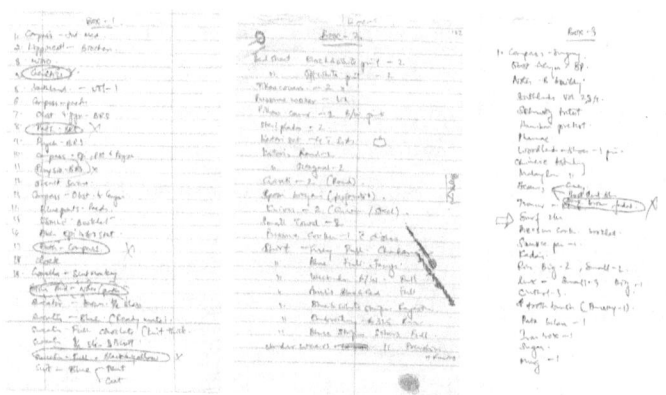

A friend of a friend, through e-mail, said Vijay could crash on his floor until he finds his own place. Vijay gives the address to his car-pool companions. They drop him at the door. Vijay knocks. The door opens and an Indian he doesn't know tells him he isn't expected.

Step one: Find somewhere to live.

We land in Delhi to change planes. I collect my carry-on totally engrossed in his story. I want to hear more. Our layover isn't long, so we grab some tea and a snack and make our way to the international terminal headed for Chicago via Amsterdam.

As the plane boards for the next leg of our flight, I follow up. "So, what happened?"

"Huh?" he says, looking up at me as we fasten our seat belts. "So, how did you find a place to live?" I probe.

"Well, since all my connections were Indian, I found

the campus Indian Association rather quickly and a group of guys who were already settled. I relied on them for advice, food and housing." I listen as he continues his story. "My new housemates told me about a computer lab in Arnold House. They said I could use the net for free. I sent my first e-mail home from there."

He would later show me the message:

Dear Brother,

I am sorry for not having called you. I have bought a phone card on the net and it is cheap (28 cents per minute) but it is cheap only because I can use it to speak with someone in a specific city in India—I have taken a card for Bangalore. I have not taken a card to speak with anyone in Hyderabad, because I can keep in touch with you people on the net. I will mail you the receipt of 170 dollars and the British Airways ticket today itself (Oh God the food on the plane was divine). I have free access to the net in my department's computer lab. My classes haven't begun yet, they will on the 5th of September. I have orientation programmes till then. I am free this weekend and I will be talking to Mummy and Daddy in Bangalore. I have shifted to my apartment, it is very close to the university—hardly 15 minutes' walk. The bus service to the university and to the places nearby from my residence is so good and reliable. The bus service is free and it is on time to the minute, if I want to catch a bus at 8:45 am I need to be there by 8:40 or so as the bus stop is 20 metres from my apartment. If I reach the bus stop even at 8:46 I would miss the bus.

I have a phone now but I am not sure of its number but I will mail it to you soon. (I think it is 413-549-1302). 413 is the code of Amherst, MA. In my next mail I will verify this number. The apartment I am staying in is a 3-bedroom apartment. Five of us are staying in it at the moment and the rent comes to about 250 dollars per person per month and the monthly charges for groceries come to about 100–150 dollars. I have made quite a good number of friends here. Two of the guys put up with me are from AP (Masters in Public Health)—one from Gandhi Medical College, the batch of 93, and another from Andhra Medical College, who has done his internship at Gandhi hospital, of the batch of 95. There are two more guys from Bengal. I haven't been able to meet any of the professors from my track, ie 'Community Health Education'. I have taken appoints with the professors in my track and will be meeting them regarding any tuition waiver that is possible this semester. I have applied for two on-campus jobs and will be applying for one more today. I think that's it for today.

Bye.
Love.
Vijay.

His new housemates show him the chore schedule, explain cooking duties and suggest he attend the university orientation.

He follows their suggestion and finds the bus stop for the new student orientation. Delighted it includes a community bus tour, he boards enthusiastically. The mall is the first stop. Vijay gets off the bus, accompanied by another Indian, Kishore, whom he had met during his apartment hunt. Kishore tells him spending money in the mall is a waste. Walmart is across the street and anything can be purchased there for less than the mall prices. He knows this information is accurate because Kishore, his new Indian informant, has a sister who moved to the States first and knows all about American consumerism.

The pair walk across the street toward Walmart, keeping an eye on the time they've been given. They pass the sliding doors and greeter, walk into the aisle-laden big-box store and stop. Vijay can't believe his eyes. He is in awe as he scans the warehouse. *So many items? All in one store? So organized?* Never in his life has he been in a store with such a variety of items to fill every possible need. This, he thinks, is amazing. He starts to convert the price of each item into rupees as he scans the products and wonders how he is going to afford to live in America. There is no time to shop in the time they've been given. They're due back at the bus stop.

Seeing a sucker in Vijay, Kishore leans toward Vijay's ear. "One dollar," he says.

"What?" Vijay asks.

"I'll bet you one dollar that is our tour guide." Kishore points at a petite blonde wearing jeans and a hoodie.

Vijay thinks about this. One dollar is forty-five rupees. That is a lot of money in India. You could have a very nice meal. On the other hand, practicing white-person recognition skills is important since he hasn't really seen any in real life before; they all look kind of similar.

"Okay? What do you say, dude?" Kishore looks at Vijay and continues, knowing Vijay will take the bait.

"Okay! I know that isn't her, *dude*," Vijay announces, practicing the word *dude*, confident in his decision.

She walks over to them, announces the bus is loading and gets on. It's the most painful dollar he'll ever lose. He has no job and had no reason for the bet. So naïve. So foolish. He had never made a bet before and will never bet again.

Step two: Get a JOB!

We're interrupted again, landing in Amsterdam. This layover is longer. We're back in a land of carbs and dairy. I can honestly say, while I didn't miss this stuff during our stay in India, it sure does hit the spot.

"So Kishore taught you to say *dude*?" I ask Vijay as I lick my double-scoop mint-chip waffle ice-cream cone. "That is hilarious! It always struck me funny that a house full of Indian guys, living on the East Coast, walked around calling each other *dude* all the time."

Vijay smiles and eats his single-scoop strawberry ice cream in a cup. "I think it's a movie influence. All the Hollywood movies have that word in it, so we just picked it up. I guess it was part of learning an American vocabulary," he concludes.

"I get it. I want to hear more!" I tell Vijay.

"Okay. Let's take a break a while. I have more stories," he agrees. "I'll pick up again on our next flight. Let's walk around a bit."

Our final flight takes off, Chicago bound. I don't give him much time after takeoff to get started again. "So, what's next for the FOB?" I ask.

Vijay rolls his eyes "Thanks, babe."

"Just testing out my vocabulary, practicing what I've learned," I tease.

Converting Rupees to Dollars

His housemates arrived a few months before he did. They're the experts. Sitting on the floor of his living room, he is eager to learn from them. A recurring topic is transportation. It becomes clear early on that life would be easier in the U.S. with a driver's license and a car. There aren't any rickshaws to take you around town. Aside from the bus, there is no other affordable transportation.

"All Americans drive five miles over the speed limit," he's told. "That's the American driving habit. It's expected. Just add five to whatever is posted and stay there! You'll never get a ticket as long as you're within those five miles."

Taking this information, he borrows a car from a driving school and heads for the Department of Motor Vehicles across town. He's nervous about the test. The administrator asks Vijay to start the car. He remembers the advice he was given by his housemates and consistently drives five miles over the speed limit. The test administrator observes and jots notes as he drives.

Vijay completes the test and pulls into the lot. He turns off the engine and sits silently for a moment. The administrator turns to him and begins . . .

"You know, you are very fortunate that I am going to give this to you today." His eyebrows furrow as he speaks. "You did everything very well, but consider yourself lucky. You need to hold your horses when you drive. You should always follow the posted speed limit. You drove five miles over the limit the entire time, which is illegal," he explains sternly.

"Oh. Okay. Well, thank you," Vijay says anxiously.

He is given the license!

Step three: Learn the laws and try to follow them as written.

"Oh my God!" I interrupt. "Are you serious? That is so funny. I remember the first time I took you driving in my car. You must have just received your license before I joined the program. I probably wouldn't have given you the license. I'm a stickler that way," I tease. "I understand, though, after seeing what it's like to drive in India! The rules and order of driving here versus there are absolutely incomparable. Did you drive a car in India?"

"Thanks, Liz," he responds to my teasing. "No car. I actually used a motorbike," he says. "I have another driving story for you if you liked that one."

"Okay!" I tell him. "I'm happy to hear stories about you. Anything from before we met."

He continues: "I went to Louisiana to visit a friend, Raj. He is a medical school friend who was working on a PhD at Tulane."

Vijay convinces Raj to buy him a ticket to visit Louisiana, which will be his first domestic flight and a new state to experience. Vijay wants to learn all he needs from this experienced, Americanized Indian he knows he can trust.

Hearing about the beach in Biloxi, Mississippi, they rent a car and decide to take a small road trip. Along for the ride are a couple of Raj's friends, a Pakistani guy and his wife. The guys take turns driving and eventually the Pakistani guy gets pulled over. After stopping the vehicle, the officer walks up to the driver's-side window of the car.

"Please hand me your registration and driver's license," the officer says through the window.

As the window is lowered, Vijay, sitting behind the driver, also rolls down his window. "Hello, Officer, how are you?" he says, excited by this new experience. He had heard that Americans are exceptionally friendly people.

"Put the window up, sir—I am not addressing you." The officer backs away from the car, hand at his waist, assessing its passengers. "Roll up your window," he repeats sternly. Vijay does as he is told and realizes this isn't an opportunity to make a new American friend.

"Where are you boys from?" the officer asks in a fresh 9/11 tone.

All four in the car identify themselves and start to take the situation more seriously.

"How long have you been here?" the officer then asks.

They all provide the information requested. As they continue to talk, the officer loosens up, runs the plates and IDs, then makes his way back to the driver's window.

"Do you think we could take your picture with us?" one of them asks.

The officer agrees.

"It's Christmas Eve after all. Holiday cheer prevented the citation," Vijay tells his friends as they pull away from the side of the road.

All the occupants agree.

Step four: Review step three and share with your friends.

"That is too funny!" I tell him. "Do you have the picture?"

"I can try and see if I can find it. It wasn't my camera, but I can send them all an e-mail and see if anyone has it."

"The captain has begun our descent into Chicago," the steward announces. "We want to thank you for flying KLM with us, as we know you have many options in your travels. Have a good day and welcome to Chicago."

"Welcome to Chicago, honey," I say. It really does feel

good to be back home. "I am so glad you shared these stories with me. I want to hear more about your life!"

We collect our luggage, go through customs and head for the L.

Standing next to my bags, watching the skyscrapers pass us, on a crowded L, I hold onto the handrail as the train turns.

"Where are you guys coming from?" a young man in a polo shirt asks.

"India!" I respond, excited to share.

"I figured something like that with the henna on your hands," he says, smiling.

I look down at what should have faded long before. I realize I'm going to begin a new job with henna all over my hands. And, in all likelihood, it will be there for several more weeks, judging by how clear the pattern still is.

I survived India. I think his family survived me. Also, I'm starting a new job soon! I'm ready to explore Chicago, dive into my new job and get to know this guy even better. Now that he's opening up and I've seen his home, I feel even more confident.

CHAPTER 5

We Do. Yes, We Do!

Jet lag be damned, Vijay goes back to work the very next day. I begin preparing for my first days in health care administration. Shortly after returning home, I join the administrative team of a long-term care facility, as their operations and finance administrator. I am excited about the opportunity and hopeful it will be a good fit.

I sit attentively in the administration office and stare at my new engagement ring as I wait for a meeting with my new boss. It overshadows the henna that was supposed to last two weeks. I'm so pasty I'm not sure the peacock design will ever go away.

"We need to order business cards," the owner says, sitting at his desk.

"Yes. We should order them with my new last name," I suggest.

"When are you getting married?" he asks.

"In November."

"Okay," says, nodding in agreement. "Shoot." He waits, hands on the keyboard, ready to type my new name onto the template.

I begin. "C-h-e-n-n-a-m . . ." He interrupts.

"Wait a minute," he says, turning his head to look at me. "It sounds like you are going to keep on spelling." With a slight smile and apprehensive tone, he looks across the desk.

"Yes. It's a little longer than my maiden name." I smile back and continue spelling, "c-h-e-t-t-y."

"Is that it?" He smirks. "I don't think your name will fit on one line." He pauses, then highlights the type he just entered on the template. "Yep. I'm going to have to change the font size." He looks at the screen and then at me. "Do you want to consider keeping your maiden name?" He smiles as if joking.

"I want the same last name as my kids," I say and smile, thinking about how cute they're sure to be.

Astrologer consulted and stars aligned, our wedding day is fixed via Atha Garu, my soon-to-be mother-in-law. It will be November 27, the weekend of Thanksgiving. This is apparently the most auspicious time. The date's been provided reluctantly, as the astrologer has had to overlook the certain catastrophe of this bad match.

After submitting what feels like our entire printable life to Homeland Security for a visitor's visa, it is official: Atha Garu (mother-in-law) and Mama Garu (father-in-law) have been granted visas to come to America. I view their first visit with optimism; all my American friends voice skepticism.

"A month?" a colleague asks, as we stand in the workroom, doubt in her voice.

"Yep." I smile, looking down at the financial packet. "Six weeks, actually."

"You have a studio apartment. How is that going to work?" She continues to look at me, concerned.

"I guess we'll make it work. I'm nervous, but also excited. It's totally going to work," I say, half trying to convince myself it doesn't sound like a lot. A hectic job that I love and Vijay busy with residency—time will fly. It'll be fine.

Later in our apartment, I ask, "Do you think your parents would like it if we booked them a room at an extended stay? They could have privacy, and it would be easier in the morning when we are all trying to use one restroom."

"What?!" Vijay asks me, shock on his face. "No," he responds quickly.

"What?" I ask, sensing he's insulted. I'm not sure what I said wrong. "It isn't a problem. They have a kitchen there and everything. It's just like an apartment. We can find the money. Are you worried they will think it's too expensive?"

"That is insulting. They will be isolated. It is a very rude suggestion," he explains.

"Why? I was just thinking they would have a proper room, more space and a kitchen. I thought maybe they'd welcome some privacy."

"They must stay in our home. They would rather sleep on the floor than be placed in a hotel," he tells me.

"Oh? Okay. I wasn't *placing* them anywhere. I was just

trying to be practical. We live in a studio apartment. I was actually asking out of respect," I explain. I drop it and start brainstorming sleeping arrangements in our furniture-less studio.

Back at work, other co-workers ask me questions.
"Is the rest of his family coming?"
"No, they weren't granted visas," I explain.
"Not even his brother?"
"No." I had no idea how hard it is for an Indian with funds, a sponsor and reason to visit America on a tourist visa.

Vijay's Indian friends have the opposite response when we tell them his parents are coming.
"They're only staying a month?" a sympathetic friend asks in disbelief.
"My dad has a job that he needs to get back to. He only gets a month off," Vijay explains.

We're on a budget, having just graduated. The studio apartment we live in has stairs and his mom recently had hip surgery. Also, it's literally one room, without furniture. So, Vijay suggests we move from Oak Park to Bensenville. I'm not going to lie: I'm pretty bummed. Our studio is just off the L, the first suburb west of downtown. But we're priced out of one-bedroom apartments in Oak Park. The complex we can afford in Bensenville does not have a direct transit link to the city and is right under O'Hare International Airport's flight path. But, it's affordable and has a bedroom, and the building has parking, an elevator and a laundry room. We haven't accumulated furniture yet. We're using a twin mattress on the floor as a couch, and our bed is some sleeping bags on an inflatable mattress that always seems to deflate halfway through the night. Moving will be a breeze, but we'll need an upgrade on amenities before Vijay's parents arrive.

On the weekend, we drive to Devon Avenue to purchase some Indian spices for their arrival.

"Don't forget to get a pitcher and bucket," Vijay tells me.

"For what?" I ask.

"For the bathroom," he says.

"Why will they need that?"

"They aren't going to be comfortable with toilet paper," he tells me.

"That's stupid," I say, intolerant. I don't understand.

"I didn't know how to use toilet paper when I first got here," Vijay says to me, a little defensive.

"What is there to know? I don't get it," I tell him.

He reminds me he didn't use toilet paper in India either.

Of course in India I thought about using my finger when faced with pooping in a hole, but I had brought baby wipes with me. I assumed it was a resource allocation issue. It never occurred to me that given a choice, toilet paper would be dismissed. I accept this rationale and purchase a bucket and pitcher for wiping and cleaning in the bathroom. I place them at the foot of the toilet, hoping this is where they belong.

Aside from arranging the new apartment, I also start to think about weekend entertainment and my Indian cooking. I learned a few things while in India and hope I can use what I've learned for some of our meals. Vijay doesn't seem to think his parents will want to leave the house while we are at work.

I don't believe they will want to be cooped up in an apartment all day.

October comes quickly and we head to O'Hare to pick up Vijay's parents. We watch as they exit customs wide-eyed and exhausted. As soon as we leave the terminal, Mama Garu fills his lungs with the tobacco of India. We push the luggage cart to the car and cram their bags in the back every which way.

Mama Garu and Atha Garu settle into our apartment quickly. Four hundred square feet doesn't take that much effort to familiarize oneself with. I assume because I enjoyed Indian food when we were in India that they would like to try an American-style breakfast. I proudly make an American breakfast of potatoes, eggs with salsa, toast and orange juice. The disappointment is immediately obvious, but they eat the meal politely.

"This is so sour!" Mama Garu says, scrunching his lips.

"My father has always been sensitive to sour tastes," Vijay tells me.

"Sour?" I say.

"The salsa and orange juice, babe," Vijay tells me.

"Vijay. Is this what you usually have, son?" Atha Garu asks.

"I usually eat cereal, Ma," he responds.

Her eyes look down and lips narrow. I look at Vijay, then back at as his mom. I wonder what she is thinking, but don't ask.

There is a pause in the conversation as they finish what is on their plates. I think about what I could make instead.

"I can cook when you are at work," she offers, looking at me. "Living in America, you are both master and servant. How do you make time for everything?"

We Do. Yes, We Do!

"I never thought about it this way before," I think aloud. "I guess it does kind of seem like that . . . Servants, or you can call them housekeepers, I guess—they would be too expensive for us," I continue. "I don't mind chores." She watches me. I'm not sure what she is thinking, but I know we've settled who will be doing the cooking for the remainder of their visit.

Within two days I realize Mama Garu and Atha Garu really aren't explorers. Vijay wasn't exaggerating. In my preparation for their arrival, I ignored the dependence factor completely. Having cable installed can't solve this. The beginning of winter in Chicago is cold, and they are nervous about the neighborhood and uncomfortable driving on their own or using public transportation. I didn't believe Vijay when he said his parents wouldn't leave the house without us. Every evening, when we arrive home from work, two pent-up visitors greet us.

Aside from a lack of activities or any social outlet, Mama Garu is also an eighty-cigarette-a-day smoker. His supply from India is gone quickly. He needs a constant supply, which one of us purchases daily on our commute home. Between the cost of a carton of cigarettes and the taxes associated with smoking in Illinois, it's turning out to be a pricey habit, one I did not budget for. We both have master's degrees in Public Health, so aside from the expense, we also know it isn't a healthy habit. I did a major project for my degree on "The Development of a Student Based Tobacco Policy Coalition," for crying out loud. But in this case, what can you tell a physician that he doesn't already know? Atha Garu is happy that these new circumstances are making her husband smoke a fraction of what he was smoking in India.

Bangles, Bindis and Babies

The apartment has decidedly become theirs. Not that they are invasive, but the apartment is extremely small and there is no getting around the fact that four grown adults are staying in it. Our cheap, white laminate countertops are yellow with turmeric, our bathroom is significantly wetter than usual and our living room has become a full-fledged bedroom. It's hard to have a private moment. In the mornings I wake up and sneak into the bathroom and out the door, hoping not to wake anyone.

Every night, over dinner, Mama Garu shares stories of what he saw from the three-by-five-foot balcony they spend a significant amount of time watching the world from. Mama Garu tells us about the dumpster pickup, the tractor that cuts the lawn as it's ridden and the machine that blows away all the leaves. I ask Vijay to encourage his folks to rent a car or take city transport to go explore. Vijay tells me they won't and not to worry, they're fine.

Throughout the evening, Mama Garu fills us in on the presidential election. It's an exciting time in America: Bush vs. Kerry 2004. They find the statistics fascinating and the debates amusing. They continually search for news programs that cover anything outside of the United States and wonder why we only report on U.S. news when we have a twenty-four-hour news cycle. Even with limited news in India, the entire world is still covered.

Taking the Eisenhower Expressway east into the city, his parents sit in the backseat, holding on to the grab straps tightly, observing their surroundings from the window. They don't say much, but when they do speak, it reminds me of how I felt in India, excited and confused.

We Do. Yes, We Do!

"We are going really fast, Liss"—a suggestion to slow down perhaps. "How many kilometers per hour are we going?" They watch as we pass shopping center after shopping center on our way into the city.

"Well, the speed limit is fifty-five miles per hour," I say, glancing in the rearview mirror at them and then down at the odometer for a conversion. "So that's about eighty-eight kilometers per hour."

"Oh . . ." They both stare out the window.

"Don't worry. We are safe," I assure them. "Just wait until we get to California. The speed limit is even faster out there."

"We know you are a good driver, Liss. Will you be driving tomorrow?" Mama Garu asks while looking at Vijay, as if skeptical that Vijay can drive at such speeds. "This must take practice."

A couple of minutes pass, then other questions pop up. "There are so many rules in the U.S., Liss. What happens if you don't wear your seat belt?"

"Then you'll get a ticket," I respond.

"It is very organized, Liss. Everyone follows the rules here?"

"Yep . . . for the most part . . . We're an orderly bunch," I say, reflecting on various traffic scenarios I encountered in India, mainly the lack of any direction *or* order.

Once safely downtown, his parents stare at the skyscrapers. We find street parking right off the Magnificent Mile. This particular part of Michigan Avenue has stores as far as the eye can see. Vijay and I had decided earlier that this area is a good example of American consumerism.

Holidays approaching, the sidewalks are filled with colorful banners and lights. We walk down the street, looking into the windows of the storefronts, finally deciding to go into Crate and Barrel. They study the organized merchandise lining the shelves, comment on the sheer volume, check prices of various items and convert the price quickly into rupees. In the center of the store is an escalator that zigzags up to the third floor. They tell me they have never been on an escalator before. I watch the hesitation in Atha Garu's step and cautiously stand behind her, just in case there is an issue as we each take a step onto the moving stairway.

We all step off without incident and I wait for a reaction. There really isn't one, but she asks, "How much electricity must this city use?"

We take them to Rainforest Café because of the large, predicable menu and ask for the spiciest item available. We're told there really isn't anything on the menu that is very spicy and so resort to steak. Meat of all kinds has become a fascination and something Mama Garu has really come to enjoy.

Vijay quite frequently has overnight call at the hospital, so he often doesn't return until the following day. One such evening I ask his parents, "What would you like for dinner tonight?"

"We would like to go to the McDonald's," they agree.

"Really?" I ask. "*Why?*"

They look at me blankly.

"I mean, I can take you somewhere nicer," I offer, having a hard time figuring out if they really want to eat at McDonald's.

"Everyone knows of this place," Mama Garu says. "We want to try one of these hamburgers."

I'm surprised. "Okay," I say. "Let's go."

We drive up to the golden arches and park. We walk past the plastic booths, supersized meals on plastic trays and children bouncing around like kangaroos.

We Do. Yes, We Do!

"What would you like to eat?" I ask, pointing at the menu above the line of cash registers.

They stare in amazement and uncertainty. "Um. What do you suggest, Liss?"

"Well, let's go with the standards," I suggest as I look up at the backlit menu and wonder what the standards are. I haven't been in a McDonald's since the french fry/lard scandal of the nineties. It's not exactly a vegetarian's delight.

"We'll take one cheeseburger, fries and a Big Mac," I tell the cashier, while keeping in mind meals in India are portion appropriate. The small coffee I ordered them earlier in the week had to be split in two and shared.

Two minutes later, the food is handed to us in the classic McDonald's bag. We drive our dinner back to the apartment and settle down at the dining table. I get out a place setting and ceremoniously remove the food from the bag and wrapping. As we unwrap each item with care, I get a knife so the burgers can be split and shared. Once the burgers are exposed, their faces drop.

"Is this what they look like?" Atha Garu asks.

"Yes," I respond, watching their reaction.

"They don't look special," Mama Garu says, looking up at me.

"I know." I take a deep breath. "If you want something after this I'll make something."

They take their first bite.

"It's okay, Liss. We will eat this," Atha Garu reassures me, swiveling her head from side to side, with clear dissatisfaction on her face.

Mama Garu puckers his lips, "The tomato sauce is so sour."

From now on, whenever food comes up, we discuss the

fact that America has fat, juicy cows, chickens and vegetables available at all times, yet we choose to eat "these things."

The night before we leave for California, Vijay and I lie in bed and talk about our upcoming trip.

"Do you think your brother is sad about having to stay in India?" I ask Vijay.

"I guess so," he says.

"How come Thatha didn't come?" I ask. "He got a visa, didn't he?"

"It's such a long trip and he is so old. He would have come if my brother had gotten a visa," Vijay tells me.

We're silent for a while and I think about how sorry I'd feel if my brother couldn't come to my wedding. I also think about what our apartment would have been like if they all came.

California bound, the four of us board our flight out of O'Hare, six days away from our wedding. Vijay starts to worry about what his parents will eat while we're staying with my folks. Bland American food is not very appealing to them and the week ahead is going to be packed with Thanksgiving, our wedding, and people in and out of my mom's house and the hotel. Cooking Indian food is time consuming. We won't be able to make fresh curry or sambar for every meal.

After an uneventful flight and drive to my folks' house, my soon-to-be in-laws settle into the guest room. Mama Garu begins watching a flurry of television, mainly focusing on Thanksgiving Day traditions. My mom and I focus on wedding-day preparations, making lists of everything that needs to happen for the entire weekend. We're going to need to make more food than usual, with an emphasis on spicing things up.

We Do. Yes, We Do!

"I'll buy jalapeños to make everything really spicy." She thinks about this a while. "I'll buy some antacid for the rest of us," she adds. "I made some chili for tonight. I added a whole bunch of peppers. It turned out about as spicy as I can take it, so I added some more."

"That should work." I smile, knowing full well that it definitely will not be enough.

Three days until the wedding, Vijay and I leave for the county clerk's office with one final question remaining. What should my last name be? Vijay's full name is quite long, Vijay Kumar Naidu Chennamchetty Jayaprakash. Should I take Chennamchetty-Jayaprakash? Should we abbreviate and choose Chennamchetty? I'd like the same last name as our children, but adding a last name with twenty-three letters to a first name with nine doesn't seem very appealing. Handing out business cards at work has already given me a glimpse of my new long-named life. Hasta la vista to saying my name correctly. Sayonara to my short, simple last name. Goodbye, one-lined driver's license. No one feels the need to discuss the origin or spelling of Palmer. I may never go anywhere again without someone making a comment or asking a question. We can't get any closer to marriage than a license. Giving up part of how I identify myself makes it start to feel real. *Tick-tock.*

The sun comes up and we lie in bed, talking about our fast-approaching day. I'm task-focused, outcome-driven, running through all the things that we have to get done. Vijay stops me.

"Do you remember the first time we met?" He's lying on his side, looking at me.

I turn my head to look at him. "At a pub night for our department?"

"No. At our teaching assistant orientation. In Arnold House . . . room 312," he responds.

"Not really." I'm surprised he remembers this.

"Well, I do. You were so put together. So professional. So elegant," he says.

"Elegant!?" I say. "That's not a word I've heard used to describe me."

"Yes. Elegant. You were dressed professionally and your hair was straight back in a bun." He looks into my eyes. "You were taking the opportunity very seriously." He smiles and pauses. "Anyway, do you remember the ice-breaker we were given?" he continues.

"No."

"We were told to give an adjective to describe ourselves. We went around the room stating our adjectives and when it was your turn you said, 'I'm organized.'" His smile gets wider as he recalls the memory.

"Oh yeah?" I say. "I don't remember this at all, but I'm not surprised that's what I said." I start to smile too.

"Yeah! You did. I remember thinking, 'Organized? I'm organized. What kind of descriptive word is that? That's all she's got?'" He laughs. "Then, I got to know you!"

I look at him and wait for the punch line.

"You are the most organized, elegant, grounded person I have ever met. This wedding is going to be great." I lie there silently. I don't have a response, but I'm no longer running lists in my head of everything that needs to happen.

I look into his eyes and smile back at him. I'm ready to marry this man.

We Do. Yes, We Do!

The countdown continues. Two days before the wedding, Thanksgiving arrives. Mama Garu and Atha Garu have spent the previous four days watching the Cooking Channel. Informed now, they can explain all the various ways to cook a turkey. My stepdad, Papi, decides this Thanksgiving the turkey should be cooked on the rotisserie grill in the backyard. Mama Garu watches as the grill is prepped, the rotisserie installed and the turkey set.

A few hours later, the men do their turkey-checking rounds. As soon as the grill cover is raised, it's obvious the rotisserie motor has burned out. The more Papi tinkers with it, the more frustrated he becomes. Pieces of the rotisserie are disassembled and the turkey, the victim of much verbal abuse, drips grease and ignites in flames.

"God damn it," Papi says, frustrated.

Mama Garu's eyebrows rise as he steps away from the grill, arms crossed, and looks at the flaming turkey.

"The turkey is burned!" we hear. Mom and I glance at each other, neither one of us willing to go outside. This frustration doesn't need a crowd.

Mama Garu looks at us through the kitchen window, somewhat amused, slightly alarmed. The rest of us stand in the kitchen, watching the growing commotion through the sliding glass door.

"I think that turkey may end up in the pool," my mom says with a smile. "Good thing we have an extra breast in the oven," she whispers to me.

Burn victim in hand, Papi says optimistically, "I was able to salvage some parts." He walks through the slider with a half-charred turkey on a platter. "I think we may have to cut off the burned part," he adds with masculine confidence.

Mama Garu walks through the sliding door, chuckling. He returns to his place on the sofa, watching the Food Network for other traditional dishes. I can only imagine what Vijay's parents are thinking. *Thanksgiving must be a time of high stress for Americans.*

The food is put out, buffet style, in the dining room. Everyone grabs a plate and finds a spot to eat.

"Remember that chili? That was good," Vijay's parents say, swiveling their heads in agreement.

The final day before our wedding, we review the steps of the ceremony with his parents. We ask my father, Vijay's father and Papi to speak and our mothers to pour sand from India and California into a vase. I can't tell whether or not my in-laws are nervous about this public task, but they gracefully accept.

The idea to have a traditional American wedding has been Vijay's from the start. When we first talked about getting married, I assumed we'd just combine a little of this and a little of that from our bicultural fusion. But Vijay really wants to experience a stereotypical American wedding without having any idea what one is like or how to plan. He also wants us to have a Hindu wedding in India at some point. So, that's the plan. He has left all decision making to me. I quite literally have ultimate bridal control with no stress of disappointing my partner.

"Here we go," I say, looking over at Vijay, as I step out of the car and walk into the club for our rehearsal.

"Here we go." Vijay squeezes my hand, walking into the country club for the first time. The sky is cloudy, so aside from reviewing the wedding we talk about rain contingencies. *Really? Rain?* It never rains in Southern California.

We Do. Yes, We Do!

The following morning, I wake up next to Kate, my maid of honor. Vijay spent the night in our hotel suite, and she spent the evening with me at my folks' house. Since I'm not one for makeup and she has fashion sense, she's a big help. After our hair appointments, we arrive at the club typically early, rain drizzling. Everything is set up inside. I haven't talked to Vijay but know if he isn't already here, he's not far behind.

The groomsmen and bridesmaids are segregated into separate rooms as we get ready for the ceremony. The bridesmaids change into gowns and take pictures. I wonder what the guys are doing. The ceremony time comes and goes and I wonder why we haven't been called. We're told two groomsmen, the Indian ones, have not made it to the club yet. Their being late is not surprising, as I've learned that *Indian standard time* is a long-standing joke among Vijay's circle of friends. So, I try to ease the jitters and remember it's not important.

Our wedding guests are a pretty international crowd, our friends and family representing a good part of the world: Germany, Mexico, India, Nepal, Iran, El Salvador, Trinidad, Scotland and Canada, as well as Texas, Illinois, Maryland, Louisiana, Massachusetts and California.

I make my way down the aisle on the arm of my mother, happy and grateful so many people were able to make it. My eyes gradually find my partner, front and center, waiting for me. His dark brown eyes look at me with excitement and his lips are nervously pursed. I recall a conversation about kissing, in public, in front of his parents. I wonder if he's still thinking about this. I glance at our bridal party, filled with siblings and childhood and school friends.

The ceremony is short and sweet. We recite our own vows and say "I do." I kiss Vijay for the first time as a married woman. It's a sweet kiss, but quicker than I anticipated. I'm pretty sure he *is* still thinking about kissing in public, in front of his parents.

Everything feels perfect. The rain can't keep us from celebrating. The red, black and white décor pop throughout the reception room and guests smile as we enter hand in hand.

"Introducing Mr. and Mrs. Vijay Chennamchetty," the DJ says. "Let's get this party started!" he urges as the music begins.

We gave our DJ a few CDs of Bollywood hits we purchased on Devon Avenue before leaving Chicago. I'm totally shocked at how much Indian men like to dance, and I don't manage to sit down to eat or drink for the rest of the night as I'm twirled around the dance floor.

"This is so much fun," Vijay tells me.

"Is this what you had in mind?" I'm curious.

He looks at me as we walk toward the cake. "This is better than I imagined," he tells me.

I have no idea what to expect of a Hindu wedding, but I am absolutely sure it will be nothing like this one.

As all weddings do for a bride and groom, the evening ends too quickly. We make sure Vijay's parents make it back to their hotel room and then meet some out-of-town guests in our hotel suite for a late-night after-party. Eventually, even the after-party has to end. Vijay and I settle in for our first night as a married couple, our one night of privacy for a few more weeks until his parents fly back to India.

We intentionally forgo a honeymoon. We spend the time with Vijay's parents since they have come so far and have only a few weeks left. My folks' house becomes home base as we spend the remainder of our trip and money taking them on a typical LA tourist tour: Wax Museum, Hollywood Walk of Fame, beaches and Disneyland. I'm proud of myself for making this choice, postponing a honeymoon and vacation time until another year. I'm making a gesture I know they will appreciate.

Since it's become a family affair, I ask my mom to go with us to Disneyland. She agrees. Except for the lack of unlimited smoking areas, I think this is my in-laws' favorite attraction. We make our way through the park, stopping at each designated smoking station as we go.

Eventually, we get on the jungle cruise. The ride is packed, so we can't all sit together. Vijay sits between his parents on one side of the boat and I sit with my mom on the other.

The safari guide asks, "Is anyone here celebrating a special occasion?"

"Oh! They are on their honeymoon!" my mom says pointing to us, a huge smile on her face. I look at her, surprised she said something. She's not the type to draw attention to herself. Everyone else on the boat turns to see who she's talking about. I sit on the bench and look across the aisle at my husband, realizing now, she's poking fun.

"Who is?" the guide asks, looking at the group, unable to figure out the situation.

"These two—they were married Saturday," she says, pointing again. "They brought their parents along." She laughs at her jab and continues to tease.

The safari guide looks at us lamely. "Oh." He pauses for a moment, then adds, "Well, that's just sad."

Everyone laughs.

And so it goes.

CHAPTER 6

DINKs

Apartment empty once again, we finish out our lease in Bensenville. It seems like everyone is telling us real estate is a great investment. Now that we're married, we agree. Oak Park is our favorite community and we watch the market closely, ready to pounce at a moment's notice. We find a condo that needs work and purchase it using ten thousand dollars Thatha sent Vijay as the down payment. We score an adjustable rate mortgage, feeling lucky for the opportunity.

We're happy to be back in Oak Park, for its ease off the L, multicultural feel and walkable village. We celebrate living our young married life as DINKs, dual-income-no-kids, and spend as much time as we can in the city. Vijay says he loves Chicago and wants to live here forever. I remember him saying the same thing about Massachusetts. He is so adaptable.

Vijay's residency keeps him very busy. He is fascinated with human behavior and finds this year of his psychiatry residency even more interesting than the last. He comes home excited to talk about psychoanalysis. I spend a significant amount of time commuting to and from my job and take this first professional opportunity very seriously. I know I'm good at it and love my responsibilities. I try to involve myself in as many opportunities as I can to learn, grow and eventually, move up the corporate ladder.

"How's psychiatry going?" I ask Vijay as we sit down for dinner.

"Fine," he tells me.

"So, are you happy now?" I ask him. He looks at me, puzzled. "I mean, are you happy you are a doctor now?" I've been hesitant to ask this, worried he'd say no since he told me he never wanted to be a doctor when we first met.

He surprises me, though. "Yes! I love my residency. This year we're focusing a lot on psychotherapy and I love it!"

At home, Bollywood films become a new obsession, with over-the-top drama, parampara (tradition) and amazing dance scenes. I dive into Indian cooking, trying to make anything and everything I can, and encourage Vijay to tell me his favorite dishes. Weekend trips to cultural events become more appealing. He is indifferent toward participating, but our Indian friends love my enthusiasm. I assume he's also enjoying it, even if he's not very expressive of his opinion.

Vijay critiques the food I make and shares what he'd do differently. Usually, a lack of salt is the biggest issue. I can now make rice, chana masala, palak paneer and aloo matar. We've attempted samosas (little Indian potato pockets) and parathas (an Indian layered bread somewhere between a tortilla and a croissant), both delicious but more complex. I plaster the condo with Post-it notes, labeling everything with Telugu words, and ask Vijay to teach me how to pronounce the alphabet on our evening walks around our neighborhood.

For the first and probably only time in our married lives, I earn slightly more money than Vijay does and feel great knowing that I am making a contribution to household expenses. Right out of graduate school neither one of us is making a ton of money individually, but together, $80,000 a year feels like an amazing start.

Most of our income is going straight into the adjustable rate mortgage we just secured. The housing market took a hit right after we closed, but our realtor tells us Chicago is resilient, so we feel confident and lucky.

All of my downtime is spent working on our home. My dad flies up from Texas for a long weekend to help us replace our linoleum kitchen floor. We tear up the stained, worn carpet, put new tile in the kitchen and update the bathrooms. I work alongside him, learning and planning our next projects as we go. I recruit Vijay to help paint the walls. As soon as he dips the roller in the pan, I can tell he's never done any manual labor before. He glides the roller over the wall in zigzag fashion, skipping parts, leaving giant holes and streaks on the wall.

"What are you doing?" I ask, arms crossed.

"Hmm?" He continues to roll, totally oblivious.

"How are you going to cover the wall that way?" I move closer to him.

"What do you mean?" he says.

I don't want to micromanage a paint job, but I'm pretty sure when he's done I'm going to have to do it over. "You have to cover the whole wall. What about all these holes?" I point at the wall.

He just stares blankly at me. He is sweet. Innocent. Completely oblivious. He has clearly never painted a wall before. I didn't think instructions were necessary. I just thought manual labor was something everyone was born knowing how to do.

"This is not for me," he quickly decides. "It's too much work."

"Work?" I say. "It's saving us money." I grew up pinching pennies. There is absolutely no way my mom could have afforded to hire people to fix anything in the home she rented. I have vivid memories of her plumbing the kitchen sink, painting the house, mowing the lawn, pruning the trees, fixing broken cabinetry, rigging the car door with a coat hanger so it would continue to work. India may be a developing country, but Vijay didn't grow up in it as a poor person. He had access to things, to staff, to amenities. I seem to have lumped the two—poor person and developing country—into the same pot. They don't go hand in hand, though. They are two different things.

We're lucky to have close friends in Illinois, since neither one of us has family around. Saraswati, my housemate from graduate school, joined a PhD program at Purdue. We drive to Indiana to visit her as often as we can. Another colleague from UMass, Pinky, who married a Turkish man, Moto, also lives in Oak Park. It's nice to have them in our lives. We are free to do what we want, when we want, and go where we want. It really doesn't get much better than this.

Vijay teaches me more about India through visits to Devon Avenue, a heavily Indian/Pakistani street in Chicago. We drink coconut water straight from coconuts and fresh-squeezed sugarcane juice from a street vendor. It feels so exotic to me. I've never lived in such a large city with micro-communities. I soak in the sari- and salwar-kameez-wearing people as we order tasty Indian food at snack shops and restaurants. I ask for my meals as spicy as they'll make it and shovel the food onto my fingers, proud I've mastered the South Indian eat-with-your-hands technique.

"Babe, only South Indians eat that way," Vijay tells me. "This is a North Indian restaurant."

"But we're South Indian," I whisper back with a smile and take another scoop. I'm pretty sure he likes it.

It doesn't take long before I discover Delhi chaat (Indian nachos), and for a while forgo all other Indian fare for this new favorite snack.

Vijay rises every Tuesday and chants his Hanuman Chalisa, forty little prayers. Before coming to the United States, an astrologer told him that Tuesday is an unlucky day for him. Since I've known him, he's taken this news quite seriously. Every Tuesday morning, he kneels on the floor, holds his prayer book, even though the words were memorized long ago, and chants his Chalisa. He very rarely misses a Tuesday prayer. This, he is confident, will counter the fated bad luck of Tuesday. He has also decided to give up meat on this day. He loves meat and believes this added sacrifice will be appreciated.

DINKs

On the off chance he misses a Tuesday prayer, he'll punish himself with a week of vegetarianism. He constantly toys with becoming a vegetarian full time, which he tells me will boost his karma.

I plunge into a book, *Am I Hindu*, my brother-in-law gave me. I take understanding Vijay's religion seriously. By chapter two, however, I discover that Hinduism, according to this book, is a patriarchal religion. Even if I wanted to, I couldn't convert to it. Realizing I'll always be an outsider, I close the book.

Our Indian base grows and all of a sudden I am part of the Diwali/Deepavali (festival of lights) celebrations, Dandiya Raas (a traditional folk dance party) and temple visits. I feel comfortable in Indian clothing and with Indian slang, calling Indians "Desis" and offspring of traditional Indian immigrants who raise American-born children "ABCDs" (American-born confused Desis). Vijay tells me I should probably stop using that acronym.

"It was cute before you started using it in public," he tells me.

"Well . . . *you've* used it. I didn't think of it as derogatory," I retort, realizing he's right; it is insulting.

I'm obsessed with integrating Indian life into our home décor, make increasing amounts of Indian food and use every excuse to wear Indian clothing whenever possible. I review Telugu words, written on Post-it notes and stuck to furniture, appliances and rooms in our condo, hoping the subliminal messaging will rub off on me. After work, Vijay and I take walks and practice the Telugu alphabet, which I know I will never pronounce correctly but try anyway. I buy writing workbooks and practice writing each character of the alphabet in them. I know how ridiculous I may seem to everyone else walking around town in a sari, but I feel proud and culturally inclusive. Vijay is supportive of my new passion, but seems less interested than I am in maintaining a full-throttle Indian lifestyle.

After binge-watching Bollywood films, I romanticize a custom depicted in one called Karva Chauth. Basically, the *event* lasts a day. To my understanding, I should not eat from sunrise to sunset. This sacrifice is for the safety and longevity of my husband. It takes place on the fourth day after the full moon in October. I find the lucky October day and plan my Karva Chauth. I envision the simple sacrifice and Vijay's appreciation of my dedication to him and his culture.

I arrive home before sunset and make dinner, waiting for Vijay. I had cereal before the sun came up and otherwise only drank water. I am hungry! Vijay walks through the door about an hour after me.

"Hi, honey!" I excitedly say to Vijay, keenly aware he's a little later than usual. My mouth is watering and I'm excited to share my latest cultural gesture.

"Hi," he says to me.

"Would you like to bless me?" I ask.

"What are you talking about?"

This is already more lame than I envisioned.

"It's Karva Chauth. I've fasted the day for your longevity and safety," I explain, smiling. "And I'm crazy hungry!"

"That's a North Indian festival," he tells me, laughs a little and heads to our bedroom to change. I'm a bit surprised. He's kind of dismissive. I thought he would be excited, or maybe proud of me. The part of my fantasy where he whisks me into his arms with love and admiration, then together we stare lovingly into the moon, as shown in the movie . . . that part isn't going to take place. I grab a plate and scoop palak paneer and rice onto it, then obstinately sit on the couch.

Vijay sits down next to me. "Thanks, babe." He puts his hand on my knee, as I realize maybe I took this whole thing too seriously.

"Sure," I say, with little enthusiasm. I want him to feel my hunger.

He gets up to grab a plate, then returns. We eat quietly for a minute. "You know, it's cute, but it isn't a South Indian custom," Vijay says.

I look at him, waiting for more information. "I didn't know that. I thought it was a Hindu celebration. There are Hindu North Indian and Hindu South Indian things?"

"In India I grew up all over the country, but my family is from the South. We didn't participate in all Hindu festivals," he says. "This isn't something my mom did growing up."

I am trying to embrace his culture and religion, following the lead from our Indian friends. It's a diverse group, though, and without help I have no idea what practices his family would participate in. It's like pulling teeth to get some involvement from him. I haven't put my finger on what's going on, so I tell myself to just enjoy Hindi films and try to relax my drive. He'll tell me if he's in need of cultural acknowledgment of some sort.

"Babe," he says, breaking my thought process.

"Yes?" I look up at him.

"I was going to wait for our anniversary. It's one year next month." He holds out a small box. "But, this was sweet. You can open it now," he says to me.

I look down at the box and back at him. I take the box and open it. Inside is a wedding band that matches my set.

"It's for the other side of your engagement ring. I know you like symmetry," he says with a wink.

"I do!" We kiss. I examine my finger. "It's perfect!"

He doesn't know each anniversary doesn't have to include jewelry and I'm not going to tell him.

We continue to explore the city and adopt a lifestyle that fits. Vijay grew up with a housekeeper, a stay-at-home mom and access to military base perks, like riding clubs and staff. I grew up in a single-parent home without any extra perks. We're both working long hours and Vijay understands I don't have a lot of time left for housework after work. So, we divide household chores, laundry and meal preparations.

My parents tell us not to rush into having kids too quickly. Vijay's parents tell us we're getting old and had better start. We consider having kids and overanalyze the consequences and benefits of such a choice.

"Well, if we have a baby now, we can send it to India. My parents can care for it while we work," Vijay tells me.

"WHAT?" I'm shocked that this is even a consideration.

"Well, what would we do with a kid right now? We can't care for it with the hours we work. We can't afford for you to stay home and take care of one. A child would have full-time support in India. My parents could look after our baby until it is older, and then we won't be so busy and we could send for it." He says this as if this is actually a real thing that people do.

I stare at him. I don't think child-rearing means the same thing to him that it means to me. I guess we've never had this conversation. I grew up without any extended family around. My mom worked hard and made sacrifices for my brother and me. Not having a partner to help her may have been less than ideal, perhaps, but there is no way she would have left either one of us! Similarly, I'd never ship my kid to India to live there because I don't have time. I'm flabbergasted. "What are you talking about?" I interrupt his little brainstorming session.

"Well, sure. My cousin, who lives in London, sent her kids to India. And you know my friends Krishna and Sharmila in Florida? Their baby is in India. They work long hours too," he explains. "Family units are tight; we support one another. Even if they are so far away. It's good for the baby."

I think he's making an argument in favor of shipping our theoretical baby to the other side of the planet because we don't have time for it. "Well! I can tell you right now that will never happen! I will never intentionally have a child and then miss its life on purpose." I'm horrified. "What's the point of even having a child?" I demand.

Vijay is calm and collected. He doesn't get all hot and bothered about the idea. It's cultural. It's logical. It's not emotional. This is shocking to me. I hope his psychiatry residency includes a rotation on child development. Where's the biological, psychological and emotional stability for the child-parent relationship in his *send our child to India* plan?

"Part of the luxury of living in a developed country is the right to have abandonment issues when you go through adolescence and young adulthood. Sending my child to India to be raised by its grandparents would definitely entitle said child to therapy once reunited with me," I tell him.

Vijay hears my utter terror. "It makes more sense to wait to have children until we have a better foundation."

"I totally agree." I'm not ready to have a kid right now anyway. I need to think this parenting philosophy through a little bit and we clearly need to talk about our parenting approach more in general.

"Let's wait until after residency is over," Vijay continues. "Then we'll know what kind of job I'll have. We'll have a better idea of what we can afford so you can stay home with the kids."

It's that simple. We really just went on a cultural child-rearing roller coaster, came back around to the loading dock and ended the ride. No more conflict. No arguing. He listened to my reasoning, albeit frantic, and agreed with me. That's the end of it. I'm happy we are so blunt with each other. Simplifies things. No wondering what the other wants. It works.

We keep the birth control in check.

Two more years sneak by with the city as our playground. We save as much money as we can and focus on paying off debts accumulated in graduate school. Vijay's residency program is almost over. He needs to find a new job that will sponsor a new visa so he can stay in the country. Right now, he has a J-1. Marrying me doesn't change his visa status, and now that he has it, he's stuck with it. The only way to get out of it is to find an employer who can sponsor a waiver.

Taking a J-1 waiver job will allow us to stay in the United States. If he doesn't find one, we, or at least he, will have to move back to India for two years. It's called a home stay requirement. Although it would be an exciting adventure, I'm not exactly ecstatic about putting all our things in storage and moving to India. It would be a professional and financial setback for both of us.

With six months of residency left, we know we have to find an underserved community to sponsor Vijay's new visa.

DINKs

Since I don't know anything about immigration and Vijay doesn't know anyone who has transitioned this way, we consult an immigration attorney to explain our situation and find out what options are available.

"Why didn't you just get married in school?" the attorney asks as we sit in her office. "The immigration process would have been a lot easier if you had sponsored him on his student visa." She's looking at me as if I was the shortsighted one.

Yeah, why didn't you just marry that guy? I think to myself, looking out the window at some random pedestrian. "We weren't ready to get married at that time," I explain, a little irked that I'm being perceived as the cause for this situation. "We had only known each other for a year at that point," I conclude.

"Well, you would have been able to get through the immigration process a lot easier," she continues. Vijay's I-told-you-so eye stares my way as she talks.

Finding this less than helpful, we end our visit. We walk down the street hand in hand. I think back to that horrible marriage proposal in the stairwell of Arnold House and cringe.

We don't completely understand our predicament, but know Chicago is not considered an underserved community for our purposes. Concerned about where we'll end up, we put our condo on the market. Vijay starts a job search. The housing market in Chicago has really taken a nosedive and our perfect investment begins to feel more like a liability.

Vijay hears about a conference designed for people who are trying to convert out of J-1 visas. Turns out there are a decent number of them. I walk into the room pretty sure that aside from the presenting attorneys, I'm the only citizen there. I begin to feel what it's like to live with the pressure of an uncertain immigration status. The stress and complication of doing it right and the fear of making a mistake start to irritate my gut. By the end of the conference, we're a little intimidated and I'm definitely anxious we might actually end up living in India for a while.

According to these guys, there are only thirty waivers per state, regardless of the state's size. You have to file as soon as the file date *opens*, you have to do it correctly, obtain a medical license in the state where you are applying and have an offer of employment ready.

"Do you think we should hire these guys?" I ask Vijay as we walk back to the parking garage.

"I think the process is pretty straightforward." Vijay's confident.

"Yeah, but if we mess it up, we'll be living in India," I tell him. "Not that it would be bad to experience living in India for a little while, it's just not great timing. Don't you think?"

I know he thinks this is less of an issue than I do. But I want to make sure we are really careful, and he understands how worried I am about processing this visa correctly.

"The attorneys presenting the information want you to hire them," Vijay says to me. The conference was designed to create this take-home, fear-based message. The pieces of the puzzle are falling into place more clearly now. Vijay feels like if we follow the rules and read the instructions we could save a lot of money, money that we don't have.

To continue our stay in the U.S., the visa waiver we seek requires Vijay to work in a medically underserved area. We know this will mean a three-year contract in a community that

DINKs

has been looking for an American to fill the position for six months without luck. After those six months are up, they can open the position to J-1s. We start looking in medical journals for job postings. Then, Vijay stumbles upon a national website that lists each opportunity by state. He investigates options every evening after work. Everything we see seems to be in the middle of nowhere.

CHAPTER 7

Serving the Underserved

"How about Alabama?" Vijay asks, staring at the classified section of a medical journal.

I turn up my nose. "We don't know anyone in Alabama, babe." Looking at a map, I add, "Do you really want to be a biracial couple in rural Alabama?" I want to support him and be positive, but I also want to find a location I'm comfortable with.

"It looks like a good job." He looks up, sees my face and realizes there is no way I will move to rural Alabama. He needs more guidance.

I print out a simple state map of the United States and highlight the states I'll consider living in. I also rank them by preference, writing a huge #1 to #10 in the middle of each state's outlined border. He knows to look for jobs in the highlighted states. California is my number-one choice, as I want to end up there permanently.

He tells me I need to be flexible. "Thirty slots, babe. California is a big, desirable state! Each state only gets thirty slots every year."

"What if we don't find a job in any of the states I've highlighted?" I'm nervous now.

He puts together his résumé and starts e-mailing inquiries. It doesn't take long for him to receive responses. He's able to schedule interviews and narrows down the search. We're hopeful he'll not only get a job offer, but also one of the thirty J-1 waiver slots the State of California can give this year. Without the waiver slot, there is no job, and no stay in the United States.

He begins with interviews in Victorville, Modesto and the outskirts of San Francisco. He interviews with a cursing medical director, a patient mill and business partners who are trying to make the most money off the system by having their foreign medical graduates drive all over kingdom come. He is lukewarm about them, but realizes his options are limited.

The final interview we think he will take if offered, so I fly out too. It's in California, but it's in the desert, a place called Imperial Valley. I grew up in Southern California, a little north of Los Angeles, but I've never heard of Imperial Valley. I Google it. It's in the southeast corner of the state, between San Diego, California and Yuma, Arizona. It literally sits in the middle of the desert on the border of Mexico. The website is inviting enough, but I still want to go and see where we may live before we actually sign a contract.

We fly into San Diego and my mom drives down from Los Angeles to meet us. We head into the desert, thrilled the closest town is San Diego. My brother lives near UCSD; the area is gorgeous and there is so much to do. This is going to be great! Vijay pulls out the new GPS I bought him for a graduation gift. It loses signal when we get to the mountains. I'm not sure I've ever lost cell or satellite signal on a major highway before.

After an hour and a half of looking at boulders and sand, and a sarcastic discussion about how much it would cost to invest in a helicopter, we approach what looks like the beginning of a town. We pass a rest station and our first off-ramp. I pull out my map.

"This is it!" I exclaim. We pass exits two and three. "Oh, wait. That was it! I think this is the last exit. We'd better get off here." I can't believe we drove across the entire city diameter in one minute, but we did. I count four off-ramps—total.

We look out the car windows; there's not much green. Tract housing lines the south side of the freeway. The ground is radiating heat, a clear sign of the 110-plus-degree weather we just drove into. It is May and the beginning of summer. Chicago as my reality, I can see *underserved community* will also mean culture shock. Dirt and asphalt surround us. No one is walking on the streets or riding bikes. I don't see anyone in front of homes or milling about. It's too hot for outdoor activity.

We get off the freeway and head north on Dogwood. We pull into a gas station and I jump out to ask directions to Main Street, our first stop. The man behind the counter stares at me like I'm from Mars and points at the street next to the station.

"Oh, thanks," I say, feeling rather silly that I didn't look at the street sign. I'm used to so many more streets, traffic, congestion, frantic merging when you miss your turn. This is simple. Off-ramp. Street. Turn left. You are here.

Before we arrived, Vijay was introduced to a local physician via e-mail. He suggested a realtor on Main Street. Convinced we'd hit the bottom of the market, this physician and realtor told Vijay the Valley was growing and now was the time to buy.

Vijay drops my mom and me off to meet with the realtor while he attends his first interview. We walk toward the glass doors of the real estate office. The dry, brown grass crunches under our feet and I wonder why grass is grown in this climate.

"What are we doing here?" I ask my mom for reassurance.

"You have to be supportive. He doesn't have many choices." She pats my back. "When he gets back from his interview, be positive," she encourages.

"Okay," I murmur to myself. "Positive. I can do that." We swing a heavily tinted door open and walk into an office. Our new realtor greets us and shows us to his car. As he drives around the Valley, he tells us about the friendly people, how easy it is to get to San Felipe, Yuma and San Diego and emphasizes, "Except for the summer heat, it's a great place to call home."

As I sit in the backseat of the realtor's car, passing one sand-colored, terra-cotta-tile-roofed house after another, I can't help but reflect on our situation. I'm not sure I can do this. Giving up a profession that I love, with growth potential, and a huge city with an active social life to become an isolated housewife is making me uncomfortable. Trying to be supportive, I remind myself it's not Vijay's fault that his visa status has this catch or that a J-1 was the only type of visa his residency program sponsored.

Time passes, the realtor is still talking and it still all looks the same.

"Do you have any streets with green trees on them? Maybe a street that looks more established, or a street that has been here a while?" I ask.

"Oh yeah! We have a street like that," he responds energetically.

"One street?" I repeat.

"I'll show you a house on Sandalwood. There's one currently available," he says.

He starts to emphasize the county's growth. They have traffic, a rush hour even and a new mall. I listen and think, *Really? What does he mean by rush hour? A five-car line of traffic or fifteen-minute drive to work?* We're used to hour-long delays in Chicago.

We pull onto Sandalwood and sure enough, there are trees, established homes and a neighborhood that resembles what I had in mind.

We thank him for his time and call it a day.

"Let's check into a hotel." My mom looks beat.

"Okay," I say. We get dropped off at a Howard Johnson's and walk into the lobby.

"Hello." I stop at the reception counter. "Do you have any rooms available?"

"I'll be with you right now," a young girl says and then picks up the phone to make a call. I later discover this is a common sentence to use in the Valley when you actually mean, "Can you give me a minute?"

Moments later, she puts down the phone and looks up. "Yes," she says in the slowest high-pitched voice I have ever heard. She is dressed straight out of the eighties with two-inch nails, rainbow bangs and eyeliner to match.

"We need a room for the night." I glance at my mom.

She confirms two queens, nonsmoking.

"Follow me." She walks toward the lobby door.

We follow.

"You need to cross that street and then walk up the stairs." She points her very long acrylic nail toward a building across the way. "Follow me."

The key card doesn't work. She fiddles with it a while and then slams her hip into the door. It flies open and bangs right into the bed. We file in sideways, pulling our luggage with us.

"Are you fine?" she asks, while a very distinct smell of smoke pours into our nostrils.

"I think this is a smoking room," I say.

"No, it isn't," she insists.

"Oh, okay," I say. "I guess we're fine then." She walks toward the door to leave.

"Is there an air conditioner?" I ask, as a stream of sweat runs down my temples. I realize my clothes feel like I just took a jog in Kanpur.

"Yeah. It's over there." She points to the window unit.

Air conditioner humming, I sit on the bed and look at my mom slouched in the corner armchair, reflecting silently. An hour goes by and Vijay walks through the door.

"Interviews are complete for the day," he says.

"How did it go?" I ask.

"It was really nice. These are the nicest people I've met yet. I really like them," Vijay says. "The director was polite and even gave me a personal tour of the area in his car. He seems to know everyone."

"Well, that beats the last few interviews," I say, studying his face to try and figure out how he's feeling.

"They will even pay for our move and the immigration attorney fees when we convert from a J-1 to a J-1 waiver!" he says.

I look at his sweet, hopeful face.

"This sounds like a normal job, in an office with a regular patient load and staff. They seem to have a real team approach to patient care," he continues.

"So do you think this is it, then?" I ask.

"Well, no one would choose to move to a place like this," he says as he wipes his forehead. It's easily 110 degrees outside. "But the team seems really nice and very accommodating!"

"Well?" I say, as I hope the AC starts working more efficiently. "Looks like this is it." My eyes dart between Vijay and my mom. She doesn't say anything; I think she is trying to give us space.

One more meeting is scheduled for tomorrow, but this is, by far, his most favorable review. My stomach grumbles. I call down to the front desk for a recommendation on where to eat. I assume, since we are right on the border, that the Mexican food will be amazing.

"Hi. What would you recommend for dinner? Which restaurants are good near the hotel?" I ask.

"Well...um...like...most people close their restaurants during the summer. Because...well, you know...it's like really hot right now. 'Cuz it's like summer. But...um...well ...a mall was just built last year. They have food there." The girl hangs up the phone.

"Okay. Wow!" I say into the dial tone of the receiver. That was not a Chicago concierge call. "We are going to the mall, guys!" I say, wondering how you get to the mall and if it is true that restaurants close and people actually leave town when it's hot.

Over dinner, which turns out to be in an actual restaurant, at a nice new mall, we decide to accept the job if an offer is made. I mentally begin planning.

Back in our bed in Chicago, I ask, "Do you really think you can move to the Valley?"

"I can move anywhere," Vijay says. "I never really had roots. As a child I moved from place to place every three years. I'm flexible." He doesn't ask me if I can move, but I'm starting to tell myself that the break will be nice. I can travel, craft, read, rest and raise children. Maybe I can even learn to chill out a little. Stop and smell the roses. Do roses grow in the desert?

I give notice at work and prepare myself mentally. We fly back one more time to look at houses, but don't find one. We finish up our last few months in Chicago trusting our realtor to find us a house. He does and we purchase it via fax. Who knew home ownership is so simple? The housing market is down. According to everyone we've talked to, the Valley is growing. A perfect time to buy, so now we really feel we've locked in a great deal. And, turns out, loans are easy to come by too. We don't have any money to put down or a paycheck yet. We still close, no problem. 2007, what a year! We take our condo off the market and decide to rent it for a year, hoping the Chicago market will pick up.

The moving van arrives. The movers load our home into their trailer and head west. I pack essentials and our cats into our Honda CRV. My mom flies to Chicago to make the road trip with me. In two weeks Vijay will fly out to join me. He'll arrive on Friday and start work on Monday. I have those two weeks to create a desert oasis.

We purchase a tract house next to an alfalfa field in a small town called Heber, instead of the fixer in the established neighborhood. Our realtor assures us it's a bargain, and we convince ourselves this house is large enough that people will visit us and we'll forget about city life. Vijay's clinic is about twenty miles away. The locals tell us it's a crazy commute, but coming from Chicago, it'll feel like a breeze.

After a few weeks, the last of our boxes are unpacked and I'm restless. I start to look for work. There aren't many health administration listings. The local hospital has fewer beds than the skilled care facility I just left. I'm not sure the job market is big enough. After a couple of interviews, I realize it may not be my qualifications, or the job availability, but the fact that I'm not from the area that will be my stumbling block.

"Well, your résumé is great. I'd love to hire you. You'd make a great addition to our administrative team, but let's just say our board likes to hire from within. You know, people they know. Locals." *Really? Did I just hear that?*

A little discouraged, I decide to look for charity work instead. Everyone needs volunteers to do something. Vijay and I also think my quasi-forced break is a great time to start a family. This will keep me occupied while Vijay completes his contract. By the time three years is up, we'll move back to a city and the kids will almost be ready for school. I'll go back to work. It'll be perfect timing. We discontinue birth control and in typical Indian fashion, share this private news with his parents.

"It's about time," we are told. "Finally a child to carry on the name."

"We aren't pregnant yet," Vijay reminds them.

They are thrilled we are finally complying with their grandchild request and are sure to reiterate how little time there is to waste.

Daily tasks, like going to the local post office, keep me pretty entertained for the first few months.

"You're from where?" the postal worker says, looking at the return label.

"Here. Heber. I live down the street," I say.

"No!" he says, looking at me in disbelief.

"Yep." I grin.

He looks down at the package and back at me. "Well, I don't recognize you and I know everyone in this town. You live in one of those new houses down the way?" he asks while looking at the return address label, and then pauses. "How do you say that name?"

"It's phonetic. I know it's intimidating to look at. You say it just like it looks." I say my name. "Chen – num (like your leg is numb) – chetty."

"Oh! That's not so bad!" he says with a sigh of relief.

I have this exchange with him more than once.

Vijay's new job splits his time between two clinics. His staff is happy to have a doctor without an overinflated ego. He is happy to have staff that is friendly, competent and helpful. It's a good fit.

The culture shock subsides gradually as I try to fill my schedule. I get involved with a local nonprofit and hospital. I work on decorating the house and become totally engrossed in new hobbies like scrapbooking, sewing, small construction projects and painting furniture. We begin to find our groove, but I long for the social outlet I had in Chicago.

I gradually become resolved to the fact that being accepted in a small town may be harder than trying to blend into a crowd in India. Vijay's acceptance, it seems, comes with his degree. He's needed here. It seems the majority of families here were born and raised here. They have real roots, and it's obvious I don't. Getting more and more lonely and bored, I look forward to a positive pregnancy test.

A few months roll by. We talk to Vijay's parents about visiting them again and finally having our Hindu wedding. They ask about our children, or lack of children. We tell them we're trying. They ask if I've been tested.

"It's been too long, son. Something must surely be wrong with Liss."

We talk about whether or not to get tested. I tell Vijay in a world as crowded as ours, adoption could be a consideration. "My mom told me if she had married the right person, she would have loved to be a foster parent and adopt children." This concept is foreign to Vijay. But I think taking the pressure off of creating a biological child and starting our family this way could be a wonderful fusion. He isn't sure his parents will understand why we'd jump straight to that conclusion.

A few more months go by. I have become an excellent sale finder, online shopper, cook, interior designer, handyman, house cleaner and accountant. I have a budget worked out down to the penny. Our focus is to pay off all loans accumulated since graduate school, build savings and have some fun. I know exactly which days Dillard's, my new favorite department store at the new mall, puts their newly marked-down items on their sale rack and have an entire walk-in closet of nice clothes with nowhere to wear them.

I start cooking with butter and savory ingredients, like truffle, that I pick up on monthly trips to San Diego. My new wardrobe is getting tight. I desperately need to get in the water and exercise. The only gym with a pool in the county was installed too short. How can I swim in a fifteen-yard pool and get anything out of it? By the time I kick off the wall I'll be at the other end. I'm getting lazy and can come up with lots of excuses. It's hard to get motivated in the heat! I don't like our treadmill. I hate running anyway. Driving two hours to San Diego, each way, to swim on a team isn't worth it. I'll use every excuse I can come up with.

I'm eager for the day we get pregnant. I've never been able to sit around and wait for anything. I want to be productive and do something meaningful while we wait for this sentence to end. My *relax and smell the roses* plan is failing. The internet becomes my outlet. I search adoption agencies, investigate Peace Corps locations, consider nursing school and a PhD program. I look into moving to Washington, DC, to work on a political campaign. I become a poll worker and make sure my volunteer commitments are solid. Really, I have the time, energy and eagerness to do anything . . . but my husband is here. He's the one with the sperm. How will we get pregnant if I'm in Jordan volunteering or away working on some political campaign? So, I clean and cook and wash and organize.

Maybe it would have been a better idea to marry Vijay while we were in graduate school. We wouldn't be here. Maybe that attorney's glare was justified. She saw the long road ahead. Between a big fish in a small pond and a small fish in a big pond, I'm a small fish kind of girl.

I start to become more introverted. Vijay comes home from a long day of listening to people with *real problems*. I go an entire day without talking to anyone. Dinner is my main interaction with a person. I'm told my meals have become quite tasty. I'm reluctant to complain about my boredom because Vijay will quickly remind me that he spends his days helping people with serious functional issues, which I do not have.

A house can only get so clean. So when the opportunity to travel presents itself, I leap every time. Fortunate to have the ability to get up and go, I encourage trips that take us new places and get us out of the Valley as often as we can. Mostly, we go for short weekends to Los Angeles to visit my mom and Papi or San Diego to see my brother. But also, I plan a vacation to India.

After a few more months, Vijay starts to feel the pressures of a bored wife and childless marriage more strongly. He suggests I get tested. I tell him if I have to get tested, he does too. We schedule appointments with an infertility doctor and get the standard sperm count and tube inspection done.

"So everything looks good," I'm told by the infertility doctor.

"Really?!" So what is taking so long, I wonder?

"Well, if you want to take some ovulation pills to help, I can prescribe them," he continues.

"Okay. Well, what would that mean?" I ask.

"Well, we'd start simple and go from there. But, I have to tell you that will increase your chance of having multiples," he says. "The chance of having twins is about three percent. Or, one in thirty births," he explains.

"Oh my God! That high?" I say.

"No, that's naturally, without drugs," he corrects me. "If you think those odds are high, I don't recommend medication at this point." He chuckles a little.

I leave the office sure I will never take medication and call Vijay at work to share the news.

"Our sperm, eggs and tubing are all okay," I tell him.

We got the all-clear.

Where is our positive pregnancy test?

CHAPTER 8

Wife of an Immigrant

Our years in Massachusetts and Chicago were so carefree and fast paced. In the Valley we are isolated. Vijay has taken up golf. I bought him lessons for his birthday and he hasn't looked back since. He spends most of his time at the club after work and on weekends. I don't blame him. He needs to have some downtime between work and a bored wife. Golf isn't a hobby we share, though.

As Vijay's identity changes from an Indian to an American immigrant to an American, he struggles with cultural identity. With all my newfound time, I begin to think more about identity, inclusion, culture and race, spending quite a bit of time reflecting on Vijay's experience.

"You're turning white," a family member tells Vijay over

the phone, after he gives a response that doesn't agree with tradition. "Stop talking like an American. Don't speak English. Have you lost your language? What happened to you?" he hears time and time again.

"Why does it have to be *acting white* or *talking like an American*?" I ask after the phone call ends. How does one *act white* anyway?

I share how frustrated I feel for him. He doesn't act out or raise his voice when he tells me about these encounters. My reaction feels so much stronger than his.

"Should I just keep it to myself?" he asks with a shrug.

"I've just never had to deal with anyone talking to me that way and you, unfortunately, have." I can feel the wrinkles in my forehead as I try to explain.

Before marrying Vijay, I never felt what it is like to be an immigrant or a minority living in the United States. Loving Vijay gives me new respect for the struggle, the sacrifice and the so-called American dream. I have begun to feel his added burden of cultural discrimination, racism and isolation. Not having friends or family nearby adds an element of discomfort I hadn't noticed in Chicago.

"I don't understand," friend after friend says. "Doesn't he become a citizen because you are a citizen?"

"No. It's a little more complicated than that." I explain his visa status, the way the J-1 waiver position works and our eventual goal of citizenship. "It's a long process."

"Wow! I had no idea!" I hear repeatedly.

Comments and questions present themselves regularly, either based on fear and racism, or many times because they are from

Vijay's paranoid patients. Yes, I'm lumping bigoted people in with paranoid schizophrenics. I'm pretty sure that's an insult to the mentally ill, though.

"Are you a Muslim?" one patient asked with a concerned tone, sitting across from Vijay in his office.

"No," Vijay replied.

"No! That's all you said?" I ask him over dinner. He doesn't feel the need to give a lecture or take a stand; it doesn't get to him. He just sticks to the facts, calmly. "Why didn't you ask what that question has to do with anything?" I retort. "I would have married you no matter what. Black, white, brown; Hindu, Christian, Muslim, nonbeliever; girl, boy, transgender—I don't really care. I married a person, not a census classification." I feel my face turn red with frustration. "How can you stay calm all the time?"

"I'm used to it," he tells me. "I grew up all over India."

"So?" I say.

"So I'm from the south," he continues. "When we lived in northern India I was usually the darkest kid in my class."

"You mean there's discrimination in India based on shades of *darkness*?" I ask.

"Yep," he answers. "Racism is everywhere, Liz. It's not only an American thing. I was called all kinds of derogatory terms because I was darker than the other kids. That's just how it was growing up in the north," he continues. "Anyway, I'm not going to challenge a scared person in my clinic."

"How did that make you feel back then?" I ask him.

"I felt bad, of course. I was a kid. No one likes to be marginalized, but this is a lifelong experience. I'm used to it. I'm not as sensitive as you are. Honestly, I don't even pick up on it as much as you do; it's just part of my reality."

As we talk, I think back to a vacation we took in the Midwest. We found a nice-looking restaurant on a lake. The hostess took one look at us and said, "We don't have a table available." I was surprised as I scanned the half-empty dining room. It was open. People were eating, talking and laughing.

"You don't have tables available?" I asked.

"If you want, you can sit over there and order off the appetizer menu." She nodded to the corner of the restaurant.

Her attitude is really strange, I thought as we agreed, passing all the other patrons. Something didn't feel right. We sat down far from others and ordered a drink and talked about what we might want off the limited appetizer menu. I knew I'd never been refused seating in the dining room before. I was taking some time to process what the hostess meant. *Why can't she seat us at a table? The dining room is half empty.* Other people were walking in and being seated. There weren't reserved signs anywhere. We were sitting in a dark corner, far away from everyone else. I scanned the room again, taking note of all the white patrons for the first time. I wondered if we were sitting in the corner because of race.

I never ask a lot of questions when faced with these kinds of circumstances. I should. I should have given the hostess the opportunity to refuse service and tell us why. But I'm never prepared because I'm so surprised it is happening in the first place. I don't do *on the spot* well. After I have time to reflect, I can always come up with useful dialogue. Yeah, next time, when I'm in the exact same situation, I know what I'll say. Yet the situation is never the same. The players and vocabulary are always a little different.

We decided not to stay for appetizers . As we walked away from the restaurant, Vijay just went on talking about where else we'd like to go. "What else looks good, babe?" he asked.

"What else looks good?" I knew he wasn't the least bit concerned. "*What else looks good?* Do you know what just happened? I think they were hiding us!" I was shocked that he wasn't reacting.

"What? It's fine. We'll find something else," he continued. He didn't let it control him. He didn't rage. "I think you're probably right, but what are we going to do about it?" he concluded.

Sometimes racism isn't blatant, but it's present.

Another time, in Florida, as we were entering a mall hand in hand to purchase a wedding gift for a friend, two older white men passed us as we approached the glass doorway. I could see their reflection in the mirrored door as we reached to open it. They both turned to stare at us, eyes narrow with disapproval, watching us walk in. I felt it. Vijay felt it. We squeezed our hands a little tighter and kept walking, not looking back. It was an insecure feeling, a strange feeling, one I can't explain and one I had never experienced before. I could feel my heart beat harder because I felt vulnerable. For those few moments I felt very insecure because of the way those two men were staring at us.

I listen to stories Vijay shares with me, the daily interactions of his life. He doesn't come home angry or frustrated. I would. I guess that's the comfort of being squarely grounded as a white citizen in the United States. With my race, citizenship and passport to freely roam the world comes ignorance, entitlement and a feeling of absolute security.

Sure, I've had little moments that were *unfair*. I've written letters about my displeasure with a service or an outcome. I've stood my ground in traffic court after being given a ticket I didn't feel I deserved. I've argued that I didn't receive something I earned. I've been misunderstood. I'm not talking about those moments. I've never had someone blatantly discriminate against me because of my race. I've never felt insecure about my safety because of it before. I didn't grow up with strangers asking me what ethnicity I am, what nationality I am, what religion I practice or if I'm a citizen. I haven't been asked these things by anyone before marrying Vijay because I am white. It's that simple.

My mind wanders to another experience. A time race educated me without Vijay present. I flew home to California to make arrangements for our wedding. After finding my perfect wedding dress with Mom and Papi, we decided to visit a few hotels for ideas and pricing. We were in an old minivan my mom had bought when my brother and I were kids. It was in pretty bad shape. We drove by a Four Seasons and I thought, *What the hell, we have to start somewhere, right? This will be fun!* There were extra security cars and suits milling around the registration turnabout. There was clearly someone important staying there.

"I'll just jump out and get a packet," I told Papi.

"What?" he asked.

"Pull up to the curb and I'll jump out to get some information," I said, thinking it would be entertaining.

"Oh sure," he said to me sarcastically.

"What? Why not?" I asked, kind of surprised by his tone.

"Do you see all that security?" he said. "I'm a brown man."

He paused and looked in the rearview mirror. I look at him, shocked. "I'm not going to sit idle, in a beat-up car, as a brown man, on the curb of a Four Seasons."

That was the first time I ever heard Papi say anything regarding a feeling of insecurity associated with his race. He said it in jest, but it made my mom and me both stop and look at him. It shocked us because we don't define him as a brown man. We don't see him as someone to fear or as a threat. We see him as a kind man, a man we love, a man we admire, a confident, educated, successful assistant superintendent of schools.

My gut dropped as I looked him in the eyes through the rearview mirror. How evidently ignorant I was of the reality of others! This was a man I'd known for years, and yet I was completely shocked by this.

This wasn't active discrimination. No one told us we couldn't be there or questioned Papi. His response came from somewhere, though. The sentiment is organic. It is an ingrained emotional response where only white elite society is allowed. To be fair, I don't belong to it either. The difference is, I wanted to pretend I could have an elaborate wedding. A fun idea and a fantasy. I never questioned what we were driving, how we were dressed or if they would talk to me. I was confident I could request and receive any information I wanted. Papi, on the other hand, was worried about sitting in a car in the waiting zone. He was worried about being profiled, and maybe targeted because of the color of his skin. He didn't want to answer questions or be asked to leave, but he had an intuitive feeling that he would be.

I think back even farther to my undergraduate studies. My brother and I didn't grow up with any extended family in

California. It was always just the three of us. When my mom finally started dating, fell in love and moved away from my hometown, I decided to move to Baltimore. Both my mom and dad have family in Maryland. I wanted to feel what it's like to walk into the house of an aunt or cousin and be welcomed simply because I am a relative, to be loved for no other reason, forever welcomed, through thick and thin. For me, having never lived that made for a powerful experience.

With the love and inclusion of my Maryland experience, another thing happened. For the first time ever, I noticed a huge racial divide in society. For one thing, I was in Baltimore, which is pretty obviously racially divided. But also, my East Coast family is ultra-white. What I mean is, everyone is married to other white people. Some of the loving arms that greet me unconditionally are the same people who make jokes and comment about how *certain people* are moving into *our* neighborhoods. Or explain how everything is going downhill now. I was so surprised to hear openly prejudiced conversations. Oftentimes I'd leave the room when someone made a crude joke, mainly to process, but also because I had absolutely no idea what to say.

My own grandmother would shock me. One morning I missed my morning statistics class because I was sick. It was the first time I missed a college class. My friend RJ knew I took all my classes seriously and e-mailed me to say he'd bring me notes. After sleeping all morning, I walked down the stairs of my grandmother's townhouse. I could see her sitting in her armchair, looking worried. I walked over to her, wondering what was wrong.

"A black boy came by the house today. He said he had some notes for you from class," she said to me.

"RJ brought me notes!" I responded, surprised and grateful he was so prompt. I looked at her little body sitting in her chair, feeling uncomfortable with her words.

"Is that black boy your friend?" she continued in a fearful tone.

"Huh?" I responded.

I was flabbergasted. I stared at her and my mind started racing. This woman is a lover of children, family, food and gatherings. She is a kind, generous self-proclaimed good Christian lady, referencing the Bible and saints in conversation. She has had a hard life and lived extremely sad stories, but survived. She's a tough cookie. I started compiling this list of everything she is in my head as soon as she asked me that question, because I didn't want to believe she'd asked it. I love her deeply.

"Of course he's my friend," I finally said, angry at the question and angry at myself for not having a better response.

When I hear Vijay talk about his experiences, I am reminded of my own experiences that are so easily forgotten because they didn't truly affect me. I don't have to live with any of it. I think every family has these stories in varying degrees and every family dismisses them.

Back in his office, another patient educates him. "I know about you people in the Middle East."

"Oh?" Vijay says.

"What part of the Middle East are you from?"

"I'm from India. It's in South Asia, actually," he clarifies.

The patient stops and thinks about world geography for a moment.

Now that we're married and I share Vijay's name, I get questions too.

A cashier looks down at my receipt before handing it to me. "Thank you, Mrs. . . . um . . . Where is your name from?" I'm asked.

"It's Indian," I answer.

"Dot or feather?" he asks.

"The country India," I reply. *That question really isn't as funny and clever as you think.*

"So did you convert? Do you wear one of those head things?" he continues.

"A head scarf or a bindi?" I ask for clarification. I also think the question is silly, the guy is standing in front of me, looking at my head.

"What are those?" He realizes he doesn't know what he's asking. "You know, one of those head things that cover your head."

I explain the difference between a bindi, a head scarf and a burka. "My husband is from a Hindu family, so if I dress for a family celebration, I wear a sari. Sometimes I'll wear a bindi, a little dot on my forehead."

"So what are you guys?" I'm asked.

I don't even know what that question means, but take a wild guess and answer, "We don't practice Hinduism or Islam."

At least once a week I have an opportunity to provide an inclusive cultural viewpoint. Usually it's with someone whom I have never met. I'm guessing the comfort in approaching me comes from the fact that I look like the person asking the question.

"Last name, please?" I'm asked, as I drop off my car at the mechanic.

"It's quite long. I'll spell it for you, okay? Write small," I suggest, seeing the man is about to write what I'm saying. "C-h-e-n-n-a-m-c-h-e-t-t-y," I spell.

"Oh yeah! Thanks for the heads-up! I would have run out of space!" he says with a laugh. "What is that? How do you say it?" I'm asked.

"It's intimidating to look at but it's actually phonetic if you sound it out," I explain.

"Oh." A pause and smile. "It's like the Dick Van Dyke movie my daughter watches! You know which one I'm talking about?" His excited face looks at me.

"*Chitty Chitty Bang Bang*?" I offer after a couple of seconds and nod.

Then the singing begins. After several lines are recited joyously, a follow-up question always remains. "Has anyone ever told you that?" His smile lingers, eyebrows raised, in hopes he is the first to think of this.

"I have heard that before, actually." I smile. "I also on occasion hear 'Chim Chiminy, Chim Chiminy, Chim Chim Charoo,'" I add.

"Oh yeah! It's like that one too."

"Good old Dick Van Dyke!" we conclude together.

"Where is your name from?" I'm asked after my number is called in a city administration building.

"It's Indian," I say.

When the woman behind the counter looks at me confused, I clarify. "It's my married name."

"What tribe?" I can tell she is really interested.

"It's from the country of India, actually," I explain.

"Are you sure it isn't Italian?" I'm briefly challenged.

"Yes, I'm pretty sure," I respond. "My husband is an Indian, from India."

"Is India in the Middle East?" I'm asked.

"No," I say. "It's in South Asia."

"So, what religion is your husband?"

"He's from a Hindu family," I respond. "But he doesn't practice Hinduism himself."

And just when I start to think I am making some progress, the Disney plot is exposed. "Is he, your husband, a prince or something?" I have to break it to her: "No, he's not a prince in India, but he is *my* prince."

"Aww! How sweet," she says in a singsong voice, then helps me correct our bill.

As she works, I think about the prince scenario. I'm pretty sure a prince could do a lot better on the socioeconomic ladder, but I'll take it as a compliment.

Vijay is unfazed by what I consider cultural challenges. He comes from a place where you make it work or you don't make it. You keep your head down, do what you have to do and get through life. It isn't a pleasure cruise. He doesn't know what it feels like to live a life without these questions, assumptions and curiosity.

I do, though. I never had any of these conversations when I had the last name Palmer. I tell Vijay it's unfair his life experiences don't start on an equal playing field. I come from a place where you fall in love, get married, have children and communicate mutual desires in blissful ignorance of any racial struggles. I've lived a life free of assumptions about who I am. The reality of how people interact with him because of how he looks and the curiosity about our foreign name is strange to me.

We talk about 9/11 and how it may have shaped American awareness of the Middle East and South Asia. Vijay arrived in Boston a few weeks before 9/11 happened. He tells me about a friend in the physics program being questioned uncomfortably by his professor regarding his whereabouts that day, and the insecurity everyone felt because of those questions. We talk about how Sikhs he knows have removed their turbans for fear of being killed in America. Sikhs had nothing to do with the terrorist attacks. But people went around after 9/11 attacking and killing Sikhs anyway, simply for wearing a turban. I start to *really* think about racial tension in the U.S. differently. How powerful can fear and hate be? The justification people feel in their own actions absolutely terrifies me.

This seems to be the truth of our culture. By excusing it, the problem remains. By ignoring it, the problem remains. By defending it, the problem remains. By denying history, the problem remains. I am not color-blind and neither is the rest of the world. Pretending otherwise is an injustice to everyone. The problem we face comes from ranking people as more or less desirable, for any reason. What is the perfect combination of understanding, patience, education and demand for change? What is the magic equation?

CHAPTER 9

The Bollywood Effect

With a surplus of time, a trip to India feels right. Vijay and I decide to go ahead with the traditional marriage ceremony we planned on having three years ago. We tell my family so they have time to get visas if they want to come. I decide to leave early, on my own, and stay with my in-laws for a month. I want to live *like an Indian daughter-in-law*.

Traveling to India, for me, is like being a star in a Bollywood film. There is drama and confusion, more drama and emotional upheaval, and in the end a touch of happiness. Someone inevitably gets hurt or misunderstood, while another expresses his or her love. An awesome wardrobe change always takes place at least once. Before I arrive, I have that jittery feeling the female lead of a Bollywood flick is believed to feel when she sees her love interest for the first time. No trip is the same and every day surprises the hell out of me. I wonder how much Bollywood I'll experience this trip.

The idea to stay with my in-laws, by myself, is my own. I think it's a good growth opportunity and look forward to having a better understanding of Vijay's origins. I constantly ask him for stories, family history and trivia. He has always been slow to divulge these things, which frustrates me. I'm hoping this trip will bring me closer to his parents and give me some background on my husband. I like the idea of telling our future children stories about their dad, his family and country. Hopefully I'll learn some family history and traditions while I'm there.

There is a bonus to traveling alone. I know that if I go without Vijay, I won't have to deal with the TSA's "random search" of him and all our belongings. Call me crazy, but I don't believe random searches are as random as the word would imply. Maybe enough time hasn't passed since 9/11, but when we travel together, I am left carrying our luggage through baggage screening in order to avoid the more thorough search. If he carries the bags, I spend time explaining why I picked them up at the other end of the conveyor belt and what the mysterious little round balls are in our luggage, usually while having to empty out the entire contents of our bag. Yes, he is my husband, and they are golf balls, people. They are just golf balls.

I pack all the Indian clothing, bindis and jewelry we purchased on our last trip to India, knowing I'll use it to immerse myself in Indian culture. We also pack wedding supplies and family gifts.

Before I know it, the day has arrived. Vijay drives me to LAX from the Valley, a four-hour trek. I'm anxious saying good-bye to Vijay but also excited about this solo adventure. I check my bags with a direct flight to Singapore.

I arrive in Singapore fifteen hours later, collect my things and head for the flight display to check the timeliness of my connection. I can't find my flight. Other flights leaving at the same time are already posted, so I decide to check with an attendant.

"Excuse me. Do you have an update for flight 2356?" I look over at the board while I talk to the terminal attendant. "I don't see it displayed."

"That flight path doesn't exist anymore for this airline," the gentleman sitting behind the counter says.

"What do you mean it doesn't exist?" I ask. "I checked in at LAX and no one said anything to me."

"It's your responsibility to check your flight status, ma'am. This airline doesn't fly that route any longer," I'm told.

"Oh. Well, how will I get to Hyderabad?" I'm a little frustrated that no one would mention an entire flight path being cancelled.

"We can put you on a flight through Chennai," he suggests.

I grab my bag and head to an internet terminal to let Vijay and my in-laws know. I'm hopeful Mama Garu hasn't begun the eight-hour drive, a day early, to Hyderabad. Vijay confirms the e-mail and gets the message to my in-laws.

If I have to be stuck in an airport, this isn't a bad one, so I decide to be grateful. It's a multicultural hub for the planet. I love the atmosphere, the people-watching, the clothes and most of all, the food! I begin with a Singapore transit visa and take a tour, suggested to me by Sanjay. I see the clean city, the impeccable landscape, the iconic merlion statue of Singapore and take the water taxi tour.

I'll be spending the next night in Chennai and am hitting thirty plane and airport hours since my last shower if I don't take one, so I rent a stall. I have another twenty-four hours of travel time if everything goes smoothly. Spic-and-span, I find a lounge chair, grab some Asian food and settle in for a nap before my next leg.

Twenty-four hours later than I was originally scheduled to leave, I say good-bye to Western toilets and board my flight for another layover. I travel the 1,800 extra miles to Chennai, arriving at midnight, collect my luggage and go through customs. I exit the airport and head to the domestic terminal.

A man stands with a large gun blocking the entrance of the building. He won't let me pass.

"I need to get into the airport. I have a flight in the morning," I say sleepily, not anticipating a problem.

He doesn't budge.

I recognize this look.

It's the bribe look.

Welcome to India.

I'm tired. I'll be damned if I will give him money to enter an airport.

"Please let me in." I tower over him. He stands about five feet tall, and for whatever reason, I am not intimidated by the very large gun he is holding.

"You need a ticket for your flight," he smirks, knowing he has the upper hand.

"Yes, I know I do. I was told to pick it up from the airline booth inside. I'm confirmed on a flight for tomorrow morning to

Hyderabad." I explain my flight had been changed in Singapore and I don't have a boarding document yet. He continues his *I can make an exception if you give me some money* face.

"I'm not giving you money. I'll be right back." I drag my oversized luggage, filled with random gifts and Costco-sized bags of candy, back down the sidewalk and find a little-league-style snack bar window. A gentleman sits on a stool on the other side.

"Can you get someone to let me in?" I ask. "I need a ticket and I am not going to sleep on the sidewalk." I look over my shoulder at the honking, goggling rickshaw drivers and cabs on the curb behind me as I talk. It's the middle of the night and I'm by myself. I need to get into this building.

With a smile and slight crook of the eyebrow, he briefly tries to convince me to take a rickshaw to a hotel. I may be a little naïve, but I'm pretty sure that isn't such a great idea, plus I only have six hours.

"I don't want to chance it," I tell him. I'm not sure traveling at midnight, alone, in a rickshaw, as a female, to an unknown destination, without a cell phone, is the wisest option. I'm adventurous, but that's just one too many uncertain factors.

His smile fades slightly. "Yes, ma'am. I will get the airport administrator." He swivels his head from side to side in agreement and disappears.

I meet the gentleman and an airport administrator at the door. The defeated security guard gives me the evil eye and lets me pass.

"Thank you," I offer.

"Right this way," the airport administrator says as he corrals me to a large common room with sleeping Indian passengers. Multicultural Singapore is long gone. I am now squarely in India. I scan the room and see I'm the only non-Indian passenger sleeping here this evening. The seats are lined in rows and everyone looks equally beat. I join them, make my luggage into a bed, and consider whether leaving it to use the restroom is a wise choice. I decide to leave it and, as I squat on the concrete floor of a well-used hole in the ground, I wish I had a bigger bladder and a fresh pair of underwear.

Finding my luggage bed, my body tries to get as comfortable as possible. I doze in and out of sleep until the sun shines through the windows of the terminal. The flight board, which is literally a board with slide-in words and numbers, is right outside the common room. I whip out my camera, only to be interrupted by an excited airport employee. "You may not use a camera in an airport, ma'am! That is a security issue!" he yells at me, arms flapping. His tone softens when he gets closer and explains the no-photo rule.

I board my flight, hopeful Mama Garu will be in Hyderabad to pick me up.

The sea of people waiting for loved ones is vast as I exit the Hyderabad airport. I'm so relieved to see Mama Garu, I don't think about what I'm doing. I feel my legs start to skip as I get closer to him and throw my arms around him. Everyone starts to stare. I release my death grip of relief, feeling self-conscious and sorry that this giant white girl made an inappropriate public display of affection right off the bat. I back off quickly and try to remind myself to keep my body parts to myself while I'm in India.

He takes it in stride and introduces me to his brother, Balaji, who has the longest pinky fingernail I've ever seen in real life. I can't stop staring as we walk through the crowd and make our way across the congested street. Balaji is quiet and soft-spoken. The two men discuss something for a moment and then we cross the street, dodging cars and rickshaws as we go. I am intrigued by this new family member.

The sounds of India fully greet me; honking rickshaws, cars, buses and people going about their noisy, chaotic day fill my senses as I look around the parking lot. We pile my luggage into Mama Garu's Maruti 800, a compact red hatchback. He ties the biggest bag to the roof. I wonder how Balaji's one extra-long nail hasn't broken off by now. I'll have to ask Vijay what the deal is.

Next thing I know we're at a tea stall for chai. We don't dawdle, drinking our tea quickly and spending most of our time staring at my luggage tied to the roof of the car so it doesn't get tampered with.

Vijay's parents moved back to southern India a few months before I arrived. Mama Garu retired from the military and felt his roots calling. They said good-bye to all their military staff and moved to what I'm told is a *small* town of 520,000 people called Anantapur.

It will take eight hours to drive from Hyderabad to Anantapur, so we stay overnight in the family condo before making the journey. The two-bedroom condo is located in a neighborhood called Ashoknagar. I enjoy the hustle and bustle of the city. This is much different from my previous experience in the military compound of Kanpur. I can *feel* the city here. We pull up to the condo and a security guard opens the gate for us. He returns to a little office on the ground floor. It is a small room, about six by six feet. There is a television and a little bed on the floor. I wonder if this is his home, but don't ask.

We walk up the stairs because the elevator is out of order. My luggage clunks up each step as we go. Atha Garu is waiting for us at the door and greets me warmly as I enter their apartment.

"Oh Liss. You must be tired from such a journey! Are you hungry? We will fetch some food for you." She smiles and looks me over.

About an hour later a family friend, Krishna, stops in. We walk down the stairs with him on our way to pick up dinner from a street vendor. As we approach the parking lot, I see his motorbike sitting in front of our car.

"I want to go for a ride!" I say.

"Sure thing." Krishna seems up to the task and excited to show me around.

"Oh! No, Liss," Vijay's parents protest. They are protecting me. I'm disappointed. "It is not safe, Liss. You need to travel in a car. Vijay would be very upset if something were to happen. Sometimes thieves will just reach out their hands and snatch your necklace right from your neck," I'm told.

I'm shocked this problem is so common that they are fearful it would happen to me, but I choose to believe what they say and forgo the experience.

"You could be hurt in an accident. It's not a good idea, Liss," they agree.

The sun sets. Mama Garu and I pick up dinner from a street vendor. The curry is ladled into clear plastic bags, the kind Americans use at the grocery store for produce, only thinner. They're filled to his specification, tied in a knot and passed to us across the cart. The bags meld into one another in a larger bag and I can smell the curry. My mouth starts to water and even though I know this method must work, I wonder how the bags haven't melted or leaked by the time we get home.

After dinner Atha Garu calls Vijay to tell him I've arrived. She tells me calls are expensive so I don't talk for long, but I share my adventure so far. Vijay wishes me well and tells me he loves me, which feels good to hear from so far away. He says he'll call each day to check in.

We wake the next morning, eat breakfast and leave the capital. I excitedly watch out the car window as the landscape changes and the smog lessens to a more tolerable level. My head hits the roof of the little Maruti 800 as we bounce our way down the partially paved road. Cigarette smoke pours into the backseat as I attempt, unsuccessfully, to stick my nose in the direction of fresh air.

I am just as awestruck this visit as I was on my first. Large trucks play chicken with us, uniformed children walk to school in the street and field workers begin their day. The extreme poverty reminds me how lucky I am. Shacks with satellite dishes line the streets as I watch out the window. Halfway to Anantapur, we stop for a routine chai break in a little village. I have to use the restroom and debate how badly, as I know finding a Western toilet is going to be like asking to find a ski resort. Biology persisting, I tell my in-laws. We stop at several street stalls in a passing village to ask if anyone knows where there may be a *Western toilet* area. Prepared with my supply of wipes, I tell Atha Garu I can really go anywhere. She, however, is confident we will eventually find something.

We get back in the car and I sit silently, wondering how Atha Garu does it. She's a lady in India. She never seems to have a public need. She obviously plans well, but the woman must have a bladder of steel. About twenty minutes later, we're referred to a service station. It's in the early stages of construction. As Mama Garu pulls the car into the dirt lot, he explains, "Service stations are becoming more popular in rural India, just like in America, Liz."

I get out and walk toward the building, sandals kicking up dust. The restroom has no door and as I walk toward the toilet area, Atha Garu in tow, I see a tile room with a grate in the middle of a slightly slanted floor. I am to go there. I'm confused by the grate. I've never had to aim with precision when using a toilet. Atha Garu stands guard by the doorless opening. This is definitely a *take my pants off* occasion.

After a few more hours, we reach Anantapur. The streets are paved and there are many homes and businesses. We eventually pull up to a two-story concrete building with a locked wrought-iron fence surrounding it. A staircase leads to the second-floor entrance. We unload the car and make our way up the stairs to the second floor.

The receiving room is lined with portraits of family who have come before us. Draped in strands of flowers, they stare down at us as we walk through the entryway into the family room. I look up at them and wonder who they were.

A pooja (prayer) room is visible from the family room. I can see the family god prominently displayed as I pass and smell sweet incense. Offerings of flowers and coconut lay at the feet of a god sitting in a small wooden temple inside the room.

I continue to follow my in-laws and am directed to what Mama Garu and Atha Garu refer to as Vijay's room. I pull my things into his room and investigate my new environment.

It's a comfortable size. A Jack-and-Jill-style restroom connects my room to another. A large carved teak bed sits in the center. Mosquito repellents are plugged into the outlets and a ceiling fan provides additional comfort. A small television sits on a stand at the end of the bed. I unpack my bags, excited to settle in.

As the sun sets, Mama Garu fetches me. He tells me we're going to town to rent the latest Bollywood films. I'll catch up on all the Shah Rukh Khan hits I've missed since my last visit. Shah Rukh Khan is like the Brad Pitt of India and probably my favorite Indian actor so far. Atha Garu tells me she will stay home to make dinner.

Spices hit my senses and my mouth waters as soon as we walk in the house. I don't know what she's made, but I can tell it's going to be good. We sit together silently in the dining room. The mound of fluffy white rice sits prominently on the table. I scoop it onto my plate along with fresh curry and begin. A powder concoction I've never seen before smells like peanut. I sprinkle it over my eggplant. It is light and fluffy and dry. After tasting it, I'm sure it will go perfectly on everything I eat while I'm here. The tastes linger in my mouth as I overeat during my first of many meals. You just can't beat the real stuff.

I spend the next several days reading, sleeping, eating excellent Indian food, visiting with my in-laws and meeting the occasional pop-in guest. With each new visitor, I learn how to appropriately greet guests with a platter of tea and finger foods in the living room. Daily home delivery services, such as the milkman, the ironing girl and the tailor, are foreign to me. I enjoy watching the interaction between Atha Garu and the service providers. I assumed door-to-door prices would be fixed, but even here, there are negotiations to be had. I don't know what she is saying to them, but I can tell she drives a hard bargain.

Each evening Vijay calls. I fill him in on what I've learned and what I've seen. I look forward to his nightly calls and start to miss him.

Every morning Atha Garu prays to the gods in the pooja parlor. Every Hindu family has at least one designated god to watch over them. There are millions of Hindu gods. It seems that nobody prays to all of them. Our family god is Venkateshwara (a form of Lord Vishnu). Venkateshwara sits prominently in the middle of the room, incense and offerings surrounding him.

Atha Garu asks me to join her as she rings a bell, lights scented incense and prays. I am instructed to follow. Praying isn't a natural instinct for me, so I feel like an imposter. I'm sure she doesn't feel this way, though, so I try to participate as respectfully as I can. Satisfied I've listened to the instructions, Atha Garu swivels her head from side to side.

"Good. Now you know, Liss," she tells me, walking out of the room. "I don't have to worry now when I die."

I watch her walk away and wonder what she thinks will happen if I pray improperly after she dies. "I'll try to do it right," I offer, following close behind, even though I think we both know Vijay and I won't be installing a pooja room in our home.

Mama Garu is gone much of the day, tending to his farm and working in an office serving veterans. He is the district soldier welfare officer. He comes home satisfied with a day's work and shares the happenings on his farmland. They are in the process of trying to tap a well. If they find water, it will be a good season. If they don't, it will be difficult. I am fascinated with how extreme the odds of successfully tapping a well are.

I become a proficient laundry washer and now know how to hang the freshly washed clothes on the roof lines. Mama Garu takes me to the front yard to show me how to turn on the water pump. After it's turned on, the water pumps up to the roof tank for the day. As we stand there watching it work, I once again think about how many things I take for granted in the States. Once sufficient water is pumped to the roof, he turns off the pump and reminds me to use the miniature water heater for temporary hot water in the restroom. The reminder is in vain, however, as I consistently forget to turn it on before shower time, and curse myself when I'm naked and realize only cold water is going to come out of the tap.

It's a little harder to get to know my in-laws than I thought it would be. It's not because they aren't friendly, but because they just aren't very chatty. Mama Garu spends a lot of his day at work and out overseeing the fieldwork. Atha Garu spends a lot of time cooking fresh meals for her husband and in the evening, once all the work is done, watching a very dramatic soap opera. I participate in the meal preparation, but I feel as though I'm more of a nuisance than a help, since I need step-by-step instructions on how to do it properly.

Atha Garu shows me how to light the portable LPG (liquefied petroleum gas) cylinders used for cooking fuel. She tells me which spices to use and shows me how to mix and cook them, just the right way. She is methodical. My favorite thing she's made thus far is a crepe-like Indian pancake called masala dosa. I think it's because they are so extreme looking.

The huge crepe creation is filled with potato stuffing. I make sure to sprinkle more of that peanut powder on top.

After mealtime, I hurry back to my room to write down what I've learned, hoping I can come close to her cooking when I return home.

Vijay and other family will start to arrive soon, as our wedding is a little more than a week away. It will take place in Hyderabad, but some family will come stay with us in Anantapur first, so Atha Garu and Mama Garu are beginning to prepare.

A farmhand named Subbu, who works in the family paddy fields, is summoned to the house one morning. He is introduced to me briefly as we are asked to clean an apartment for family who will be staying with us from Kerala. He has a small frame, thick black hair and big brown eyes that dart around a little, unsure of whether to look at me directly or avoid eye contact completely. We walk down the stairs to the apartment behind the house and look inside. Vague on the details, I'm not sure what exactly I'm supposed to do, so I just try to generally organize and clean. Subbu and I can't understand each other, so we pantomime our tasks.

As we work together, we try to teach each other words, mine in English and his in Telugu. I point to items and tell him the English word. He repeats it very poorly and then points to another item and says the word in Telugu. I repeat his word very poorly. We laugh and practice for several hours this way before I decide we can't really do much more and point toward the house. I'm not sure if we've succeeded in the task we were given, but I'm glad I've met him.

A few days go by. Vijay, my mom and members of Atha Garu's family will arrive soon. I decide to try to help by scrubbing the marble entryway. Framed garland-adorned ancestors staring down at me, I kneel on my hands and knees and scrub. I hear Mama Garu behind me and look over my shoulder. He's chuckling as he walks away. He returns about a minute later with his camera and takes a picture.

"I shall take a snap."

I look at him, confused.

"I don't know anyone else in this situation. A white girl on her hands and knees, in my house, scrubbing my floor. This is not a very common occurrence for an Indian," he says to explain his amusement.

He leaves me to my task. As I finish the floor, I think silently about what I know of the British occupation and the humor he finds in my performing a simple household task.

I don't venture far from the house alone, but, when the opportunity presents itself, I try to explore. Excited children stop and stare when they see me approach. Some know a bit of

English; others just wave energetically. I take pictures with the digital camera we got for a gift at our California wedding. I show them their picture on the screen. I wish I had a way to print out the pictures.

My time alone with my in-laws has passed quickly. Mom and Vijay will arrive for our upcoming wedding in just a few hours. This trip is a little out of my stepdad's comfort zone and Mom doesn't want to travel alone, so Vijay and Mom fly in together.

Atha Garu is anxious to see her son. We expect them to arrive at midnight in Hyderabad. I don't think she will get any sleep in anticipation of his arrival. Vijay and Mom will travel the two-hundred-mile, eight-hour route from the airport, the same one I took a few weeks before. Mama Garu and a hired driver leave for Hyderabad to pick them up. I stay with Atha Garu at the house in Anantapur. She tells me they will sleep at the Hyderabad condo for the night.

"Oh Liss. I think they will arrive soon," she tells me.

"Yes, soon," I agree. I turn in for the night knowing she'll be up, waiting for a call from Mama Garu telling her that her son has landed.

"Liss. Oh Liss," I hear Atha Garu say.

I wake up and look at the door. She is standing in the

threshold, calling to me. "Come. Liss. Oh Liss. Come," she repeats with a wave.

It's dawn. I briefly think I've slept through an entire day. I see the car in front of our house. Vijay and my exhausted-looking mother walk through the door and receive their traditional greeting of rice, turmeric paste and prayer—the same one I received on my first trip to Vijay's home in Kanpur. I study my mom's face as rice is thrown on her.

"They came straight here," Atha Garu says as she finishes the last of the rice throwing and looks out the door for her husband, who is lugging bags up the stairs. "They drove straight through."

It's good to see Vijay, and I feel relief knowing Mom was able to travel with him. Mom, Vijay and I hug as we pass through the entranceway into the living room. Their faces are tired from their long journey.

After her thirtieth hour of travel, Mom sinks into the couch in the living room. I glance out the window at the driver. Poor guy must be exhausted. That was quite a drive, all the way to Hyderabad and back. Vijay and I sit with my mom as she begins to explain the unbelievable fact that she escaped certain death. She looks pale, and there's a hint of disbelief in her voice.

"I wouldn't believe it if I hadn't done it. I thought we might die. At one point the driver pulled the car over and took off the side-view mirror. He literally removed it." She pauses for a moment and thinks about her journey. "For a while I thought maybe he was too close to oncoming traffic. That's how close we were! I mean . . . really close! Vijay told me that's what he thought too. Then, the driver told him that the mirror had actually just come loose and that's why he took it off." She pauses and chuckles a little. I know exactly what she's talking about and study her face as she continues. "I don't know if I believe that. I can't believe I didn't have a stroke! Do you think I'm going to have a stroke?" Her eyes look at me earnestly as her body gradually relaxes into the couch.

I continue to stare at her, partly amused and partly worried this trip may be too much. I always thought of her as so tough. She raised us on her own. She dug in and did any job that needed to be done. She never relied on anyone. This is the first time she has ever seemed vulnerable to me. She interrupts my thoughts.

"I'm exhausted! I don't think I would have been nearly as scared if Vijay didn't look terrified too," she says.

"It's been a while since I've traveled any distance in India," he offers, letting her have this moment. We look at each other and smile.

We sit silently for a while longer. It's nine in the morning. Though she hasn't slept since arriving in Hyderabad, we decide they should stay awake all day to acclimate to the time difference quickly, since their stay in India is so short.

"That was the most harrowing drive ever. I can't believe we weren't killed," she repeats. "I'm exhausted."

It feels like Vijay and I are back to our Oak Park days, Amherst days even. We don't have the desert calling us home. We're so far away from our regular lives. It's fun again.

We spend a few more days in Anantapur exploring the city, shopping and trying local food. Vijay tells us his parents want us to see historical sites while we are there. They've planned a trip to an ancient city, one hundred miles northwest of Anantapur, called Hampi. We're told a car has been hired and the trip is set.

The next morning Vijay, my mom, Subbu and I get in the car knowing that one hundred miles in India is quite a trek.

It takes three hours of crawling before the conversation turns to the distance we have left. Most of the road is dirt. Giant potholes, some the size of cars, sporadically litter the road. The driver takes great care to maneuver around them. Because of these obstacles, large semis with broken axles, stranded hatchbacks and sedans clutter the sides of the road, which adds to the maze.

"This should be a video game," Mom suggests. "I don't think anyone would believe this, though."

"I don't think it's worth it for the driver . . . whatever we are paying this guy can't be enough," I agree, looking at him.

"Actually, I don't think a video game would do this justice. I don't know how you could describe this well enough for someone to understand it," Mom concludes. "Do you think we'll be able to get there and back today? How far do we have to go?"

"We'll make it." Vijay's confident. "Traveling in India is always time-consuming. Time doesn't have a price tag here."

We spend the next three hours discussing how unbelievable the road is, repeating our concern that this can't be worth it to the wear and tear on the driver's car and confirming the likelihood that we won't make it to our destination and back in one day.

We stop for a snack at what everyone is calling a restaurant. "I should have gotten a hepatitis shot," Mom says regretfully, leaning into my ear.

We order food apprehensively. We're hungry, though, so we eat. I try to eat just enough to stay strong, but not enough to have to use a restroom. It's a tricky combination. Our break is short and we continue the drive past huts, paddy fields, slums and herds of animal. The entire drive takes six hours.

Arriving at the ancient ruins, we can see they are vast. I've never been anywhere like this and am instantly grateful for the chance to see Hampi. The driver and Subbu, the watchful farmhand, follow us around to make sure we don't get lost or distressed. Even though there are people everywhere, this task is not as difficult as it may sound. We stick out pretty dramatically. I stand a good foot over the locals and my mom isn't far behind. We also now fondly refer to each other as *jumbo-jumbos*, due to the fact that whenever we ask shopkeepers if they have our size clothing, they respond with, "Ahhhh! Jumbo-jumbo!"

We could easily spend more than one afternoon walking around the ancient city of Vijayanagara. I'm most fascinated by the elephant garages. The stone structures are overwhelmingly large. I try to imagine what it must have been like when processions of jewel-adorned elephants walked the streets during royal occasions. A statue of Ganesh called Kadalekalu Ganesha is colossal and many temple sites still stand. Irrigation wells and large canals run through the city, all engineering marvels for their time. We follow the ancient canals that trace back to the main areas of the city, walking for hours.

The Bollywood Effect

A coconut stall is appealing as sweat drips from our foreheads. The coconut water instantly quenches our thirst. It's a natural electrolyte and has easily become our drink of choice.

As we make our way to the main temple, Virupaksha, street performers line up outside, ready for our donation. An elephant blesses people with its trunk, a man with a dagger through his bloody cheek looks hopefully in our direction and a woman selling trinkets urges us to stop. Mom gets swept away in an elephant blessing only to immediately feel sorry for the scrawny old elephant after receiving it. This is a reoccurring feeling that plagues us as we live our vacation in India. Our desire to try something new and exciting is usually followed by extreme guilt or a slower realization that said activity was somehow not *right*.

The line to enter the temple is packed and pushy. Leaving our shoes behind in the giant shoe mound, we're manhandled through the temple entrance. Mom questions whether the special walking shoes she just purchased for this trip will be there when she gets back. I remind her that no one else has feet as big as ours as we walk with the determined crowd of holy people. Packed tight, we try to observe the Brahman priest, deities and the overwhelming amount of donations that have been presented to the gods. The forceful flow of traffic pushes us through quickly, but we can still see the coconuts, flowers, jewelry and money thrown across the floor of the temple all in hope of a better life, health, a happy marriage or job opportunity.

We exit on the opposite side of the temple and walk barefoot on the dirt road to reunite with the shoe pile. We can see our driver is tired. As the sun begins to set, we head for the car. He can hardly keep his eyes open as he swerves back and forth on the dark road. I hope, once again, that we aren't going to die. This fear of death has become one that I no longer wrestle with, but rather accept as part of traveling in India. If it's my time, it's my time, no matter how terrifying, so I might as well get over it. We all fall asleep in the car, leaving our fate to our driver.

The next day, we're still alive and back in Anantapur. It's Christmas Day. Vijay's parents want to recognize this Christian holiday for us. They tell us they've arranged a picnic at the family farm. We're told all the farm workers are going to celebrate with us. I put on a black salwar kameez with big yellow flowers embroidered on the front.

"Oh no, Liss. What are you wearing?" Atha Garu asks, panicked.

"What? Why? I love it!" I exclaim.

I purchased it from a street vendor and haven't worn it since it came back from the tailor, who had to add a substantial amount of fabric to make it jumbo-jumbo.

"Only poor people wear such things," she explains.

"Ma, let her wear what she wants," Vijay argues.

"Ohhh son. She needs to wear a nice silk sari," she disagrees.

I ask Vijay if I should change my clothing. He says no. She is worried what kind of statement I will make going out in something of such poor quality in front of the farm help. Honestly, I'm more comfortable wearing something simple than dressing up for people who have absolutely nothing. If Vijay wasn't with me, I know I would have changed into whatever my mother-in-law told me to wear. But he said it's fine. So I feel supported by my choice of clothing.

In her defense, my poor mother-in-law is trying to do what is proper for her reality, in her culture, where she lives. She has this really tall, American daughter-in-law who sticks out like a sore thumb. I waltz in and most likely misinterpret all of her cultural expectations, and then refuse to even consider a wardrobe change. I feel guilty for not following her direction, but still much more comfortable with the choice I've made.

As we approach the farm, I can see all the workers gathered. Everyone was clearly prepared for our arrival. We are given a tour of the farmhouse and tombs erected in honor of Mama Garu's parents and brother, with empty spaces to honor the not-yet-departed. We sit with everyone in front of the farmhouse under a large canopy, trying to talk to all the local farmhands as we eat our meal. They are sweet and accommodating.

Before we leave, a holiday sheet cake is presented to us with the words *Happy Christmas* written across it. The cake is served. One of the farm workers tastes it and says "much so sweet," with a frown.

As the afternoon rolls along, Mom and I stand in the courtyard to take pictures with the farm workers. Vijay's father looks at my mother, then at me, then at a woman who tends to the crops. "She looks like a pygmy standing next to you people," he says, smiling ear to ear and chuckling loudly.

CHAPTER 10

Unexpected Company

Mama Garu, Vijay, Mom and I sit in a corner of a café in downtown Anantapur for our last night before leaving for Hyderabad. A television mounted to the wall plays a cricket match. Suddenly, a news report interrupts the match. "Benazir Bhutto got into her car while leaving a campaign rally for PPP, and was assassinated," the BBC anchor announces, followed by an analysis of what this may mean for India. Mom and I look at Vijay and his dad. Mama Garu was a colonel in the military. He had been stationed at the border between India and Pakistan. He shakes his head, disappointed, and listens to the news anchor.

We watch the news unfold and follow the ensuing riots for the rest of our meal. I wonder if this will have any effect on world diplomacy and politics in the U.S. as we, Americans, head into an election year. In my opinion, it's a big one. We're in the middle of a war and our candidates could not be more different: Obama vs. McCain. We linger in the café for a while and talk about Indian/Pakistani relations. Sitting here, watching the world news unfold feels so real, so close, so much more meaningful. Before this, any foreign news felt so distant, detached from my reality.

I don't think I'll be able to watch news in the U.S. without questioning a twenty-four-hour news cycle that cares more about pop culture than world diplomacy. Granted, I am not in the States right now, so I don't know how this is being covered there, but I doubt it would feel the same. When I'm home I feel secure and confident in our isolationism, distant and detached from the rest of the world. Here, watching the news as it's happening, I feel like I'm a part of it, like it matters, like I should be doing something.

We return to the house a few hours later and check in with everyone. Vijay's aunt and cousin arrived a few days before and are staying in the apartment Subbu and I "arranged" about a week earlier. They will be traveling with us to Hyderabad. Vijay explains that we won't be hiring a car and driver to take us. There are too many of us for one car this time. Instead, Vijay, Mom, his aunt, his cousin, her daughter and I are going to take a train to Hyderabad. Vijay's parents are going to drive separately.

The night before we leave for Hyderabad, I lie in bed with Vijay, talking about a few of the experiences I had before he arrived. I tell him about praying in the pooja room, the children who want their picture taken when I walk the streets, all the cooking his mother does, from scratch every time, and how many things I take for granted in the States. Then I remember something.

"Hey babe," I say, looking at him.

"Yeah," he responds.

"You know how Subbu and I worked on straightening up the apartment your aunt is staying in?" I ask.

"Yeah." He glances in my direction while packing his suitcase.

"Well, I saw a skin of a cheetah." I approach the subject lightly because first of all, I don't know if this is something that people talk about, or if it is even legal to have a cheetah skin. And secondly, I don't know if I really want to know.

"It's a leopard skin," he corrects me. "I think cheetahs are extinct in India, babe."

"Oh. Okay, yeah."

"My grandpa shot it." He zips his luggage shut and places it by the door.

"What do you mean? Why would your grandpa shoot a leopard?"

"My grandpa was in the police department. He told me a leopard showed up in a village and was terrorizing the people. He set a trap and captured it. Then they tied it up, putting a stud through its tendon, and walked it around the village to show the people they had captured it. He told me it was quite wild and ferocious. I'm sure it was scared and in pain as well. Anyway, he said it ripped the rod right through its leg, breaking free, and lunged at some people. That's when my grandpa shot it." He sits down on the bed next to me.

"Why were they parading it around?" My instinct was right. I don't want to know this story, but like gawking at an accident, I just go ahead and ask the follow-up questions anyway.

"That was a long time ago, Liz." He reaches for the remote. "It was the fifties, right after India's independence. Animal rights were not exactly on the forefront of anyone's mind. They still aren't really. Remember that bear you saw on the side of the road?"

"Yeah," I say, thinking about that poor bear I saw on my first trip just outside of Agra. I am a self-proclaimed tree hugger, a vegetarian who feels guilty if my shoes have leather on them.

"Oh! Speaking of bears! I should tell you the story my grandpa told me about a bear he killed!" He straightens up.

"Oh no! I don't want to hear it." I lie down to go to sleep but instead lie awake thinking about the poor terrified leopard, with a rod through its tendon, getting paraded around a village of people cheering.

The next morning, we start to organize for the trip. We won't be returning to Anantapur, so everything must be packed. Family and friends from India who couldn't come to our wedding in the States will get to celebrate with us this time.

At dusk, we are taken to the train station. We're to catch the overnight AC sleeper coach called the Bangalore Express to Hyderabad. We stand in the concrete quad of the station waiting for our train to arrive. My mom looks around, scanning the platform lights. "Are those the mosquitoes that aren't a problem?" An accusing eyeball looks at me and then back at the large swarm of mosquitoes hovering above us.

"Yep. Those would be the ones," I confirm, doubting my earlier recommendation that malaria shots weren't necessary. I hadn't been in train stations at night before. The house has plug-in mosquito repellent in all the rooms. We've always hired drivers. Standing around waiting for a train, at night, in stadium lighting never occurred to me. We suddenly feel vulnerable. My mom immediately whips out some mosquito-repellent wipes and begins a frenzied rubdown on all exposed skin. She passes them to me and encourages my participation.

About forty-five minutes later, the train arrives in the station. All the other passengers push frantically to embark. An immediate rush of excitement comes over me. It's a mad dash and we're told to hurry, as trains don't wait. Subbu, our trusty farmhand, loads all our bags and we shuffle quickly on the train. We are repeatedly reminded it won't stop long and notice Subbu's concerned face as he runs on and off our car with loads of luggage. I have absolutely no idea what made it on the train or where our bags ended up. I can't understand anything anyone is yelling, but I'm confident it will all work out. It always does.

Once we're on board, the train lurches forward. We make our way down the narrow aisle, swaying from side to side as we walk. The sleeper car is air-conditioned and little bunk beds line the walls, each with a curtain. The bunks remind me of a navy submarine I toured one time. I am sure that out of all the possibilities, this is a very nice accommodation. As we walk down the hall and find our designated spaces, curtains begin to part. I can see eyes staring out at what must be a somewhat annoying and typically loud American entourage. I find my bunk next to my mom's and settle into the very short bed. I'm grateful to have it and I sleep through the night, knees to chest. The next morning we arrive without any cases of malaria, but plenty of comments about my careless vaccine advice.

Vijay hails cabs at the station and asks the drivers to drop us in front of the hotel his parents have reserved. I still don't know where we are staying because I can't understand anything anyone has been saying. It's kind of fun. Every day is a surprise. It's also kind of frustrating. I like to control my own destiny.

We drive through a large gate and into the courtyard of the hotel, which is their parking lot. The cabbies help us unload our bags, and we carry them up to a modest lobby and check in.

Our room isn't quite ready, so Vijay and I are given what the receptionist is calling a "holding" room. My mom checks into the room she'll share with my brother when he arrives. As soon as I lay my bags on the bed and take a quick look around, a knock at the door interrupts my train of thought.

"Ma'am, your suite is now. Your guest also. Canada. In room hall." The young bellhop points as he practices his broken English.

"What? Guest from Canada?" I ask, slowly catching on.

"Down hall, ma'am. Three down," he says, his finger still pointing.

"Uh, okay." I walk down the hall knowing we weren't expecting family or friends from Canada. I get to the third door and knock.

A tall, enthusiastic white woman with short, spiky red hair opens it. "Oh hi! You must be Liz! Eh?! I'm Maggie. It's so great to be here! I'm really looking forward to this! What are your plans for the afternoon? How was your flight? Mine was a mess! My luggage was lost, but it's okay. I'll get it back. Would you like some syrup?" Maggie talks quickly, clearly excited to finally be in Hyderabad.

I look at her, confused. "Um, we're going to a museum." I'm not sure why I'm answering that question in particular. Maggie must see the confusion on my face.

"That sounds great! When are we leaving?" I stare at her as she speaks, still trying to understand.

"Where did you come from?" I ask her, still processing.

"Oh, I heard about your wedding from your cousin in a chat room! I decided it'd be a great opportunity to see a traditional wedding! Oh, here you go." She whips out a leaf-shaped mini bottle of maple syrup. "These weren't lost."

"Cousin?" I ask.

"Yeah, Vijay's cousin," she confirms. I watch her talk and wonder how you decide to fly to India, from Canada, for a wedding of someone you don't know, based on a chat room conversation with someone you've never met. I'm also shocked that she seemingly knows more about my own wedding than I do. For starters, where it is going to take place and which hotel we are staying in.

She seems friendly enough. What's the worst that could happen? I tell her we've rented a car for the day and she is welcome to join us. When in India . . .

The bellhop greets me in front of the woman's room and reminds me that my suite is ready. I collect my luggage from the room we used for five minutes and follow him upstairs to our room. It's larger than Maggie's room, more of a suite. My in-laws must have arranged it. There is a large wooden platform frame in the bedroom with a thick mat on it. The sheets are decorated with flower petals in a large heart shape. There is a tube television at the foot of the bed and a small sitting room off the bedroom.

I am told that we are in the Western portion of the hotel.

Unexpected Company

Across the courtyard, another building houses many of our Indian wedding guests. In their section of the hotel, there are no individual washrooms. Washrooms, it seems, are a luxury for the natives. Ours has a thin, lightweight toilet seat, which wobbles and creaks when sat on. I never sit with all my weight in case this jumbo-jumbo cracks it or breaks it off entirely. The shower is open without separation from the rest of the room, as are most in India. This means that showers often make the toilet and everything else in the room wet. I'm used to this and have no trouble, but my American visitors are a little thrown off by the restroom setup.

After a little sightseeing, my only order of actual business in Hyderabad is to rectify my return flight problem. The flight path was cancelled on my arriving flight and I'm assuming I'll have the same problem on my return flight, although no one told me that was the case. Mama Garu and his brother with the extra-long nail drive me to the airline office. It is a large office with open seating. The wait looks dreadful. There are not very many attendants and there are quite a lot of customers.

I am eventually called up to the counter.

"How can I help, madam?" A very pleasant woman sits across from me, dressed in a sari.

"My flight path was cancelled and I need to arrange for a flight to LAX," I tell her.

"Yes, madam, we can fly you to LAX." She proceeds to tell me what she's arranged. I will have many layovers, zigzagging across the planet to get back home.

"That isn't going to work for me," I tell her. "I purchased a ticket with one stop. I paid for that. I expect to return with one stop," I explain.

"The only airline that flies with one stop currently is Singapore Air," she tells me.

"Okay. Then put me on Singapore Air." Mama Garu looks at me. He seems rather surprised at my forthrightness, but doesn't comment.

She talks to her supervisor, then her supervisor's supervisor, and eventually comes back with a voucher for me to fly Singapore Airlines.

"You must go to their offices today," she says.

Every transaction has to be done in person, which always means driving and often a lot of waiting. We've already spent all morning taking care of this issue, but Mama Garu doesn't complain. "Come, Liz," he says and drives me to the office of Singapore Airlines.

It's near the airport. We walk up the steps and open the door to a lovely reception area with soft instrumental music playing in the background. I'm the only customer. A well-groomed, professionally dressed women in a sari greets us calmly and offers bottled water. She asks what she can do for us. I explain our situation and she gets my ticket without pause.

Mama Garu raises his eyebrows and looks at me. "We must fly this airline from now on." He shakes his head from side to side, acknowledging the difference. I think he's impressed.

Maggie joins us each day, and from now on she's family. Museum tour. Canadian lady? Yep. Pre-wedding ceremony. Canadian lady? Yep. Pre-wedding pooja and wedding henna design. Canadian lady? Yep. Prime placement at family picture sessions. Canadian lady? Yep. She is not shy about getting involved. Everyone includes her and everyone assumes we know her.

Unexpected Company

My brother, dad and stepmom land a few days later. Everyone coming from the States has arrived. I start to divide my time between my family members. My mom, the Canadian lady and I spend most of our time traveling around Hyderabad. Vijay joins us sparingly, as his main focus is to visit with his parents, since he's here for only a short time.

In the evening we return to the hotel. Hungry, we head to a restaurant in the courtyard for the first time. My mom, my brother, the Canadian lady and I walk in. Vijay, our usual translator, is spending time with his parents. As soon as we open the door, everyone stops to stare. One of the gentlemen standing at the bar says something in Telugu, which none of us understand, and then another gets up and starts walking toward us rather quickly. We are escorted out of the restaurant and I think we're told not to come back. We're a little surprised, but leave. We had no interest in causing a scene, so we walk to the other side of the courtyard, cross the parking lot and walk into another restaurant. We are escorted to a back room away from all the other patrons. *What on earth is going on?* We are so confused. Menus are brought to us along with an English-speaking staff member.

"It's because you are woman," we are told.

"Oh, okay!" I say. "No wonder. Wait? What?"

"Because you are woman," the gentleman says to us. "You cannot be a lady in the bar."

"Really?"

"Yes, madam, which is why you sit here in our private room, away from the bar," he explains with a smile.

We turn to each other; we all agree a drink would have been really nice. We look over the menu and order our meal. The food arrives and we talk about the adventures we've shared.

Maggie tells us she is a costume designer for the film industry, which turns out to be pretty interesting. I still don't know why she'd fly solo for a mystery wedding, though, so I ask.

"So, how did you decide to come here?" I put down my napkin and turn toward her. "I mean, it's quite a trip for a wedding of someone you don't know, isn't it?"

"My son is half Indian," she explains. "My son's biological parents were young. The girl is from a Mormon family and the boy is an Indian. I've always wanted to travel to India. I want to understand his roots and learn more about his culture."

We continue to talk and her adventurous spirit is contagious. I'm glad we got to know this random Canadian lady.

"So, what about you?" she asks. "What is your wedding going to be like? It's only two days away!"

"I have absolutely no idea," I tell her with a smile. "I'm just doing whatever Vijay tells me to do."

CHAPTER 11

A South Indian Bride

The day before we're to be married, I'm taken to the roof of the hotel. A curtain lines the edge of the roof and a stage is being assembled at one end. As Vijay and I walk around looking at all the preparations, he tells me everyone he knows has been invited.

"One guest called to say he is bringing fifteen people, which is a typical Indian situation." He walks toward the stage and looks at the flowers.

"Fifteen people? Who are they?" I ask.

"Friends of his, people interested in attending," he tells me. "This is actually quite common . . . to bring friends."

"So, how many people will be here?" I'm not sure why I don't already know this. But I'm surprised by his answer.

"We're expecting around two hundred people," he says.

I think this sounds like a lot, but Vijay tells me the wedding is small. "Sometimes there are more than a thousand."

More than a thousand! That is just unimaginable to me. How can someone have a thousand wedding guests? I scan the roof and look at all the preparation that is going into this wedding. I am so excited. I can remember Vijay telling me that he wanted an American wedding and a Hindu wedding. He is getting exactly that. He had no idea what to expect in the States, and now I'm in his shoes.

I wake the next morning on our wedding day. Vijay's mom tells me to have breakfast and then be in my room for a morning pooja ceremony. There, a henna artist will tattoo my arms and legs.

I wait in the sitting room for everyone to arrive. Mom, the Canadian lady, Vijay, Atha Garu and an auntie attend the ceremony. Like an American bride, the Indian bride seems to be the focus of the ceremony. Unlike most brides, however, I have no idea what on earth I'm supposed to be doing, and nothing is in English. I constantly make the mistake of not pressing Vijay for more information before things, which leads to a little bit of frustration, uncertainty and ultimately a surprise.

A bowl of bright yellow turmeric paste is placed next to me. I'm asked to spread it all over my face. *I'm white. They know that, right?* I think to myself. My face will stain the color of this stuff. I'll look like a highlighter.

"It will make you look healthy, Liss," I'm told.

This is my wedding day, so my reluctance I think is founded, but I apply the paste anyhow. I look at my bright orange face in the mirror and wonder how long I have to keep it on. Have they ever seen how turmeric stains? Bleach doesn't even get that stuff off countertops!

"It will improve and brighten your complexion." The Indian women nod in agreement.

Well, the brightening part is true, I think to myself. I try to stay calm and collected and follow instructions. Most of which are discussed in Telugu, and eventually briefly translated.

After the turmeric and prayer session, the henna application begins, on my hands first and then on my feet. A small woman sits in a hijab, working quickly on my hands. She asks for the groom's name and writes a *V*, then asks my name and writes an *E* on each palm. She brings them together and draws half a heart on each palm, so that when connected it forms the shape of a heart. The rest of the design is extremely intricate and goes from the tips of my fingers to my forearm. She is so quick and accurate. It's obvious she has done this many times before. Once my arms are complete, she wastes no time moving on to my feet and calves until they, too, are fully engulfed in design.

After the henna dries and flakes off, I'm left with absolutely beautifully dyed skin. The hours go by quickly and before I realize it, I'm told to get dressed for the ceremony. I know we've purchased two wedding saris but I don't know which one to put on, when or how. The entire process is quite literally a surprise. I am kept in our hotel suite for the first half of the ceremony. Vijay sits on a stage, on the hotel roof, as the wedding begins.

My parents, the divorced biological ones, apparently have a big role to play. They sit next to each other, on a stage, in front of everyone and try to make offerings and pray appropriately to the gods. I hope they're behaving themselves. I'm sure they are, but I'm still nervous about what's going on up there. The Brahman priest chants in Telugu and shows them what they should be doing by holding their hands and guiding them in the direction he wishes them to face.

Vijay is presented to my folks on the stage. He sits across from my mom and dad, legs crossed, facing each other. Vijay is asked to uncross his legs and bend his knees, placing his feet in a pan filled with water. Then, my parents, who haven't spoken to each other for years, are asked to wash his feet together. They respectfully proceed without incident.

As the Brahman priest prepares Vijay on the roof to receive his bride, Atha Garu and Auntie dress me in the hotel suite downstairs. We put the first of two ceremony saris on with great wrapping, folding and pinning precision. It is a gorgeous red and white silk sari with gold thread embroidery. Atha Garu took me to pick the fabric a few weeks before the ceremony. A tailor measured me and sewed it into a *jumbo-jumbo* masterpiece in time for the wedding. A jet-black hair extension is sewn into my sandy-brown hair, the length being the important factor here. Then, a floral garland is incorporated into the extension. It is so long that it touches the floor when I'm sitting.

A South Indian Bride

I am doused in jewelry: gold hoop earrings that loop from the first hole to the second, several gold necklaces of varying lengths, a gold belt, gold and glass bangles and gold arm cuffs. I stare at my reflection in the mirror as I shimmer in gold. Some is borrowed, some plated, but every bit of me is covered in it. I feel like a Smithsonian exhibit.

According to Indian tradition, a girl is given jewelry by her family. She wears it during the wedding and takes it with her to live with her husband's family. Vijay tells me this is *backup*, something to count on if the girl should fall on hard times, if the husband dies or the woman needs it. It shows her financial security, that she deserves to be taken seriously, that she has assets aside from her husband. Mine is more of a status symbol I suppose, and it all comes from his family, so the traditional aspect of our gold arrangement is a little backward, just like everything else we do. The way we waltz in and out of culture with such ease must be a constant frustration for his parents.

After some time admiring my sparkling reflection, it's my turn to join the ceremony. I am guided up the elevator to the roof of the hotel and escorted down a hallway. As I approach the stage, a large white sheet hangs vertically in front of Vijay, blocking my view of my future "mystery" husband. Floral arrangements and garland wrap the pergola, which has been constructed especially for this event. Vijay's disinterest in details and lack of translation can be frustrating at times, but this time adds to the magic. I am awestruck as I try to take in everything I'm seeing.

A hand I recognize as Vijay's passes me offerings under the sheet and I pass offerings back. Mom and Dad sit on either side of me for the first time since I was seven. The Brahman priest continues to direct us by pointing toward our next task and encouraging participation with a simple head nod. An air of mystery persists even though I already know very well who is on the other side of that sheet.

This under-the-sheet exchange goes on for some time. I'm pretty sure we've used every spice in existence by now. The Brahman priest chants religious meaning as each spice is passed. The sheet is finally lowered dramatically so that I can see, for the first time, my husband.

Vijay and I stare at each other. Am I supposed to act some special way? Shy perhaps? Like a woman who just met a man for the first time? Is it silly that I want to play that game even though it is obviously not our case? Instructed by the Brahman priest, we continue to pray together, offering the gods coconuts and betel nuts. We end by smashing jaggery and fennel-seed patties on each other's heads. The guests are invited to come to the stage to bless us with rice, which is thrown at us from all directions. As each person walks up to the stage, rice in hand, something is murmured, and then the rice is tossed at us, sometimes gently, and other times aggressively. I'm thrown off by the differences in approach and wonder what the guests are saying to themselves as they throw rice on us.

Unbeknownst to me, a television crew came to film the wedding. They interview our family members about cross-cultural marriages. We all gather for their questions and they tell us, "This will be shown in forty countries, from Germany to Dubai."

Days after the ceremony, people call to tell us they "just saw it on TV!"

We never did.

Vijay mingles with the guests, while I am escorted back down the elevator for another wardrobe change. The guests are offered rice and curry as they visit.

I can hear the Indian musicians begin to play as I walk away, catching a glimpse out of the corner of my eye. I don't know what I was expecting, but they're sitting on mats on the ground, dressed traditionally, and playing instruments I've never seen before. It's quite fabulous! The music is intoxicating and very foreign to me. I've never heard these sounds before and I can't help but smile as I walk past them, offering a slight wave.

My wardrobe change goes a little quicker than the first time. I paid attention before and now spin appropriately as my regal purple silk sari is wrapped around my body. Still, great care is provided by the women in wrapping and folding excellence. As I look in the mirror at the shimmering gold embroidery in the fabric I notice rice, spices and legumes smashed into my hair. I begin to pick it out but am discouraged by my mother-in-law.

"It's okay, Liss. Leave it," she says, waving her hands to dismiss my fuss.

I agree. It wouldn't come out even if I really wanted it to, anyway.

Back in the elevator we ride to the roof. I'm directed where to sit. A metal chair has been converted to royalty. It is covered in red velvet, with a large ornate back and silver piping. Vijay and I sit next to each other as we are introduced. An impressive queue forms as guests bring us flowers and take pictures.

With just a few days left, everyone tries to spend their time cramming in as much sightseeing as possible. I haven't been able to spend a lot of time with my dad and stepmom, so I take a day to explore Hyderabad with them. Vijay spends more time visiting with his parents.

My dad and stepmom hire a driver to tour Hyderabad. As we drive through traffic, my phone rings.

"Hello? Is this Elizabeth?" someone asks.

"Yes," I say. "Who is this?"

"This is Ganga radio," the radio show host say.

"What!? How did you get my number?" I'm confused.

"Your in-laws," the host says, talking quickly. "So, here's what we are going to do. We are going on the air in five minutes. Can you tell us what it's like to be an Indian bride? How do you feel marrying an Indian? What's it like to be traveling in India? Do you like your in-laws? Can you do that?"

"Um, I think so," I say, amused by the situation.

"Okay. Great! We're on now," she continues.

"Hello and welcome back to our show. We have a new guest. She is an American girl and was just married. We want to find out what it's like for her to get married in India. Elizabeth, can you tell us what your wedding was like? What are your favorite Hindi songs? Can you sing any of them?"

Oh geez, I think to myself. I have no idea what I'm going to say before I start talking. "I loved the wedding. My in-laws are very nice people. I'm having a lot of fun traveling around India. I don't know many Hindi songs by heart. I love Shah Rukh Khan," I add. "I know the national anthem," I say without thinking.

"That's a very patriotic song," the host says. "Are you standing?" I'm asked. By this time, we have arrived at our destination and I'm walking around.

"Yes, I'm standing," I start. "*Jana gana mana adhinayaka jaya hey* . . ." I finish a few lines. I get nervous about singing on the radio and fade quickly, bashfully. The questions continue and blur together and I answer them as best I know how.

My dad and stepmom leave for the airport that evening. Vijay, my brother and Mom had left earlier that day. All the Western guests have checked out of the hotel, including Maggie. I was the first to arrive and I will be the last to leave India, and I'll finish my visit staying in the family condo in Ashoknagar with

Vijay's parents. I get back to the house and tell my in-laws about the radio call.

"Ah yes!" I'm told. "That is a cousin."

"What?!" I say.

"We gave her your number to call," they explain.

I'll have to ask Vijay for the details of who it was when I see him again in the States. I've met so many new people and I have so many questions about all the little things.

My in-laws take me to the airport. Tears well as I walk away from Atha Garu and Mama Garu. I walk through the gate into the airport alone. I am grateful for the experiences this family has given me. I would never have seen India this way as a tourist. I know that for Atha Garu and Mama Garu, having me tag along was riddled with judgment from peers and society. They probably had to explain, on many occasions, who this jumbo-jumbo is. I can only imagine what kinds of conversations take place and the explanations they must provide.

Society and beliefs are what they are. I will never be shorter than Vijay. I will never be Indian. I will not become a doctor or an engineer. I will never understand the full extent of how to behave like an Indian daughter-in-law should. I am certain I've made many cultural mistakes along the way, many of which I will probably never be aware. Nevertheless, Atha Garu and I both tear up as we leave each other at the Hyderabad airport. We were saying good-bye to each other as family.

India has been an amazing experience, and given me a more inclusive appreciation for the rest of the world. But as I board my flight, I also know how good it will feel to be home again, in my own bed and in the comfort of the lifestyle Vijay and I have created together. A month away, for an American, may be something to be proud of, but for an Indian, it has been "just a short visit."

Officially married in both cultures, we anxiously anticipate our next big adventure.
    Babies!

CHAPTER 12

Calling All Eggs and Sperm

Weekly calls to India continually remind us a child is long overdue. The encouragement is relentless and free flowing.

"Oh son, when are you going to have a baby?" Vijay is asked.

"We're working on it, Ma," Vijay confirms.

"Maybe Liz should go get checked again. We are getting old, son. We don't want to die without a grandchild," he's reminded. "Are you even trying? You've been married for four years. When are you going to start?"

"Okay, Ma. We'll look into it."

"It's been too long. I will pray, son," his mom pleads. "You need to try more often."

"There are only certain times a month you can get

pregnant," he reminds her. "You have to time it right."

Thinking we know all there is to know about sex and how to do it, we focus more seriously on this reproductive mission. Five months go by. Nothing. The sixth month proves lucky.

We both start planning in excitement. We tell everyone we know. We paint the nursery and pick out a crib. I feel completely validated in buying tiny onesies, receiving blankets and cute little nursery decorations.

"Oh good, son!" The phone is passed to me. "Congratulations, Liss," I hear from the receiver. "We are so happy to have an heir. Finally, someone to complete the family lineage." I look at Vijay and crinkle my nose.

"Thank you," I say and hand the phone back to Vijay.

I look forward to having more purpose in my housewifery by filling my time with a crying, cooing, peeing, pooping, sweet baby. We are excited to register for baby stuff and do so before I'm even showing. The registry gun is fun. Like any woman with too much time on her hands, I rationalize the absolute need of a baby-wipes-heater unit while enthusiastically swiping the bar code, adding it to the list.

It's time to celebrate.

We decide we don't want to know if it's a girl or a boy and watch the ultrasound pictures accumulate on the fridge in excitement. A little flutter I'm told is a heartbeat, then a little bean-shaped thing. We hang each new set of photos on the fridge when I return from my ob-gyn visit in San Diego. We admire them when we get up in the morning to pour our cereal, and over dinner we talk about how our lives will change. I imagine my new busy, meaningful life in the Valley as I wait for my tummy to grow.

Bangles, Bindis and Babies

Two months pregnant, we update our Homeland Security information and review the rules for sponsoring visitors from India: take out private health insurance, send in our bank statements. Vijay's parents decide to come for a "quick" ten weeks. Their previous experience in the States was packed with travel, Thanksgiving, our marriage and both of us working in time-consuming professions. This time, I am free as a bird. I'm not going to lie: I'm a little anxious about what I'm going to do with them all day in the middle of the desert while Vijay is at work. But we know each other now. How hard can it be?

Our house has a guest room, but it's pretty sparse: a mattress on a metal frame. I drive into San Diego to get supplies. I want them to feel as comfortable as possible. Unaided by Vijay, I try to think of things that would make their stay more comfortable. I purchase new bedsheet-and-comforter set and frame some artwork from our travels. I try to pick a bucket and mug like the one I saw in India for their restroom routine. I buy travel books on Southern California and San Diego for the nightstand, hoping they'll want to do some sightseeing. I go to the Asian store and stock up on spices and mixes for the food they like eating. We buy a television and stand and order a Hindi channel, the only Indian channel we can get in the Valley. I ask Vijay if he can think of anything else. He says his parents are good with what we have.

Vijay picks them up at LAX and brings them to our desert home. Living in a small town and jobless, I have a lot of time for my two dependent in-laws who have completely different cultural expectations from my own. *Indian homemaker* is not exactly a role I have been taught. After miserably and immediately failing at cooking breakfast to their liking, I relinquish proper food preparation to Atha Garu. The strong smell of curry wafts through our home morning, noon and night.

Christmas is approaching. Mama Garu and Atha Garu watch the neighborhood lights go up and decorations come out. I put stockings on the mantel and climb our ladder in the driveway to put lights on the garage roofline. Atha Garu worries about my activity level and offers Mama Garu's assistance the next time I try to do anything *dangerous* while pregnant. I hadn't even thought about it. I feel great, but, if it stresses them out, I guess I could refrain from climbing ladders.

American Christmas traditions are new to them. There are Christians in India, but they are the minority, and materialism hasn't caught on in quite the same way there. I explain how Christmas trees are decorated and that gifts are placed under them. Atha Garu listens to my description thoughtfully. After I'm done explaining, she looks at me and regurgitates this new knowledge.

"Okay, Liss. So the tree comes in the house?" She repeats what she has learned.

"Yes."

"And you place it here . . . in your living room?" She continues looking toward the corner of the room.

"Yes," I say, nodding.

"So then . . . where do the roots go?" She looks around.

"Oh! No! They cut down the tree," I explain. "It is only used that once. Then you throw it away. Some cities use it for mulch and stuff like that . . . after the holidays are over."

She looks at me, silently processing this news, swiveling her head from side to side in understanding. I realize if India was a country full of Christians, this would not be a sustainable endeavor, wasteful even. When Vijay and I first met, he told me what a disposable society we have. I didn't really understand at the time. This was all I knew. But having been to India I know everything gets mended, fixed and reused. At this point, I'm slightly embarrassed.

I share our conversation with Vijay when he gets home.

"So, as a kid, were you aware of Christmas or Christianity?" I ask him.

"Sure!" he says. "Mom was a Christian."

"What?! What do you mean she was a Christian?" I ask, pretty surprised.

"When she met Dad, she converted and took a Hindu name," he tells me. "She changed everything for him."

That's quite a statement. I process a minute. "So her whole name changed? Her entire religious belief system was abandoned? Did she ever do any Christian celebrations with you?" I ask.

"No. She left the religion, and I never grew up celebrating anything besides Hindu festivals. But, there was this time we lived on a base and a Santa came. It was a low-ranking soldier, a really skinny guy dressed in a Santa suit. The kids lined up to receive their gift. The soldier would read the name written on each package, and the kid would walk up to get it." He pauses.

"So what did you get?" I ask him.

"I just watched." He doesn't say any more.

I look at him, waiting for clarification.

He looks at me, realizing he's going to have to finish his story. "Mom told me he was just made up and that the parents gave him the gifts to distribute."

"Ah, bummer," I say. "Were you sad?"

"Well, of course I wanted a gift, but I knew if my parents didn't buy one there was no sense in hoping. I never really thought about it after that."

The following evening, I hear animated talking downstairs between Vijay and his parents. I don't understand what anyone is saying, but as has happened several times before, Vijay comes to me with what I'll call a criticism.

"My parents are upset by the god in the bathroom," he tells me.

"What are you talking about?" I ask.

"There is a god in the bathroom," he says.

"What do you mean 'a god'? What bathroom?"

He explains to me that a black metal artifact that I got on our last trip represents one of the Hindu gods. I purchased a shadow box and had hung it on the wall in one of our restrooms, displaying the figure. I assure him I didn't know it was meant to be a literal representation of a god with placement requirements. I tell him I thought it was really cool art. It never occurred to me that the room it's displayed in matters. Our house is filled with cultural souvenirs. The last thing I want to do is insult his parents, culture or religion. Why would I purposefully cause controversy?

"They are angry," he says. "But I think it's ridiculous too."

"I didn't know. Did you explain that to them?" I'm annoyed. He agrees with me, yet still presents it as a problem. "This stuff happens all the time. How am I supposed to know?" I'm mad at him for bringing it to me as if it's my fault. That metal statue has been there for a long time and he never once said anything. Now, he's coming to me as if I should know that it is somehow inappropriate. Why didn't he do something about it? Why make it a big deal . . . directed at me?

"Why do I always have to be the go-between?" Vijay asks me. He's frustrated and getting angry too.

"Because I don't know this stuff. Like it or not, you are the Indian. These are your parents. And from the sound of it, it's become a big deal." I am frustrated. We're both on the same page and yet we're fighting over this.

I ask what he wants me to do about it. I think this whole situation is ridiculous. I know what I should do. I should take the *god* down graciously. Explain to his parents that I didn't know. But why couldn't *he* have just told them that? Why couldn't he have just said, *Oh, sorry, folks, I'll take it down*? Why is it, *Liz put it up and Liz should know better*? He lives here too.

These little cultural misunderstandings start to happen regularly. Vijay doesn't know how to handle them. He feels like he's caught in the middle and that we, his mother and I, are both right and wrong at the same time. He wants us to communicate directly. He becomes frustrated and defensive with us both. Atha Garu and I start to struggle against each other. For her, when Vijay left India, time stopped.

The Vijay that left her six years ago is not the Vijay I live with now or the Vijay his parents remember. He is not the Vijay I first met and I am not the same Liz he set eyes on at UMass. The lifestyle we share is the one we created together, and each suggestion of wrong-choice-making feels like a direct criticism of me, not us. Vijay is in a bad position between the two women in his life. I want him to support me and his mother wants the same. He's conflicted when there are differences in opinion, and I feel he handles it poorly.

Many, many things have shaped who he has become. She remembers a different time, a time her son listened, followed and communicated his day regularly.

It isn't as though this is the first time we've all spent time together, so why such a big conflict now? I've been to India twice, but my experience there was as a follower. I was directed to do as they do, and did so happily. Their first trip to the U.S. was so packed with travel and our wedding. This trip, we have all the time in the world, and our world is getting a little shaky.

Halfway through the ten-week visit, the weeks begin to pass slowly and we run out of things to say to each other. I think the typical mother-in-law/daughter-in-law relationship can be challenging for anyone, but when you add cultural differences to that relationship, it becomes a really daunting experiment. Vijay constantly finds himself in the midst of *situations and is torn between the way we do things together and the cultural expectations of his parents, both of which he understands and is comfortable with.*

We decide to break up our Valley days by taking his parents on a trip to San Diego. My parents drive down from LA to join us for the weekend. We rent a beach house in Carlsbad. I can't say for sure, but I think they are enjoying themselves. Evening conversations focus on what we are all looking forward to, our baby.

"What are you going to name the baby? It will be a Hindu name, yes?" Atha Garu suggests as she sits across from me on the couch. My parents watch the scene from easy chairs across the room.

"Maybe some of it will be Hindu," I offer, thinking that is generous, since neither one of us is Hindu. I look over at her, then to Vijay for support. He doesn't say anything or look at me. I wonder how this conversation is going to end.

"But the baby is going to be Hindu! What do you mean 'some Hindu'? It must be complete Hindu name," his mother confirms with a hand gesture that I identify as meaning *all is understood*.

"Well, the baby is going to be Indian and American," I say. "Vijay doesn't even consider himself Hindu."

A look of disappointment, blame, and then worry spreads across his mother's face. Vijay doesn't exactly disagree with what she's said or offer any input. I feel vulnerable. Does he actually agree with this? It's news to me. Why doesn't he say anything?

Back in our room, I search the internet for *Indian baby names* online. I make a list of names I like. Vijay keeps telling me the names I'm picking are Muslim and his parents won't understand that either.

"They want a Hindu name, Liz," he explains. "An *American* name would be a Christian name and they are not Muslim."

"This is ridiculous," I say. "There are plenty of people in the States that aren't Christian, Muslim or Hindu, including us. Why can't it just be a multicultural name that we like? I don't see you coming up with any realistic names! The kid is already going to be a Chennamchetty!"

I'm so agitated I could go smoke a carton of cigarettes with Mama Garu.

Another ultrasound opportunity pops up before we know it. I bring back the pictures of our ever-changing little bean, share them with my in-laws and make copies for our parents.

After the appointment, new conversation and cultural expectations about our future child creep in.

"Do you want to know what you're having, Liss?"

"No, we want it to be a surprise."

"Girl or boy, both will be fine, Liss," I'm told.

I'm sure that comment is intended to show open-mindedness, which I appreciate.

As our little being is growing and developing, the pictures get more and more exciting.

"You are doing too much work, Liss. You should be careful when walking around. Don't get up from the couch too quickly," my mother-in-law warns.

"I think I'll be fine," I say.

"The baby may fall," she says. I cringe a little. I'm not a lounger! I'm not sure what that means. This advice has got to be lost in translation, but I'm not going to engage.

"Girls in India cover their head with a shawl. They believe it is to prevent cold. The cold in your ear makes you sick," Atha Garu shares. I look out the window at the sunny desert landscape and feel pretty sure I won't have that problem.

Vijay's parents regularly Skype with his brother. He is settling into a new life in Australia with his new wife. He had decided to study abroad and is struggling to find a position since he is not a citizen. In the past he has asked us to send rent money and pay for an exam, which we did.

During a Skype conversation, he asks his parents to transfer some money. They are unable since they are visiting us, so Vijay asks me, "Can we pay for another exam for my brother?"

"Yeah. Just get the website and we'll pay it directly, just like last time," I tell him.

"Actually, he wants our credit card number," he says.

I have no problem with the money transfer. I am happy to help him. But now I feel like I'm placed in an uncomfortable position. I hesitate. "I don't think you can give someone a credit card number to use out of country if their name isn't on it," I say. "And, if it's charged out of country, won't it trigger a fraud alert or something?"

I'm concerned. Not that I am unwilling to pay for the exam; I just don't feel like his brother needs access to our credit card information. Bush is our president and he has just signed the Terrorist Finance Tracking Program and the Patriot Act. I don't know enough about either program to know how much tracking of foreigners they plan to do, but I also don't want to find out. No one in our family has anything to hide, but my brother-in-law is pretty vocal about his criticism of the United States, post 9/11. Bush makes me nervous, and my husband is not yet a citizen. Maybe I am being paranoid, but flashes of Homeland Security visitor visa forms come to mind. The consequences of one false move are severe, with the government claiming it can take all your assets and property. Governmental mistakes are no joke.

The cultural, generational and personality differences start to wear thin. Vijay goes downstairs to talk to his parents about it. There is a lot of loud discussion, all of which is not in English. Then, his determined steps come back up the stairs to our room. I sit on the bed listening, feeling very uncomfortable.

"Well, my parents are upset that you won't give our credit card information," he says.

"Me?" I say. "Isn't this something we talk about together?"

"Well, I don't have a problem with paying," Vijay says.

"Neither do I! I just don't want our credit card information being used overseas," I explain. "Why can't we just pay online or transfer money? What's the big deal in doing it that way? I'm not trying to pick a fight. I feel like I have a genuine concern."

"You are being ridiculous," he tells me. He's angry and I can see it. But, I feel like my reasons are valid. I know our credit card company would agree.

I listen, but I'm tired of trying. It shows. Vijay goes to the guest room and has another very loud conversation, in Telugu, with his parents. I can only assume it is about *my* decision.

These predicaments make his mother feel unwelcome. I am sorry it's come to this, but I'm ready for a break too. She agrees and says as much. Ten weeks is a long time. Their previous visit went so differently, so quickly. Six weeks flew by. These ten weeks have been about eight weeks too long. What's going on?

Two weeks after they leave, I feel the first gurgles of life in the bulge that is beginning to resemble a baby belly. I'll be headed to my five-month checkup in a week. Since our OB is over 150 miles away, Vijay has yet to join me at an appointment. He'd have to take the day off to come with me, so it seems unnecessary at this point. I gladly fill him in when I return in the evening.

I dutifully read *What to Expect When You're Expecting* each night before bed, making checklists in my head, writing birth plan ideas and deciding which birthing classes to take. I want to give this baby the best of me. I'm so ready for this!

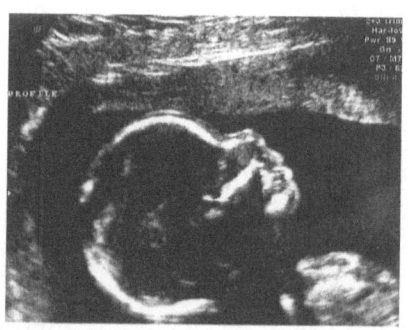

CHAPTER 13

Halfway There

Our five-month checkup is here! I drive the two hours it takes to get to our OB's office in La Jolla. The first appointment of the day, I'm assigned a room immediately. As the ultrasound wand glides back and forth over my stomach, I wait in anticipation of my next batch of pictures.

Maybe I'll head over to the beach once I'm done, soak in some sun. It's a straight shot from the UCSD La Jolla office. It'll be such a relaxing day: I'll put my feet in the water and sit in the sand . . . it's winter, but still pleasant.

My daydream in interrupted by the technician.

"Your little one is a stubborn little thing . . . Let me get a doctor to try to get it to turn around," the ultrasound tech says to me in the exam room. "You don't want to know what you're having? *Right?*"

"No, we want it to be a surprise!" I say, answering the big decision of the day. I know she can tell what gender it will be.

"Okay. Well, hold on a sec," she says, wiping the wand and placing it back on the resting dock. She walks out of the room.

It's quiet for a few minutes. I think about the surprise of who we'll have, a boy or a girl. I mull over all the choices we get to make, like whether to breast-feed, buying or making our own baby food, cloth vs. disposable diapers . . . A second tech enters the room and spends a couple of minutes waving the wand over my lubed stomach. "Hold on . . . Let me get the doctor . . . which is totally normal . . . Lots of people are seen by the doctor, so don't worry."

"Okay," I say, but now I'm a little worried.

I know something isn't right by the way the white-coated man avoids eye contact when he opens the door.

"Hi, I'm Dr. . . . ." the white coat says. I don't catch his name.

"What?" *What did he say?* The room starts to close in and the slow-motion car-crash effect begins.

"I need to see something really quick. Can you turn away from the monitor and face the wall for me?" he continues.

I do. This isn't normal.

"I see a couple of things here . . . Hold on . . . I want to talk to you . . . The first issue I see is . . ." He begins his sentence several times. "Hold on." He reconsiders, then looks at the monitor some more.

"Okay," I whisper. My heart starts pounding. I can feel it beat in my neck.

He mumbles some thoughts to himself or to me; I can't

really tell which. Then he starts talking. "So, I am looking at a couple of things here. There seems to be a serious problem." He pauses and sighs.

I begin to stare at the holes on the acoustic ceiling tiles, telling myself he isn't going to say anything really bad. His voice is distant. I know something is wrong and I am completely unprepared to hear whatever it is he is saying. I interrupt him.

"Um . . . I'm sorry. I can hear you talking, but I have no idea what you're saying. Can you please call my husband? We live out in the Valley and he's at work," I ask as I tear up. "He's a two-hour drive away," I explain.

"Sure." He puts down the ultrasound probe, gets up and starts walking toward the door. "Come with me to the consultation room," he says, as he walks out the door.

I scooch off the exam table and follow, ultrasound gel on my stomach, dazed. I call Vijay's cell phone, which he doesn't answer. I nervously sift through my purse for an office number. I call that next and ask the receptionist to have him call back right away. The doctor and I don't say anything to each other while we wait for his call. The room seems small, sterile and impersonal. All the furniture is cold and hard, the kind you can wipe anything off of.

The phone rings. I look up and stare at the flickering light on the line that belongs to Vijay. The doctor picks up the call and starts explaining.

"Hello. Dr. Chennamchetty?" he asks.

Pause.

"Yes. Well, I have your wife here. I was performing an ultrasound and I am not seeing any movement in the left ventricle," he explains into the phone and pauses.

"No, none at all," he repeats.

Pause.

"Yes."

Longer pause.

"Okay."

Pause.

"I'm recommending she go to the hospital to see the fetal cardiologist," he explains. "Would you like to speak with your wife?"

I stare at his lips as he says these words into the receiver. *Ventricle? Cardiologist? He's talking about a heart?* I reach for the phone as it's handed to me. "Babe?!" I whimper.

"This is very sad," Vijay says.

"What is?" I ask. I'm not following.

"Go to the hospital and meet with the fetal cardiologist. Then call me once you're done." He waits a minute for a response. "Babe?" he says.

"I don't understand!" I sit holding the phone in disbelief.

"Go to the hospital and then we can talk about our options," he says.

"Options?" I repeat.

"Yes, sweetie. Call me once you've met with the cardiologist," he confirms. *Call him? Isn't he on his way? No, he doesn't need to come. I don't need to overreact. I'll call once I have all the facts.*

I hang up the phone, wipe the ultrasound gel off my stomach and put on my clothes. As I walk toward the door I hear, "You need to go to the UCSD Hillcrest emergency room. Do you know where that is?"

I sort of nod. "Yes."

He adds, "Abortion is a real consideration here. Please head over to the hospital. They know you are on your way."

I don't turn around because I don't want to believe what I just heard. I walk slowly, completely dazed, out the door, down the hall and onto the elevator. Everyone and everything is a haze, a fog. I feel like I'm in a strange, cloudy tunnel. I am in shock. *The hospital? Fetal cardiologist? Drive there?*

Luckily, my appointment was the first of the day. I do know one person in town who hasn't left for work. I call my brother, who predictably sleeps in and lives only a mile away. I drive to his apartment. I tell him my news. He takes the morning off and drives me to the hospital.

Sitting in my brother's car, headed toward the hospital, my phone rings. It's a number I don't recognize.

"Elizabeth?" a woman's voice asks.

"Yes?" I can feel the anxiety in my voice and chest.

"We need you to come back to the office when you're done at the hospital. We need to give you a RhoGHAM shot because of the testing we performed while you were here," a medical receptionist explains into the phone.

"Okay," I respond. I don't know whether I'm coming or going. I feel annoyed they are calling about this now. Couldn't they have done this while I was in the office? They really don't understand the crisis I'm spiraling into. I can't just bounce around town as if running errands. I'm in shock, confused, and now frustrated.

The fetal cardiologist and a resident meet us at the hospital. They are wearing white lab coats, but I can't bring myself to really look at either one of them as they glide the ultrasound probe over my stomach. Sitting on swivel stools, they stare at a monitor, occasionally point at the screen and discuss what they are looking at for about half an hour. I lie there waiting, silently. My brother sits in the corner chair next to me. We don't look at each other and don't talk. When the attending physician is through, he walks the wheeled stool over to me on the gurney and starts drawing on a piece of paper clipped to his notebook.

"Are you religious?" he says as he draws.

"What?!" I look at the top of his head. He's still looking at the paper he is drawing on.

He looks up from his sketch. "Well, I want to explain options while respecting your beliefs," he explains, looking into my eyes.

"Oh," I say, nodding my head in understanding. I pause. "Wait . . . So you're saying nothing can be done?" I slowly realize what he means.

"Yes. I'm very sorry," he says as he hands me the picture he just drew and begins to explain the difference between a healthy baby's heart and ours.

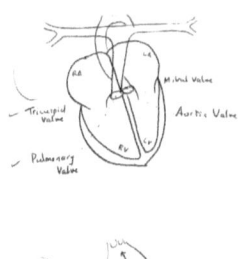

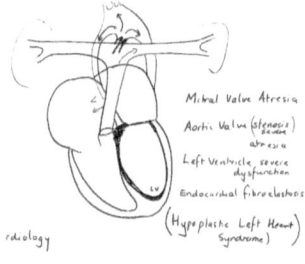

"But I don't understand. Nothing?" My voice cracks. "How can that be?" I sit dumbfounded. "How is that even possible? Nothing," I whisper.

I sit silently for a minute. I don't understand. Tears begin to roll down my face and I just stare at him.

He says, "Your baby's heart is not formed correctly. There is no movement at all in the left ventricle. That isn't the only problem, though."

"But, can't it be fixed?" I interrupt.

"Well, there are some in-utero clinical trials. One in Boston, one in San Francisco, but I really don't think you will qualify. Too much is wrong. It's just too abnormal," he says.

My brother walks me out of the ER to the parking garage. I am overwhelmed. I know we are talking, but I'm not listening to what we're saying. He drops me off at his apartment and leaves for work. I make my way to my car and go back to the ob-gyn's office for my RhoGHAM shot. *Why am I alone right now? Where is Vijay? Am I strong enough to do this myself?*

Other pregnant people sit around the waiting room with loved ones, waiting for the checkup I'm supposed to be enjoying too. I look at the newborns in strollers, with mothers who have just given birth. I sit and wait for my turn. Tears start streaming again and I can't control them. I grab a magazine and turn the pages aimlessly. The receptionist behind the counter finishes her call with a patient, looks up and calls me to the front. She checks me in and notices my watery eyes. She says, "It's all right, honey."

"No it isn't," I whisper, though I feel like yelling. I can't understand why she would say that if she doesn't even know why I'm crying. *Why did they make me drive all the way back here right now? Can't this wait? Don't they understand I need help?* I'm lost. I'm alone. I'm coming unhinged.

The door opens and a nursing assistant calls my name. "Elizabeth?"

I stand up and walk through the door and into a room.

"Are you ready for your shot?" a cheery nurse asks.

I begin to sob.

"What's wrong?" she asks.

"My baby is going to die," I whimper helplessly.

"Oh," she says, not sure how to continue the conversation. I'm a little surprised she doesn't ask me if I need help. She doesn't ask if I'm with anyone. She simply picks up the shot that has been prepped on the tray.

"Just a little pinch," she says.

I don't say anything else to her.

Somehow, I make my way back to the car. I don't know where to go now. I don't know what to do. No one has given me a task, a next step. I'm at a red light and have no idea which way to turn. I see a strip mall across the street and pull into the lot. A sandwich shop is the closest store to my parking spot. I buy a drink, sit in a booth, and call my mom. As soon as she answers she knows something's up.

"What's wrong?" she asks.

"It's the baby." I tell her what I know so far, my voice breaking.

"We'll be there as soon as Papi gets home from work tonight. Hopefully we won't hit too much traffic through LA," she says.

"Okay. Vijay is coming in tonight also. He has to drive back to the Valley to wrap some things up tomorrow, though," I tell her. She keeps talking, but I'm not listening anymore.

The first real ping of abandonment creeps inside. *Where is everyone? Why isn't anyone leaving now to be with me? Isn't this a big deal?* I sit for a little while, trying to decide where to go next. I can't sit crying in a booth all day.

I go back to my brother's apartment and call my dad in Texas. I tell him our news as well. The more I say it, the more it seems untrue. I feel like I'm repeating horrible news that belongs to someone else. I lie on the living room floor of my brother's apartment, staring at the vaulted popcorn ceiling silently. The plans I have are crumbling. The meaning in my life is slipping away. The Valley, the isolation, the joblessness all float over me and our baby rains down on me like a dark black cloud, jabbing at my heart like a bolt of lightning. What am I going to do?

I lie there the rest of the day, numb. As the sun sets, the people who love me start to arrive, offering their support, advice and opinions. How did I go from having no one to a room full of opinions? Vijay, Mom, Papi, my brother—it doesn't matter how lovingly they say it, what examples they provide or how much support they offer. I don't want to hear any of it. I don't want to believe any of it. Now, I feel invaded.

It's our baby, but it's my body. I feel like all the decision-making is ultimately my responsibility. I don't want to hear about what it's like for other parents with babies that suffer on machinery or parents that have to watch their child die after birth. I don't want to hear about the *least painful* or *quickest* death. I don't want to believe these are my choices.

Vijay is such a practical person, so clinically based. He didn't grow up voicing emotion or acting irrationally. For the first time ever, he feels distant from me. I'm sure he feels this loss. I'm sure he is sad. He says, "This is sad," but I have yet to see a tear or hear an outburst. He is grounded and rational about the decision we need to make and it's making me angry. Why are we so different? Where are *his* feelings?

"It was nothing you did," they all keep saying.
"It is not genetic. Totally random," I hear more than once.
"You can't do anything to prevent something like this."
"These things just happen," they say.

Forty-eight hours and a few consultants later, it is confirmed. The cardiologist is right. Our baby's heart is deformed. The diagnosis is catastrophic. Hypoplastic left heart syndrome, mitral valve atresia, aortic valve atresia, left ventricle severe dysfunction and endocardial fibroelastosis. A bunch of big words that basically mean the left ventricle is not working at all. The aortic valve is not even formed. It's frozen. It is deformed so severely that even if our baby makes it to full term, he won't live without an immediate heart transplant, which is not a permanent solution and is extremely improbable, risky and painful. The damage is too extensive, unfixable. He is completely dependent on my body, which is supporting his blood flow, giving him life. Once he's born, that won't be the case.

Death is really the diagnosis. It is certain. It's just a matter of when. When will our precious baby that we have been anxiously, obsessively waiting for have to die and how painful will that death be? The choice is impossible, shocking. How can this happen? What kind of choice is this?

I suppose if fetal imaging technology didn't exist, we could be asking similarly difficult questions after a miscarriage or a stillbirth. That isn't comforting, though. We have to make a decision. I don't sleep for three days straight while we weigh our options.

We finally decide to have an abortion. What an ugly word, *abortion*. Society has turned it into an ugly word.

Because of my gestation, this requires preparation. I have to be manually dilated several days prior to the procedure. I can't go home to the Valley until it's over, so I decide to stay at my brother's apartment. Mom drives back down from Los Angeles to stay with me. Vijay goes back to the Valley to wrap a few things up at work. He tells me he'll be back at the end of the week.

When we arrive at the hospital, the first dilation morning, the office doors are still locked. Mom walks into the building with me and I stand against the wall in the hallway, waiting for the staff to unlock the door. I can't talk. I am numb. I lean against the wall and silently cry. Then, my knees feel weak as I slide down the wall and squat by the door.

"What do you want to do?" Mom asks.

"What *can* I do?" I say. She holds my hand as I cry.

The office door opens and I walk in. I look around the chair-lined waiting room and pick a seat. Happy couples, the women with ready-to-explode bellies and newborn babies, arrive and sit in chairs waiting for their appointments. Why do I have to share a waiting room with *them?* Why are they blissfully ignorant of the loss I am feeling? How come *they* don't see that I am in more pain than any other person has ever been in? I have never felt such pain, such heartache. I am jealous and angry. The emotions inside me are overpowering. I want to die.

"Elizabeth. You can come in now," says the clinician behind the door. "Is it all right for the residents to be in the room to watch?" she asks.

"Yes." I always say yes. I think it's important for residents to learn from real-life experiences. Today, though, I just don't care. Nothing matters. They can do what they want to me.

Mom walks with me. We enter the room. She stands next to my head as I lie on the gurney.

"We are going to insert these laminaria sticks into your cervix to help you dilate. You will need to come back tomorrow, and we will remove them and put new ones in. You can take Vicodin for the pain and you may have some bleeding," the doctor says as she hands me some pamphlets. "Please read this packet of information and make sure you follow the directions."

"Okay," I say as I drape a paper sheet across my lap. My feet are placed in stirrups and I look away.

I don't speak for the entirety of the procedure. I lie on the table, exposed, while huge tears run down my face. Even though my mother stands by my side and holds my hand, I feel completely alone, powerless and weak. The reason I'm here breaks my heart.

They finish and I get dressed. My mom tells me I have to eat. We stop at a café for a bite. I'm not in pain, but I scoop up a Vicodin and a glass of water and order something off the menu. I sit numb and depressed as I move the food around the plate.

A half hour later we get back into the car and drive toward my brother's apartment, which has now become the crisis hub. My phone rings.

"How are you feeling, sweetie?" Vijay asks. "I canceled

clinic for Thursday afternoon and Friday. I'll be in town soon," he says.

"Okay," I respond, staring out the window at the passing cars on I-5.

"Vijay . . . I just want . . . oh no . . . wait . . . I can't see . . . My lips are tingling." I drop the phone. "MMMMMMMOOOMMMM???? I CAN'T SEE!" My blood pressure drops and I begin to lose consciousness.

"I'm pulling over," I hear her say. Her voice is distant, as my mom navigates the car through traffic on the freeway.

I must be leaning against the car door because when my mom opens it, my body follows the door. The seat belt holds me in as I dangle limply out of the car and throw up on the shoulder of the freeway. My mom supports me and I can gradually start hearing her.

"Liz!? Liz!?" I hear.

I regain my composure and look up at her. I can feel the traffic speed by.

She looks me over, concerned, making sure I'm all right. When she feels certain I'm okay she says, "You might want to call Vijay back. That probably scared him."

Mourning what's to come Friday, I don't sleep. I call the mental health department of the hospital and ask for help. I get an appointment with the director of the psychiatry department and a prescription for sleeping pills, and I ask for additional therapy. Help is scarce as it's almost Christmas. Most of the staff is out for the holidays. The department head meets with me and agrees I need someone to talk to who isn't family.

By the last laminaria dilation, we are told the baby is a boy. A resident tells me that not only does he have a defective heart, but also a chromosomal abnormality. Both random, both rare, and neither associated with the other. I sit and process this for a moment. It's like winning the worst lottery in the world . . . twice.

A social worker sits next to me while I wait on the table in the exam room. There is a small window with closed blinds. I wish the blinds were open. I wish I could see outside, a tree or the clouds, something to focus on. I don't want to talk to her, but she starts talking anyway. I hate her because she is there, because she is going to try to help me, and I'm not ready to talk. Not yet. Not to her. There is nothing she can say that is going to help me right now.

"Do you have other children at home?" she asks.

"No," I respond. I look at her like that was a mean question.

"Oh. Okay," she says. "I only ask because then you could focus on them."

Pause.

"Do you already have the nursery set up?"

"Yes," I say flatly. *How is this supposed to be helping?*

"Oh wow. Okay. Well, retail therapy is a great form of therapy," she offers, this time with a smile. *Retail therapy? Really? What kind of training do these people get?*

A few minutes of silence pass and she adds, "Did you decide how you want to handle the remains?"

I look up and stare.

We decide to have him cremated. The social worker gives me a list of funeral homes and I pick one. I call and make an appointment. Mom drives me.

"Welcome," a somber man greets us in the lobby. "How can I help you today?"

"I need to schedule a cremation," I say.

"Okay. I can help you with that." He is a fitting funeral home employee. His eyes look kind; he is mellow and consoling. I fill out all the paperwork he hands me, answer his questions and write a check.

"What was the date of death?" he asks.

I hesitate and look at him. "Tomorrow," I say.

His eyes open wide and he looks at me, then quickly adjusts his facial expression and accepts the date, without comment. I appreciate his composure.

"The hospital will call us once your baby is in the morgue," he explains. "We will pick him up and cremate him. Once we are through, we will call you and you can pick him up."

Back at the hospital, the social worker suggests a support group at a local church. "Just tell them you lost your baby," she explains. "They don't believe in abortion."

I look at her with a sarcastic eyebrow grimace and roll my eyes. *What the fuck? How is that going to help me? If I can't be honest about what is happening, what good is the group?* I call the psychiatrist's office and ask for psychotherapy. I'm assigned a psychologist and given an appointment for after the holidays. I'm totally irritated there aren't more support options. Understanding my desperation, they also place a hospice grief-counseling referral.

The day has come.

We drive to the hospital on what I refer to as *death day*. As it's still dark outside, I wear sweats and a hoodie pulled over my head. Vijay and Mom are with me in the waiting room. My name is called and I get into line with all the other people waiting to have surgery. Vijay comes in with me. My tears start streaming. I am not making noise, just crying. I feel completely exposed, helpless and sad. I don't stop crying until it's over.

The first thing I think when I see the resident in recovery is how appreciative I am that she is there. "Thank you for seeing me through this. You are the only familiar staff member I saw this whole time." It is comforting to have a little consistency. I am groggy, uncomfortable and feel a throbbing sadness. Blood is streaming from me and I feel completely empty.

"I'll bring in your husband," she says. "Your baby has been taken to pathology and will then go to the morgue. The funeral home will pick him up," she explains and walks away.

I don't see her again.

The funeral home wrote *Baby Chennamchetty* on all our paperwork. I start to wonder. Should we give him a name? We're choosing to send him to a funeral home. What do we do with this grief, these ashes and this child who will never be?

I lie on the gurney and name him.

Matthew Prashant.

A couple of days later it's Christmas. Everyone has taken back their baby-related gifts, and I sit on the floor of my living room fiddling with a stocking stuffer. I look down at my shirt. It's wet.

"What? No one told me about colostrum? I didn't even think about producing milk if I wasn't full term," I murmur and head up the stairs to take a shower and squeeze out whatever I can.

I don't sleep through most nights, and many times I awake actively crying. I dream that friends have been hacked to pieces and stuffed in a car trunk, or sometimes that I have been hit by a car and left in a ditch by the side of the road to die a slow, painful death.

The hospice grief counselor who is filling in for the holidays calls and lets me know my psychologist is on vacation. She tells me they want to check in with me, since this is a difficult time of the year. I tell her about my dreams. She says that they make perfect sense. There's comfort in telling someone, in admitting I have them.

Vijay tries to console me. He wakes me the nights I cry out loud, rubs my back and tells me we made the right decision.

I let Vijay give his parents updates on what is happening. I'm sure they are disappointed. I know they sympathize, but they give me a break from their opinions and comments. I don't really want to talk to them or know what they think right now. I know how much they wanted this. Being pregnant was something I finally did right.

The day after Christmas, Mom decides I need to get out of the house. As she puts it: "You shouldn't dwell." The guys decide to spend the weekend golfing in Tucson and leave early the next morning. Vijay calls about an hour into their drive to say that Homeland Security stopped them at a border checkpoint between Arizona and California. He forgot his passport and visa paperwork. They let him go after a strongly worded warning. He asks me to grab it and bring it along with me.

Now I have to go. How can I get out of going and leave my husband potentially stranded in Arizona without his immigration papers? I am skeptical of the notion that this is a good idea or that it will somehow help me with my grief. I wallow in self-pity as I'm loaded into the car along with my brother and mom. I ask to drive. I want to avoid having to sit quietly in the backseat, thinking. I want to concentrate on anything other than my self-loathing attitude. I speed down I-8 deeper into the desert. *What the hell am I going to do in Tucson? This idea totally sucks! How can Vijay want to go golfing?* As I drive faster and faster, it doesn't take long before I'm pulled over.

"Ma'am, do you know how fast you were driving?" the officer asks.

The truth is I don't care. "Eighty-five or ninety?" I say flatly.

"Ma'am, you need to be more careful while operating a motor vehicle," he says. "It's a big responsibility."

"I know. I deserve the ticket," I tell him quietly.

He issues the citation and asks when the last time I got a ticket was.

"Oh, I don't know. It's been years," I say calmly. But my inner dialogue is loud and angry. *I don't care! Fuck this! My baby is dead!*

He looks at me indifferently, but still adds, "Well, ma'am. Please be careful. There is another speed trap ahead. You wouldn't want to get two tickets in one day."

I sign the citation and put the car in drive.

"Are you sure you don't want me to drive?" Mom asks as I pull away from the emergency lane.

I don't even answer. I just keep driving. It feels fitting to get a ticket. I deserve it.

The raw, naked sting of pain is something I haven't felt before.

Not like this.

This changes a person.

CHAPTER 14

Swimming in the Dregs

Pregnant women seem to follow me around. Everywhere I go, I see women about to pop or infants so small they just squeak, the most precious squeak there is, but also the most hurtful when you are singularly focused on wanting it for yourself.

Breast-feeding, nursery furniture, organic baby food and clothing fade away. It all becomes insignificant. I feel sorry for myself. Disbelief and then anger set in. I go through the stages of grief many times, sometimes in order, sometimes backwards, trying to complete them like some sort of assignment I have to get through to graduate.

Denial and isolation? *Check.*

Anger? *Check.*

Bargaining? *Maybe . . . What do you have for me?*
Depression? *Check again!*
Acceptance? *Oh man. I'll have to do that?*

I go to therapy every week to try to make sense of what I am going to do with myself.

"Maybe you could plant a tree at your house in honor of your baby?" my therapist suggests kindly.

"I live in the desert," I sigh. "It's so hard to grow things there. I'll probably underwater or overwater it, and it will die," I whimper.

"Okay then . . . So, we aren't quite ready for a tree." I look up and belly-laugh while I sob, realizing how out of control I really am.

It is hard to tell people the honest, raw truth about what happened. For a while now, I've been telling people that our baby had a defect and we had him at the hospital. To say it any other way seems unfair. It may seem strange to say we chose to have an abortion out of love. But, we did it out of love. We chose the quickest end we knew and we chose it because we wanted to curb inevitable suffering for him, not us.

I'm scared of getting pregnant again. I don't know how to wait five months in anticipation of bad news. How do you nurture and love the idea of something, ask it to grow and then have to say good-bye in such a brutal way? I am shocked and saddened by the lack of resources available for a grieving parent in this circumstance. This lack of resources causes me to focus on one step in the grief process most, anger. I have become keenly aware of just how hateful the reproductive debate in this country has turned. Women have been expected to deal with abortion silently, as if it's something to cover up or to be ashamed of. But, this is my body, my child and my life.

We did everything the right way. We got married, waited, planned and saved. We got pregnant, ate healthy and got prenatal care.

How can I heal unless I can be honest? How can I be honest, when there are people living in our country ready to kill an abortion doctor, or protest in front of a clinic that helps women in need? How can we help women who can't find a support group because they are rejected, or viewed as criminals by some? I should feel secure in this healing process, not judged or secretive.

The word *abortion* is not a punch line. It shouldn't be used willy-nilly to get votes or to distinguish between those who love life from those who supposedly don't. It's something that happens to women. An abortion is an invasion of your body, mind, spirit and heart. Everyone who has one is affected forever, no matter the reason, no matter the circumstance. It's insulting to throw the word around as a bargaining chip in negotiations on legislation, to hold the appointment of officials hostage, or to demonize the person who has made the choice to have one. To limit access or to restrict and deny availability is offensive, harmful and barbaric.

I'm angry. And, I've earned the right to say this. No one should have a daughter, a wife, a sister in need of such care. Care that has been stigmatized. Care that is painful. Care that is humiliating. Care that feels shameful. Care that is devastating. Care that is invasive. Care that is expensive, even when you are insured. Care that leaves you bleeding, naked, fat and worst of all, without a child.

Some of our conservative friends have told me in hushed

tone, "Oh, I had a D&E too." As if now I'm in a secret club, where we can share our sins. A club where it's okay if you call it a D&C or D&E instead of an abortion. Is it okay if you shame it publicly, but have one privately? Is it okay if *you* have one as long as *they* don't? I've never seen or heard of anyone who skips into the ob-gyn's office to have one, thrilled for the opportunity.

I'm not ready to get pregnant again. I want a child. I just can't do it again. Not yet.

Vijay handles things differently. He's hard at work, busy helping people with *real problems*. All day he helps people combating delusions, suicidal tendencies and homelessness. He gets home from work and reminds me I have a roof over my head and food to eat.

"Liz, go live in the Salton City," he suggests in response to my gloom.

"I can't believe you are telling me that! I am really having a hard time!" I rebut. "I *am* grateful for the things we have." Still the black hole of emptiness looms heavily on my heart.

Most evenings and weekends Vijay spends out of the house, golfing. When he does come home, I want to talk, since I go many days without talking to anyone. Understandably, though, he needs a break from talking about our life. I think we love each other. I convince myself that once I find meaning in my life again, everything will get better.

He keeps in touch with his family, updating them on what happened. I haven't talked to anyone. I'm in no state to have a *try again* conversation, and I'm not ready to cope with the intrusion of opinions and advice that's often given by his family. They did wish me well, but what else can they say really? I need to heal on my own, in my own time.

On optimistic days, when all the stars align, Vijay and I talk about what our family will look like some day, and how we will get there.

"Mom always wanted four kids," I tell him. "She told me if she had married the right person, she would have adopted children too."

He listens. "Four kids, Liz? That's a lot of kids! I think two is a good number. I'm from a country with an overpopulation problem."

"What do you think of that, though?" I ask. "The adoption part?"

He doesn't respond right away. It's taking time to sink in. "Foster care and adoption is not an Indian concept," he offers.

"I really don't want to get pregnant again. Not now. I know we don't have a genetic concern . . . It just doesn't feel right. We need to take a break or consider children that are already here, who need homes now," I suggest.

"The planet is overcrowded," Vijay agrees in his typically rational way. "I think it's an option." He looks at me, concerned. "My poor parents. They aren't going to understand."

While Vijay is at work I run errands, clean the house, mow the lawn and pay the bills. Pulling into our driveway after a grocery run, my neighbor crosses the street holding a houseplant.

"Don't worry," she sighs. "If I get pregnant again, you can have our baby!" She hands me the plant. "I already told my husband!" she adds cheerfully.

"Oh. Okay," I say and smile. I haven't told her our whole

story yet, but she knows I'm not pregnant anymore. "You rock," I add lamely.

What else can I say? She gives me a hug and hurries back to her car to head for work. I watch her drive away. I actually believe her and appreciate her potential *oops baby* offer.

After what can only be described as a mediocre trip to the States, Atha Garu tells Vijay's brother about her negative experience during her visit. He is older than Vijay, so culturally feels he has a responsibility to inform me of my gaffes.

Checking e-mail one night, I see a message from him, so I open it right away. I glance at the length; it's a whopper. As soon as I start to read, my heart starts pounding.

Dear Elizabeth,

I hope you are doing well. It has been a long time since I heard from you. Of course I talk with Vijay and he keeps us informed about everyone there.

I am sure that you are now fine. Of course you will be very good, you are a doctor's wife, aren't you? I know that when a girl in America marries a doctor she is looked upon with envy. Just kidding. We are happy that you are a member of our family. Actually ever since we got to know you in 2004—when you visited us in Kanpur— we have always tried to make you welcome, comfortable and feel like a member of our family.

But of late we really feel that this feeling was not mutual and that you obviously do not share the same feeling. Of course we can attribute a part of this to the cultural factor.

When you visited Sydney, you weren't exactly very warm towards us. At least I felt that. That could be attributed to jet lag, a short and packed itinerary and also that you were with child at that time. But I am not that naive as not to get the feeling that you do not like me or that there were some underlying biases towards me. When I asked you to come to our place in Parramatta, there was no response and you even said "we will see." And to think that when one of our uncles visited Sydney on a two-day business trip, he took time to come and visit our home. Well, Vijay said that since you were seeing us pretty much every day you did not feel the need to come over to Parramatta as it was such a small trip.

Of course you might be thinking here that I have no business to talk and say all this to you. But well, you should never forget that even though Vijay has been integrating in your culture he is still an Indian who has a family. Americans might be individualistic and family might become secondary to their own self, but that does not work in collectivistic cultures where we feel that we have a say in things relating to our people.

Of course for you, your family might be your biological one and not the one that you have married into. That is no fault of yours. Vijay never took an effort to give you some cultural education. And look where that has brought things to.

When our parents visited Vijay, it should have been a learning experience for you. But as Vijay told me on the phone it was something different. He said that "Elizabeth and Mummy were living in two different universes". There were cultural gaps but as a daughter in law you should have made the effort to try to at least bridge that gap. They are elderly people and they come from a culture where respect is a part of life. However, it is tragic they found neither affection or respect. Of course you seem to forget that you have married Vijay who comes from a different culture. And obviously I feel that you have not tried to at least make the effort to learn the basics of that culture.

At least our parents were open and did not make any fuss when Vijay announced the decision to marry you. Of course, anyone would have preferred someone from a similar cultural background. But that is not how life works. They were made to realise that it was Vijay who paid their airfare. And of course there was the gross insensitivity to our religious icons. Anyone would know that placing a religious icon in the toilet is not exactly respectful. One can be atheistic or agnostic, but that does not mean that one should be disrespectful to any religious symbol be it Christian, Hindu or any religion.

However if spending money for your own was such a big deal then have you ever realised that our family happily gave Vijay money to buy the Chicago property with no second thoughts. That too when considering that the Indian currency at that time was 50 Rupees to an

American Dollar. The money that was given was a small fortune, something that an average Indian would take years to make. But like we Indians always say, it is how families function.

Everyone in our family have been trying hard to make you welcome. We even organised the wedding in India—you might be thinking here that it is no big deal because Vijay did foot a part of the bill—but who put in the effort when there was no need to. There was no need for him to give the money, we would have done it anyway. But being a westerner you will not appreciate or even understand the dynamics of how Indian/ Eastern families work.

And now there is the thing about charity. There is an old saying that "Charity begins at home". Vijay wants to get involved in fostering and even adopting which would be American children. But isn't it odd that the large heartedness did not extend when you refused to pay a few measly dollars for our parents' shopping and you split the bill. Of course it is not your fault. It is how your culture works. Where families will not pay for one another.

Of course when I asked Vijay for his credit card number to pay for the visa fees, Vijay refused to give it. Of course we all know who was really refusing. But then it is again your culture where a mother will not trust her own children. Of course it was hurtful. However when our friends knew, about three people gave us their credit card details and said that their credit card was mine to use. The three people were an Indian, a Persian and an English. Strangely I wonder aren't English westerners too. But then that is about love and trust. I still have their credit card details with me and have they been put to financial risk? Of course they haven't because they still are such dear friends.

Of course you might be thinking that why should our feelings matter in your decisions. Vijay told that to our parents about fostering and adopting, they were hurt. They don't say anything because they don't want to hurt you. Which is again an eastern trait which Americans might not even understand let alone appreciate.

Today whenever I talk to Vijay about these things Vijay says that it is easy for me to say all this because I am not married to a white person and do not know how it feels living with a white person. And so I cannot understand his position. He even called it a cultural nightmare. Of course I am not lying. It is true. When your partner does not make the effort to adapt to your culture or at least try to learn about it then it can be a nightmare. There is no one to blame except the situation. However when life is going smooth without you making the slightest effort —with us bending head over heels to try to adapt to you why would you even try.

Vijay has always said that you are different because according to him most American girls do not care for the husband's family. But somewhere down the line a tiny detail seems to have been lost. In this case that being that the husband's family is not American. Of course had you been so American you would not have married an Indian in the first place. But there were a lot of other factors in play as we all know which even includes the life that you are currently leading which includes things that you might not have done if you had not married into our family.

I would like to add here that your idea of fostering and adopting (which would be American) children has hurt our family a lot. You in your American sensibilities might not even care for this. But I feel that if you had even the slightest regard for us—your husband's family— you would not want to hurt us. I hope you have not forgotten the lengths to which a foreign family went to accommodate you and treat you as one of their own. This would be the least that you could do for them.

Of course I do not expect you to warm towards me after reading this letter. I am sure you might not even read this letter. And Vijay might get ballistic and not want to have anything to do with us. But then that would again prove that had it been someone from our culture, they would have taken it as an advice from a dear family member and not get so upset.

I have seen interracial couples who have so well adapted to each other's cultures. But in your case you have not done enough whether you like it or not. When I say 'we', it is an Eastern thing which perhaps Americans may not understand because with them it is all I - me - my - mine.

I remember you telling me that initially you were hesitant to approach Vijay because you did not want to ruin it between him and his family. But isn't it ironic that you landed your husband in a 'cultural nightmare'. It is not as if you are newly married. It has been four years and how much effort have you put in to learn anything about him or his culture except for watching some gibberish Hindi films. While Vijay has adapted so much to you to the extent of not even eating meat at home among other things, I ask how far have you gone? Have you made an attempt to learn about the culture or religion that your husband come from? If you look deep inside yourself, I guess not much. You might even say, why do you need to?

The bottom line is that we do not expect you to pay heed to our feelings. You will conveniently put it to cultural gaps. But since Vijay wouldn't convey our feelings and we feel since you are a member of our family—we think of you as one of us—we have the right to let you know what we think. I sincerely hope you do understand that. Had you been someone from our culture or even an Eastern person there would have been no place for this letter either.

When I said that I hardly ever hear from you, Vijay said that if I want to keep in contact with you I should be on facebook and that you are not much of an email person. What can I say to that? Of course like I said before we will try to adjust to your ways and shrug it away. I wonder how much effort or time would an occasional email take.

Of course Mummy did join facebook. I wonder if you would realise the significance of that.

I hope you take what I have to say in the right spirit.

If I have said anything inappropriate do forgive me.

With love,
Sanjay

I've never read anything like this before, definitely not something directed at me. I knew Sanjay didn't like the U.S., but I had no idea how displeased he was with me personally. My heart continues to pound as I reread it, hoping maybe I've taken it too seriously the first time through. I'm not in any state to receive this. This e-mail is one more disheartening blow to my quickly dissolving self-image.

I have to respond. I have to explain. I'm angry. No. Sad. No. Frustrated. How can he be related to Vijay and be so incredibly different in approach and view? Maybe I could explain my side of each allegation. All of his references happened, in varying degrees, but the reasoning, the explanation, the outcome is vastly different in my reality. I guess you really can have three people experience the exact same thing and have three totally different interpretations of it.

I care deeply about Vijay's happiness and I care about his family. Maybe I could reason with Sanjay. Maybe I should tell him to buzz off. Maybe I shouldn't respond at all. No, I have to address this. I press reply.

Dear Sanjay,

I am sorry that your life has been this disrupted because I am a member of your family. Vijay and I share a loving, strong, happy life partnership and do not live it trying to cause any hurt or anxiety to anyone – let alone our family. I am aware of the cultural differences we have. For you to think that I am completely unaffected by them is ignorant. The fact that you feel I don't care about culture or do not want to learn from experiences (positive or negative) shows how very little you know about me.

I do not think you understand the intense sadness losing a child can cause a person. I would appreciate if you would refrain from advising us on how or who we should parent in such a hurtful way again. I am aware that you are upset; it is obvious from your e-mail. I hope you are able to find happiness and peace in your life Sanjay. I am happy to correspond with you but I don't want to play this game and will not participate in this sort of attack in the future.
Peace,
Elizabeth

I cc Vijay and his parents, just so we are all on the same page, confident that everyone will agree this was a bit over the top. No one says anything. I'm shocked that Vijay's mom confirms her feelings as accurate to Vijay during the next weekly call home, and even more shocked that Vijay completely understands her view. Before this, I was oblivious to the depth of our miscommunication. But it's clear now. Crystal clear.

One final response sits in my in-box. I click open,

Dear Elizabeth,

If you feel that I am attacking you and playing a game, then you have not understood me. We all belong to one family and so I thought that as an older brother I have the right to tell you what I feel. There is no place for games or attacks. Because I think of you as one of our dear family members, I thought I could tell you about this. I hope you understand that. We should all live happily together.

Love
Sanjay

I don't reply to this e-mail. I'm actually surprised he felt the need to send any of this. We've only ever met twice and we don't communicate much otherwise. Once was on the first trip I ever took to India. The second time, my brother, mom and stepdad went with us to visit them in Australia before Atha Garu and Mama Garu came to visit.

"I won't be coming to the United States again, son," Atha Garu tells Vijay.

What is Vijay supposed to do with this news? What am I supposed to do with this news? Vijay says he understands both sides. He understands his mom's frustration and where she is coming from. I don't know what to do. I take the letter and my response to the next psychotherapy appointment and ask for advice. I don't know how to move forward from this and be true to myself. I feel rejected by Vijay and his family. I feel so alone.

Vijay starts to pull away from me more directly, too.

"Good night. I love you," I say, as I pull the sheets up and snuggle into my pillow.

"Thanks," he tells me. I open my eyes to look at him. "What?!" I ask, "Thanks?"

He glances my way. "What?! I can't tell you I love you if I don't feel it," he says to me.

What have I done to justify this new behavior? Who says that to his wife? I'm grasping at straws now. There are only two choices. Fix it, or don't. I'm not sure how much more *broken* I can get. I make sure my therapy appointments are confirmed and try to figure out what to do with myself and my grief, alone, in the middle of the desert, with absolutely nothing to do.

It always gets worse before it gets better. I start sleeping in, wearing pj's all day, and watching an extreme amount of musicals while Vijay's at work. Musicals are my chocolate. *Evita* becomes a regular, twice-a-day choice. I stand in our living room belting out Evita's song as she dies at the end of the movie.

After two weeks of this . . . I realize I can stop. I'm tired of crying. I'm tired of all of this. I need to figure out what to do. How do I make something out of the dregs of this barrel?

With fifteen pounds of pregnancy weight, on top of a lazy body that needs to move, I must redefine myself in the Valley. I must find meaning again. Since there aren't any women eagerly lining up to hear my plight in an *I had a late-stage abortion too and now my marriage is going to shit* group, I must create a normalcy rehabilitation program for myself.

An acquaintance, Sarah, agrees to start walking with me for exercise. We become morning mall walkers. I've never envisioned myself as a mall walker. And, I've never seen another thirty-year-old mall walker. But when life gives you lemons . . .

Each morning we walk five miles around the mall. These early mornings become life analysis sessions and for me a new exercise partner who becomes a desperately needed companion and friend. We discuss the volunteer work that unites us and eventually share our lives. Sarah shares her stories with me and listens to mine without judging.

It feels good. I have someone. Someone local. Someone who cares about me.

One day, after a morning walk, I sit at my desk sorting the mail. Amongst the medical bills that have started to stream in comes a letter from our condo board in Chicago. They inform us they will not grant a waiver for our unit to be rented another year. The prior year, the board allowed us to rent our condo in our all-owner-occupied building, since the market was in such bad shape. The market is still in bad shape, but they won't allow the waiver for a second year. We can't afford the mortgage without renters. Now, we'll have to sell, and we're negative on equity.

We have a realtor check the condition of the condo in the city I dearly miss. She calls to tell us it is in pretty bad shape: the restrooms are filthy, the carpet is destroyed; we'll need to fix it up before we put it on the market. I decide flying to Chicago to do the work myself will be a good break from Vijay and give me a project to focus on. I tell Vijay that instead of hiring someone, I want to go paint the unit, fix what's broken and clean it up myself. Not shy of construction projects, I'm looking forward to the trip. Also, I still have friends in Chicago. Friends who are excited that I'll be in town for St. Patty's Day weekend.

My flight takes off and I'm immediately renewed. I leave behind my sorrow and embrace this project. I have a purpose. Something important to work on when I arrive. Aside from journaling in India, I've never been a writer, but for some reason I pull some paper out of my bag and begin. I use the front, the back and the sides. Smaller and smaller I write so as not to lose a thought. I'm on a roll. It's honest, angry and raw. I have something here. I feel empowered. I write until the captain announces our descent and I am forced to put the tray table up. I know I have more to say.

I write what's wrong with abortion policy and the health care system. I write about losing our baby and my depression. I write about what could have helped me process my loss: a national support site, resources, groups or a hotline, somewhere to go, something for people like me to grasp at. I know what I needed that awful week of my life, and I want that wrong to be righted for others. I've found a voice on the privacy of my paper, and it's clawing to get out.

In baggage claim I feel a rush of excitement when I see the *Welcome to Chicago* sign. Along with the enthusiasm of seeing the city again, I feel some control. I take the L to our condo, enter our home and lie on the floor. It's so nice to be back here! I wish I were staying. I unpack my suitcase filled with painting supplies and random tools, survey the damage and make a

Home Depot list of anything else I'll need while I work. I hit the ground running, painting rooms as efficiently as I can.

Friends from UMass, Pinky and her husband, Moto, who also moved to Chicago, drop off a sleeping bag for me to use while I'm in town. I work hard until the condo is presentable and ready to list, all the while thinking about my new outlet. Writing everything out felt good, a way to control the narrative and hopelessness I've been feeling. I scrub the paint off my skin and my friends pick me up.

St. Patty's Day weekend in Chicago is FUN! There will be a lot going on in this city that never sleeps. The three of us head downtown. It feels amazing. I'm back! I'm alive! It's St. Patty's day in Chicago!

I've heard people say that drinking doesn't solve problems. Generally, I'd agree with that. I'm not an advocate for binge drinking, and two of the three of us going out tonight have advanced degrees in Public Health, but a night of bar-hopping with Pinky and Moto is the perfect distraction. Beers flow down my throat like water, one after another. I am buzzed and energized quickly. Moto, who is an immigrant from Turkey, starts claiming he's part Irish and we begin a drunken debate about our definite heritage, making claims one is more Irish at heart than the other. We go from bar, to bar, to bar. We pause briefly to throw beads into the air and cheer at the night sky. Pinky, our designated driver, guides us on our path.

The night is young. Moto and I decide to reenact "A Night at The Roxbury," Will Ferrell and Chris Kattan style, on Pinky in the middle of the street as we cross. I can hear her laughing her intoxicating Pinky laugh, yelling, "What are you guys doing?" as I encourage Moto, who I am now calling Two Percent because we both agree he has to have at least 2 percent

Irish in him somehow, to take our reenactment really seriously. We thrust, club style, at Pinky's small, delicate body in dancing delirium in the middle of downtown Chicago, singing "What Is Love" badly. We know we're totally nailing the scene as Pinky says to someone, "Oh hi!" and laughs as she recognizes a colleague from her PhD program.

Next bar, the night is still young. Pinky is a good sport and a responsible designated driver. At least our shared degree rubbed off on one of us. We head closer to home, stopping in Forest Park. I don't remember these bars as well as the first few. I am now throwing beaded necklaces into to the air and running up to random pedestrians, giving them, in my drunken opinion, a friendly spank on the butt as a greeting. I'm so drunk, so uninhibited, and feel so free. What is completely inappropriate in every way is an instant release and a welcome departure from the reality that has been my life the last three months.

Moto and I cheer when we hear "Last call, people," as if the bartender announced he's pouring free drinks for everyone, and Pinky tells us, "Okay, you two, it's time to go home." She laughs as she loads us into their car. Pinky and Moto drop me off at my condo. They call the next morning, Pinky chuckling as she retells the tale of Liz and Moto, the Irish twins, living it up in Chicago for St. Patty's Day. She can laugh harder than we can; we're both milking some pretty big hangovers.

I pack my bags, give my friends back their sleeping bag and hug them good-bye. Leaving Chicago, with a clean, repaired, listed condo and a sizeable headache, I know now it's okay to move on, to live, to do something. Chicago, and its terrible reason for coming, has reminded me who I am. I am a fun-loving person who seeks adventure, humor and friendship. I want to be that person again. This trip has fixed something I wasn't sure I could get back. Chicago has fixed something in me that was broken.

An offer comes in several months later well below asking price, but we take it knowing we might not get another one. It is $25,000 less than we have in equity. Wanting to do the responsible thing, and not wanting to hurt our credit with a short sale, we take out a loan. It's sad to know we are going to have the same problem with the house we're currently living in when we leave the Valley, but we'll deal with that when the time comes.

As timing and luck would have it, a local charity needs a consultant. I'm offered the job. I use the money I earn to pay off the loan on the condo and feel good knowing I am doing something productive. I reexamine my *that was easy* attitude about owning property. We are real estate idiots!

Weeks turn into months, and the pieces are all starting to come together. Vijay and I begin to communicate better.

"It sounds like you want this to work. So, just make time for each other," my therapist says. "Go to the movies together. You don't have to talk to each other. Just go do something together. The rest will come with time."

We start skeptically. But, you know what? It actually works. We start to date again. We start to interact with each other. We start over. I try to remember all the things that brought us together in the first place. He tries to be more patient and present. We both want to fix this. We both want a family. We talk about what to do with the nursery and spare rooms in our home. Should we try again? Should we adopt first? Should we foster?

On a confident day, I'll peek in at the crib and baby clothes in the nursery, but for the most part, the door remains closed. A routine starts to take hold and I am more successful at keeping busy. One afternoon, as I stand in front of my dryer folding laundry, my eye catches movement out the window. A young high school couple stands under a streetlight. They look upset. Is he breaking up with her? Did she make him mad? She is crying. His school binder, resting at his side, gradually makes its way around the front of his body to cover his crotch. He looks uncomfortable and starts to squirm.

I continue to watch, fixated on the drama unfolding in front of me. They are in a deep discussion. They look like sweet kids. It hits me. I know what's happening here. She is pregnant. I can help! I desperately want to run across the street to offer room and board. On lap three of our morning mall walk the next day, my girlfriend says to me, "Yeah? You know, Liz, you used to have to worry about pedophiles sitting outside your kid's school. Now you have to worry about crazy baby ladies," she snickers.

"I know, right?" I laugh too. "At least I have enough sense to realize I'm cracked." We finish up our routine and head our separate ways.

The direction Vijay and I decide to take next, foster-adopt, is a very non-Indian approach. The desire to help heal a battered heart seems very fitting right now and we know there is a serious need for foster parents in the Valley. As we work through the paperwork, inspections and classes, Vijay's parents ask questions.

"What do you mean, son? You are going to do this foster care?" His mother is worried. "Where do these children come from? What is foster care? Are you keeping these children? What about getting pregnant again?" They are completely confused.

Vijay tries to explain. "We can get pregnant if we want to; we're just taking a break," he offers. "If it happens, it happens."

"Okay, son, whatever you want," she adds. "You and Liss are going to get checked out again? Aren't you?"

"We don't want to get poked and prodded," he says. "These are children who need a home while their parent(s) try to get back on their feet," he continues in his mellow, matter-of-fact way. "We want children. We just aren't going to focus on getting pregnant right now."

His mom listens but doesn't quite understand the concept or agree with the rationale.

We meet with Child Protective Services, go through registration, background checks and orientation, accrue the necessary education hours, become CPR certified, participate in home inspections and fill out medical and behavioral questionnaires. We didn't think about being asked to narrow down exactly *who* we are willing to accept, in such detail. The questionnaire surprises us. Race, sex, age, behavioral challenges and different types of trauma are all included. We are optimistic, resourceful and educated, so feel we can be flexible. We keep our options completely open to all children under five, for a short term or permanent stay, with the exception of children who require special home licensing for medical equipment.

I'm ready to do this. I know we'll be good at it. I know we'll make great parents. Everything we are will change. I can't think of a better way for us to spend the rest of our time in the Valley. It could be a short-term placement. Or, it could be our lives, if it's a child who will make us a forever family.

Finally, the phone rings. It's the call we've been waiting for. The call that will make us parents.

CHAPTER 15

Temporary Love

It's July 7. Midday, midweek. Vijay is at work.

"Hello, Elizabeth?" a caseworker says on the phone.

"Yes?" I say, feeling the excitement in my voice.

"We have a baby in the receiving home for you," she says.

"What?! Really?" I exclaim. "A baby?"

"Can you come and pick him up?" she asks.

"Yes! Right now?" I feel my voice squeal.

"Yes. Right now."

"How old is he? Do I have time to go to the store and get some supplies?" My mind is racing.

"Yes, if you hurry," she says.

"How big is he? I mean, what size car seat do I need to bring?" I ask as I look over at the zero-to-five-year-old range of car seat options piled in our closet ready for any situation.

I install the car seat, rush to the grocery store for diapers his size and head to the receiving home. Vijay doesn't get a heads-up call.

I park the car and rush to the waiting room of the receiving home. A caseworker is standing at the door holding a fifteen-month-old baby boy with big brown eyes. He stares at me, nervously.

"Is this him?"

"Yep. This is him. Here you go." The caseworker passes him to me with a Ziploc of meds and a green folder containing his records.

"This is Carlos," she says. She doesn't really explain anything to him as she passes him my way.

He looks scared and holds onto me, uncertain of what's to come. He glances at the caseworker for some sort of reassurance and holds out his hands to go back to her. I rub his back and talk softly. "Hi, Carlos," I whisper.

That's it? I think. *Just like that? Oh my God! Oh my God!* My heart is pounding and I hold him carefully. I can't believe it! I'm his mom right now. I need to take care of him. I sign the log, put him in the car and head home slowly, carefully.

I call Vijay.

"Guess who's at our house?" I say into the phone.

"Did your mom come for a visit?" he asks.

"No! A baby!" I say, smiling ear to ear.

"A what?" He repeats, "Baby?"

"Yep! I can't wait until you come home! He is fifteen months old. I'm holding him right now!" I pause. "He's such a little guy. I can't believe this." We've been waiting for this day for such a long time. I am ecstatic!

Carlos has pneumonia and is anemic. He doesn't understand what being nurtured feels like. Cuddling, being rocked and affection are all foreign concepts. His coping mechanism is banging his head against the wall and floor. He also practices incredibly tense eyebrow grimacing, trying to look tough.

Vijay gets home from work and meets his new foster son. "This is Carlos," I tell him. Vijay holds him close and talks to him about his beautiful brown eyes. Carlos is quiet and mostly stares. He'll be trying to figure us out for a while. We are sure to give him love and space to do that.

At bedtime, we take him up to his room. We read him stories and sing him songs. He doesn't seem to respond to them. We warm a bottle, which he guzzles down quickly. He hands it back to me for a refill, crying. We aren't sure what to do. I rock him in our rocker and talk to him quietly. He doesn't stop shaking the bottle in my face. So, after a brief conversation about it, Vijay and I decide to grant his need for this first night.

He can sense our lack of knowledge about him or what his routine may or may not have been. This bedtime may be a bit early, we may be overprotective and it must feel scary to have two hypervigilant adults staring down at him. Second bottle down, his eyes start to close and he eventually falls asleep. We congratulate each other on our success and go to bed shortly thereafter, only to be awakened two hours later by a screaming baby. We jump out of bed, go to his room and see the diarrhea phenomenon that two bottles of milk will create.

"Well, that was a mistake," we acknowledge to each other as we clean him up and try to console him from the trauma of a messy crib. He doesn't let go of me. We bring Carlos into our room and take turns sleeping. Vijay takes first shift and I take second, watching his little innocent body sleep in our arms.

Carlos continues his head-banging routine the next morning. We have a brief conversation about whether he needs a helmet. But, I think he's slowly realizing head butting hurts and is not going to get him the attention he seeks. If it continues, I'll be sure to bring it up at his first doctor's appointment. By lunchtime, I've managed to turn his intense eyebrow grimacing into a funny game by mimicking him and then giggling, which makes him laugh too.

Lisette, who previously promised me her future *oops* baby, comes over to meet our new little guy. He ceremoniously poops. I think it's important to note that I've always been a gagger. As a toddler, I trained myself to use the toilet because I couldn't stand my own diaper. Even so, I don't think changing a poopy diaper is something that anyone particularly enjoys. As I gag my way through the poop heap, changing the diaper and wiping his sweet little butt, I can hardly contain myself.

"Oh Elizabeth! Get a grip! It's just poop," Lisette says, watching me gag while trying to turn my head so that the baby doesn't think I am reacting negatively to him.

"Yeah. That was totally a man poop. I think you should get to work your way up to that kind of thing!" I say, looking over at her, totally traumatized.

She leaves a bunch of toys that belonged to her son, Miguel, when he was small and goes to pick him up from preschool, promising to return shortly.

Moments later, the doorbell rings and little four-year-old Miguel bounces into the house.

"Hello, Ms. Littlebitts," he says, unable to pronounce my name yet. He gives me a hug.

"Hello, Miguel," I say.

"So where's the baby?" he asks, hopping into the family room. He stops when he finds what he's looking for and stares. "So, can I play with him?"

"Yes, but he is a baby, so you have to be careful," I say.

"Okay." He squats next to Carlos and stares.

"OH WOW!" he exclaims. "I used to have toys like these!" He looks over at me, eyes sparkling.

"Those are your toys, Miguel," I tell him.

"What?" A look of concern crosses his face. "How did you get them?"

"Your mom brought them over while you were in school for the baby to play with," I explain.

"What do you mean?!" he says, thinking about the scenario.

"When you were at school, she came over to visit the baby and brought these toys. Since you aren't a baby anymore, we thought Carlos could play with them," I explain.

"No, I'm not a baby anymore . . . so, it's okay with me," he says slowly, while processing how something could have happened without him present.

I spend the next couple of days reviewing the folder of information I was given, trying to figure out medical care needs, determine what doctor to follow up with and plan a schedule for our days together. I wonder if all Child Protective

Services departments are the same, or if it's different in the Valley. It doesn't seem like I have enough information about this little guy. The system seems strained, and resources must be scarce.

I continue to meet Sarah for our mall-walking routine. As soon as she meets Carlos, he gives her the biggest eyebrow grimace I've seen yet. After exerting all the bravery he can muster, he falls asleep in the stroller. Day after day I bring him with me to walk the mall with Sarah. He gets used to the routine, but realizes quickly the sliding doors are the way out. Every time we pass one, he fusses. His displeasure gets more and more elaborate until, before we know it, we're parking-lot mall walkers. Carlos gets up early, so exercising before the hot desert sun comes up is not out of the question and Sarah is agreeable to the predawn routine.

According to the caseworker, reunification doesn't look good. Kelly, Carlos's mom, is struggling with substance abuse, is in and out of jail regularly and has not complied with her appointed plan. I follow the guidelines the caseworker gives me and begin the visitation schedule with the knowledge the mother is not very reliable. All the visits will be scheduled during business hours, Monday through Friday. Vijay has to work, so it won't be easy for him to come to them. Vijay and I talk about whether or not he should attend these visits too, but we decide, for now, I'll go on my own.

The first visit with Kelly gives me a sense of the baby's situation. Carlos and I sit in the lobby together, without a caseworker, waiting for Kelly to show up. She walks in with another woman, who I learn is Kelly's mother. They smile and tell me they recognize me and that they are glad Carlos was placed with me and Vijay. I instantly question the confidentiality of his placement. The family is not supposed to know who we are. I don't know anything about them. They tell me they recognize me from a prerequisite parenting class that Vijay and I were in.

Carlos sits with me. He does not go to Kelly, but climbs off my lap to see his grandma. Then he immediately starts butting his head against the wall.

"Oh. He does that," Kelly says, unfazed. "Hey Carlito! Come here."

"What did you call him?" I ask.

"Carlito," she says.

"Oh, okay." I nod. I've been calling him Carlos and he hasn't been responding. I assumed it was because he was still nervous with us.

"We'll call him Carlito until he turns two. Then, we'll call him Carlos," she explains.

I try to digest what I am seeing and learn from this experience. I feel myself mutter an "Okay," but let the rest sink in for now. At the end of our lobby visit, a caseworker joins us and says visits will be scheduled once a week from now on.

I get him home and try out "Carlito." His little face truly lights up for the first time since we have had him. Knowing his nickname could have made things a lot more comforting from the get-go! I can't believe his reaction. He looks at me as if to say, *Oh my God! She knows who I am!*

A few days pass and I discover Carlito has sleep apnea and has not received most of his vaccines. We've also noticed his inability to speak. He makes only a few sounds and no real words yet. We schedule a follow-up appointment to see the doctor who's been treating him for his pneumonia.

Mom comes to town the day of his first appointment. She and I open the door to the waiting room and are instantly taken aback. There are many people waiting; the chairs are old and stained; there are exposed wires sticking out of outlets, paint chipping off the wall and a dirty corner with broken toys. I've never been in a medical office waiting room this run down. I feel like I'm in a developing country.

We get there a good fifteen minutes before Carlito's appointment, just in case I need to fill out any paperwork. Two hours later, we are called in. A nurse takes Carlito's temperature, and after another forty-five-minute wait Carlito starts to freak out. He is hungry and has eaten all the small snack items I brought for him. My mom rushes out to find him some milk and I poke my head out the door to ask an aide if the doctor will be coming soon.

She comes about fifteen minutes later. She doesn't make eye contact, answers minimal questions and won't touch him. It's the most bizarre appointment I've ever had with a medical professional, and I instantly have new respect for the underinsured and uninsured people in this country. This is an outrage.

After an experience I wouldn't subject a stray cat to, we discontinue care at the patient mill of a clinic that is not treating him adequately. I immediately recruit Vijay to find a more appropriate, permanent family doctor. He investigates options and finds a pediatrician with whom he has mutual patients. Vijay has had a good working relationship with him and he'll take Medi-Cal. I finally start to feel more comfortable with Carlito's immediate health needs and begin to focus more on the cause of his sleep apnea and possible developmental needs.

Before we got Carlito, Vijay and I had a trip planned to attend a friend's wedding in Chicago. We've already purchased the tickets and booked the hotel. It's been only two weeks since Carlito came to live with us, but we feel confident enough to go. We decide to keep our plans and ask child welfare services if we can bring him along. Traveling with a toddler is a little stressful if your parenting experience consists of a few weeks. People who are parents already know the preparation that goes into loading your kid on a plane and packing all the stuff that needs to go along with that child for a trip. Having a more established relationship with your child would also be helpful in controlling potential in-flight tantrums.

First things first: I need to obtain a court order to be able to leave the county. Once approved, I need to figure out what to pack and how to plan our trip with a toddler. I call the caseworker to ask for a court order and begin a list. I start with Google. I type: "What to pack for a plane trip with a toddler." Bingo! That was easy and amazingly accurate.

I call the airline for an additional ticket.

"Sold out?" I say.

"Yes. But, he's less than two years old. You can hold him on your lap," the agent explains.

"Sweet! That's awesome! I'll do that!" *Excellent idea*, I think. *I got this!*

The day before we leave, I check my Facebook news feed. A friend from high school has posted, "Chicago flight tomorrow." What are the chances she's on our flight? I e-mail her to see. Our flights are the same! She'll get to meet Carlito!

And so it is done. We meet on the plane, she switches seats with the all-too-happy-to-move stranger sitting next to us and we are on our way. Carlito bounces between the laps of Vijay, myself and my friend. He coos, takes a nap and is fairly happy for the entire flight. I consider it a success and congratulate myself for good luck and good planning.

In the following weeks, we try to give Carlito diverse opportunities that encourage development. We have a couple of concerns about his delayed speech and his quick-to-anger response to some situations. Days are full and busy. I have meaning and I am in love with being a mom. The longer he is with us, the better we get at our routine. We make family time, plan outings and vacations.

Scheduled visits continue every week with Kelly, and anyone else she brings. Sometimes she shows up; sometimes she doesn't. She has shown up high, late and a half dozen times not at all. One visit was cancelled because she was in jail for breaking and entering. I wait in the stark waiting room with Carlito each time, anxiously anticipating the outcome. The plastic chairs are lined in rows and we watch as other foster children greet and say good-bye to their family members. I try to keep Carlito happy and busy in case she doesn't show. Vijay misses these meetings, but we talk about them when he gets home from work.

Each visit is different and each one tests my emotions. As visits become more common, Carlito begins to recognize the parking lot and gets agitated when I park. He becomes apprehensive about going into the waiting room. I try to stay upbeat and fun while we wait. I have to remember that what I do and what Kelly does are two different things. I constantly remind myself that my parenting style is not the one that matters and that if I had an addiction, I might not be able to make good choices either.

The day he holds onto me for dear life as Kelly walks through the door, I realize I also need to change my relationship with her. She walks up to me and snatches him into her arms. Enormous tears fall from his cheeks and he looks at me in that classic one-year-old way that is both pathetic and convincing.

"You are my baby!" she says forcefully, as she grabs him in the waiting room.

I watch her as she unsuccessfully tries to console him.

"Do you want me to hold him and calm him down?" I ask as kindly as I can.

"Yeah," she says, handing him to me.

I hold him and rock him side to side. I whisper in his ear in my nighttime voice. "It's okay. You are going to have a fun visit with your mommy. It's okay. Shhhh. It's okay. Shhh, shhh." I rock him some more. The tears subside and his breathing becomes calm.

I look at Kelly. "He is such a sweet boy," I say. "You are his mom. I know that." As I rock him, I look in her eyes so she can see I mean it.

From that moment on our relationship is different; she realizes I'm not trying to steal her child and I'm not the enemy for caring for him. We form a partnership of sorts. We are interested in the same thing: loving this child in whatever way we can. In that moment, we bond.

Five months go by and she starts fulfilling more and more of her requirements. I start to make even more of an effort in our relationship, sharing stories about Carlito with her. She starts getting more time for visits and eventually gets to take him for an hour or two unsupervised, off-site. I know she is excited for her alone time with him.

On her first unsupervised outing, Carlito hangs onto the door frame of the office, screaming as she walks out of the building with him. I feel sorry for her that she has to drag her child away and sad that he doesn't understand what's happening. It is confusing for him and I worry about the visit.

I also leave, about five minutes after she drives away. I go to the mall about a block from the office and roam around, wondering how he is doing and how she is managing. I come back a little earlier than pickup time and sit in one of the chairs, watching out the large glass door for her car to pull up. Carlito sees me as soon as he gets to the door and runs, arms outstretched, with a huge smile on his face. I give him kisses and talk to him about how much fun he must have had with his mommy.

The more successful she is at showing up for visits and complying with her goals, the more time she gets to spend with him. He gradually becomes more comfortable with the schedule as he spends time with her. He starts to realize this is part of his life and that visits will be okay.

As his time with us, his temporary family, grows longer, our love for him grows too. We begin to feel a sense of sadness in realizing that the life Vijay and I want to give him isn't the life he will be living. In the beginning, I watched as Carlito's mom missed visits with him, as she identified the wrong man as his father, showed up high and got arrested. Toward the end, I watch her get pregnant again, attend rehab, fulfill class requirements and start to show up for visits regularly. Over the months, I've learned more about her: her situation, her own experience as a foster youth, her addiction and the inevitable cycle she finds herself in. I applaud her as she tries to get better and remind her of how amazing her son is.

I don't agree that she is back on her feet, but she has a chance for a new beginning. I need to start a transition for Carlito and prepare myself. I ask her for pictures of the people in her life and make a family book for Carlito so he can see his family when he is with us. I tell him it is going to be okay, even though deep down, I'm not sure I believe it. I'm certain my idea of *okay* is a bit different from the system's idea of okay.

I talk to him about his family when they aren't around. I make his mom a scrapbook full of all the things he's done with us. I want him to have happy memories and know he was cared for. I also want her to be able to see all the things he is doing with us, so she can ask him about his adventures when he visits her, even if he isn't talking yet. She tells me she loves the book and that Carlito is proud to show her all the pictures of himself.

I tell her she can do it, that he is worth it, and that she is strong. I tell her that he is an amazing gift in my life and although not the best situation for her, my life is better for knowing them.

Carlito has been receiving in-home developmental and speech therapy, and we are assured it will follow him to her home should he be returned to his mom. We have him on a schedule that he understands for naps, meals and a nighttime routine. He is learning how to express himself, form words and show emotion without a temper or self-destruction. He is gradually realizing that hugs are nice and affection can be comforting. I cautiously share these things with Kelly, wanting her to know, but not wanting her to feel I am pushing things on her. When overnight visits are introduced and become more and more common, I try to show her how to incorporate these routines in her life.

Kelly comes back from her first overnight visit with Carlito, impressed.

"We were at the park and got McDonald's," she starts. "We were just sitting wherever. You know?" I watch her as she shares her story.

"Uh-huh." I nod my head yes.

"Do you know what he did?" she asks, looking at me. "He took his food and went over to the picnic bench and ate at the table," she laughs.

"Oh yeah?" I say and smile. "What a good boy."

"You have him on a good routine," she offers. "He has nice manners!" She smiles, proudly. "We are glad he is staying with you!"

I'm not sure she'll be able to continue what we've started. Her instincts are not strong. The reality of her life will be hard and we understand that.

As we get more and more comfortable with our temporary family, we get an unexpected call.

"Mrs. Chennamchetty?" a woman says.

"Yes?" I respond into the receiver.

"Hello. I am a placement worker with Child Welfare Services," she continues. "Would you be willing to take another child? I can see on your license you can accommodate two children."

I stand silently for a second and think about my answer. I wasn't expecting this call. "Can I give you a call back tomorrow?" I ask. "I'd like to talk to my husband about it once he's home from work."

"Sure." She gives me her contact number and some general information. I promise to call the next day.

The initial information is minimal. We're told a five-year-old Caucasian boy, whose parental rights have been terminated, needs a home. He has had multiple placements and has siblings in different homes, none adopted. He has a few behavioral challenges, which seem to be ADD related. Also, if we are interested, the caseworker would like us to have several trial visits over the next few months before the placement becomes permanent. He is a potential adoption placement.

The last sentence is the most exciting. We take this information seriously, and also consider the effect two young boys will have on our household, how parenting dynamics will change and how bringing in an older child may present different challenges for Carlito. We are eager, confident and ready for another child. We're excited the parental rights have already been terminated. The termination process seems to be a long one. Also, we feel like there won't be as much emotional distortion for us, playing a waiting game that we may not be on the winning end of. But, most of all, this is a child waiting for a forever family now.

We anticipate sibling rivalry. We think it's a good thing for Carlito, whose mother just gave birth to his sibling. He will have to learn about shared time anyhow, so this may be a good introduction. We also know we can handle whatever comes our way.

Vijay's learning curve has been steep. One benefit of having a child from birth may be to grow and learn how to become a parent along with your child's developmental growth. You ease into parenthood. Having children who are already walking and talking and who have also been traumatized in some way adds to the challenge of parenthood for the inexperienced. Vijay has professional, clinical experience with children in his clinic, but in a psychiatric setting. He has never been around children full time prior to Carlito, not as a parent or even a babysitter. What he's told me about his own childhood in India is minimal, but also radically different from how I grew up or my experiences around children here. Child rearing and child development are viewed very differently in each of our cultures.

He assures me he is confident with the new challenge another child will bring. We have some normalcy now. Why not add another little person to the mix?

CHAPTER 16

And Then There Were Two

Our lives are busy and that's just the way we want it. Every day is bustling with excitement and toddler drama. We know we want more than one child and we have plenty of room, time and resources. We are eager to learn more about Jon, this new little boy who may enter our lives.

Vijay doesn't share the latest news with his parents just yet. We think we should wait until we are sure of our decision. Weekend calls home are more of the same. "Is Liss feeding you? How is your health? Are you trying to have a baby? When are you coming to India?" Vijay's asked. "You are looking old, son. Your Facebook snaps . . . you are losing your hair!"

And Then There Were Two

Before we agree to a permanent placement, the caseworker suggests scheduling a few weekend visits for Jon to meet us and visit our home. A pale, skinny little thing, with sandy-blond hair, he's cute, charming and exceptionally friendly. He seems to know just what to say and how to say it. He is also excitable, animated and has a lot of nervous energy. We are told he has ADHD (attention deficit hyperactivity disorder). We watch him bounce around the house, flapping his arms like a little bird. We can see he's hyper, and so badly want to believe we can help him. We decide to take him.

Carlito finally has a diagnosis for his sleep apnea, and surgery is scheduled at Rady's Children's Hospital in San Diego. His surgery date happens to coincide with Thanksgiving weekend. We'll drive into San Diego for the in-patient procedure. We rent a townhouse by the beach so we aren't too far away from the hospital. My parents meet us for the long holiday weekend. I drive into San Diego with Carlito early, since I'll be staying overnight with him. Vijay goes to work for the day and plans to meet the caseworker in the afternoon to pick up Jon. Vijay will bring Jon to celebrate the holiday weekend with us.

The morning after surgery, Carlito and I return from the hospital and meet Jon and Vijay at the rental house. Vijay snuggles in with Carlito and I promise Jon I'll take him to the beach. It's November, so a little overcast, but that doesn't stop us from heading straight to the water. Jon's skinny little body runs up and down the beach asking all the children to be his friend, flapping his arms wildly as he goes. He doesn't stop moving the entire time we're at the beach and is extremely excited. My heart melts for him. I am so happy he is with us and so excited for him. I desperately want him. I want this to work.

"Are you sure he just has ADHD?" Mom asks as she watches him play.

"Vijay thinks he has ADHD," I tell her defensively, even though my gut tells me maybe she could be right. I just see a happy, excited, energetic kid who's had a terrible start. He deserves a shot and I want to be his chance.

"Well, I'm no expert, but I think there's something else going on with this kid. I know how bad you want him, but I'm just saying . . . are you sure there isn't something else going on? I work with ADHD kids at the school library and they are hyper, but I haven't met one quite like this," Mom says. She doesn't add anything else. I know she knows I'm annoyed by the comment and don't want to hear it. Some little part of me agrees. She's right. I don't say that, though.

"He's probably nervous! This is a big deal! He knows what's going on," I say, as I watch him run up and down the beach letting the white water chase his feet. "Poor thing probably feels like he's auditioning," I tell her, defensively. "Also, he's never seen the ocean before. Can you imagine? How would you act if you'd never seen the ocean?"

"Okay." She doesn't say anything else about his potential challenges the rest of the weekend.

After several scheduled weekend visits go well, we agree to his placement. His foster parents bring him to our home with all of his belongings. You can tell they want the best for him. They are an older couple and tell us they are unable to care for children long term. Their wish for permanency is palpable. His foster mother sits on our couch and watches the interaction between Carlito and Jon. She looks a little concerned as Carlito shows his jealousy and demands attention by whining and flailing around. I'm a little surprised by this behavior. He didn't do it when we had Jon for visits. He must sense the shift in focus.

Jon runs around the house and takes charge immediately. His foster mother watches anxiously from the couch. "So you think this will be a good fit?" she asks. "I just want the best for him," she says, looking apprehensive.

"Well, he certainly seems to be excited," I say to her. "He knows where everything is." I smile as I continue to hold a fussy Carlito, who's jealous of the shared attention.

They have brought bins of clothing and toys with them to our house. I carry them all up to Jon's room and tell him we'll help him unpack a little later. He jumps around, running up and down the stairs. When it's time for his foster mother to leave, he doesn't even say good-bye. I notice her disappointment. After all, they've been taking care of him for over a year. After we encourage him to say good-bye, he still has no response. He's a kid. They do stuff like that, but a little antenna went up noting it anyhow.

An instantaneous life with a toddler and a five-year-old gets hectic fast. We hit the ground running. We've never been this busy. I go to the elementary school in our district and register Jon for kindergarten. Vijay and I begin to identify needs and manage them. Both Carlito and Jon have very different developmental and behavioral issues that we know we have to address. We are full of hope and anticipation of what's to come.

Carlito knows his schedule but is not using many words or actions to let us know what he needs yet. We rely on routine for him, which works well. He needs to be free of negative influences, to learn behaviors that will help him express his feelings, since he is still not talking and gets impatient easily.

Jon, on the other hand, has a lot of energy and seems to know everything we want to hear, using it to his advantage. He requires constant guidance and redirection. I wonder what kind of structure he's had in his little life. The only time he's still is when he sits in front of the television. He continually asks to watch shows from the Adult Swim network and video games that are much too sophisticated for him. The moment there is any interaction with anyone, he starts to spiral. The caseworker suggests we make a behavioral chart to help him make good decisions when challenges arise. We are glad for the suggestion. Vijay, Jon and I sit down to create it. We ask Jon to help us add his ideas on goals he thinks he can handle.

"Can you call me Whiskers?" he asks me.

"What?" I say.

"Well, when I behave I want to be called Whiskers," he says.

"Okay, Whiskers, but you can be good anytime!" I encourage.

Within a month, *charming Jon* is too hard to maintain. He can't control his behavior. He can't follow rules or expectations without destruction. His behavior quickly goes from charismatic to challenging. We go through six more "I'll be good if you call me" names: Fluffy, Rex, Boe, Sally, Sam and Matt. I'm pretty predictable and he knows this. I'm becoming less and less effective at redirecting him. He begins to tell me graphic stories of abuse and death in his life. He tells me the story of his mother's death, and that his best friend in his old school was killed. He tells us other stories of abuse while living in past homes. His behavior continues to deteriorate. So rapidly, I start a journal for his protection and ours. Every time he shares a story, we ask his social worker if she has any information. She says she doesn't think any of it is true. She reviews his file, but can't find anything to match his tales. What is in his file? Did anyone ever report anything? He is only five years old. This poor child. If any of his stories are real, no one knows. And, if none are real, his imagination is damaged. Either way, something has happened to him.

When manipulating me directly doesn't work, Jon turns to his foster brother. He sets Carlito up to fail often and finds comfort in his failure. Now if I leave the room, I take Carlito with me. I worry about Jon's interaction with other children in general, at school, the playground and in the neighborhood, and begin to pay close attention to his interactions with people outside our family.

"Call me Lucky. Okay, Mom? Lucky! Say it, or I won't talk to you anymore," he announces.

"Okay, Lucky," I say, confirming his newest name.

I realize I need to identify reoccurring behavior and log what I'm doing that is successful and what isn't. My success column is pretty bare, while negative behaviors are growing daily. I search the internet looking for guidance and solutions, and call the caseworker and his previous foster parents.

On the phone with his previous foster parents, I decide to give an example of what happened after school. I need guidance from them on what has worked in the past. "Jon was misbehaving, so I asked him to come in for a while. He threw down his new bike Santa brought him for Christmas, kicked the stand and broke it," I explain.

"Yeah, he does that," they say. I tell them he set up our neighbor Miguel, encouraging him to climb the roof of a play structure and fall, twisting his wrist. "Yeah, he's a handful," I'm told.

"What worked for you guys? I mean, when you had a conflict," I ask them.

"OH! Time-out usually," his previous placement tells me.

"Well, I do try to use time-out. They say one minute for each year they are old," I offer. "I just need him to calm down so we can talk about it."

There is a laugh on the other end of the phone. "Oh no! Five minutes is not long enough. You have to have him sit for at least thirty minutes." I don't respond right away, but I'm not really comfortable with a thirty-minute time-out. I only want to use it long enough for him to calm down, so we can talk about what happened. He'd be in time-out all day if he sat for a half an hour or more.

Jon has two biological siblings. Both of them have been placed in separate homes. I'm encouraged to get the kids together and to start with his brother, because his sister is still having some adjustment challenges and is quite a bit older. Maybe meeting his younger brother will help Jon with some of his behavior challenges. Jon's younger brother has been living with a family for about a year. I call his foster mother to plan a meeting for the boys, hoping it will help Jon. After the first five minutes I can tell the woman is a mess. She went from homeschooling her four children to placing them all in school because she could no longer handle Jon's brother. She feels like a failure and began taking antidepressant medication. He hits her. She is barely hanging on. The stories she begins to share with me over the next few weeks are mirror images of behavior I'm seeing in our Jon.

What on earth happened to these children? My notes help me reflect later in the day on issues we've had and on my reactions to them. They don't tell me his true story. I guess that's not really the goal, though. I just need to be better prepared for tomorrow. Do better. Try to help him navigate through life a little easier. When Vijay gets home, we talk about the challenges I'm having while he is at work. He gives me suggestions on how to manage them. I know he has clinical experience, but sometimes textbook facts aren't helpful in real-life parenting. I need a class or something. I am missing a step here and I don't know what it is.

We try to get the boys out of the Valley as much as possible to experience other things. We take them to LA and San Diego. We go to zoos, amusement parks, plays and the beach. We want them to experience activities that will challenge their development and expose them to other children their age. We regularly walk to the park two blocks from our house to spend time outdoors. Once we arrive, it doesn't take long before parents gather their children.

"Come on, Sally, we have to go home now." Sally's mother looks at me annoyed, again. I look up to see Jon running behind Sally.

"Come on! Go down the slide so your butthole rips open!" he yells at her, sure all the kids can hear him.

Families we used to see regularly start to avoid us at the park.

He makes announcements that concern us. He wants to be a cop when he grows up so he "can shoot people." He says things like "I don't like Indian people" and "I don't like Chinese people." We go for walks around our neighborhood and see a fence spray-painted. His eyes light up because he wants to be a "bad boy" and "spray-paint stuff." He asks me if we can go to a gun store to "buy a gun," because he knew a guy with a gun once who would take him hunting. He starts *hunting* Carlito in the house. We walk through all of it. We redirect him every time. We have conversations about culture and about helping people instead of harming them, but I don't think it's sinking in. It's not enough. I have a bad feeling about what's brewing in that little mind. And it's a little scary.

He can be superficially charming at times, but at other times he throws things around the room and makes demands that are unreasonable. He talks of abuse from people that were never really *documented* in his life.

There is much more to Jon's life story than anyone knows. Our expectations of what it would take were not realistic when we met him. We have been able to get Carlito the treatment he has needed, but Jon's problems are so much more ominous. To rehash the full extent of our days together or even regurgitate my journal would in itself be a book, and a very hard read. It's important, I think, to understand that this child does have, and will continue to have, very real challenges on a daily basis that include lying, stealing, incontinence, manipulating adults and other children, sexually acting out, throwing, running away, alternative personalities and hitting.

Driving up Dogwood Avenue, I listen to Jon talk about "a hosing" he got one time. I look at his innocent little face in the rearview mirror and probe a little.

"You know! When you get in trouble you go into the yard and get hosed," he explains in an upbeat tone.

"We don't hose people in our house," I say, even though I don't know what exactly he means by "a hosing."

I'll investigate more with his caseworker, but I have a feeling no one would report himself hosing this child.

He refuses to eat anything, telling us, "I'll get fat," "My arm will fall off if I eat" and "It's not nice to eat, I'm just a kid," all frustrating for so many reasons. Carlito weighs more than Jon does and they are three years apart.

Jon is destructive and talks about friends and family dying that aren't really dead or that never existed. He talks about my death.

"Hey Mom!" Jon says.

"Yes," I respond.

"See that canal?" he says, staring out the car window.

I say I do.

"What would happen if the car flipped?" he asks.

Giving him the benefit of the doubt and deciding it's the inquisitive kid in him, I respond, "Don't worry," to reassure him. "That isn't going to happen."

He begins, "No, Mom! I mean you will go in it!"

"No we won't. Don't worry," I repeat.

He begins his story. "When you are driving the car will flip. The sides will fill with water. Slowly . . . slowly."

I watch his face light up in the rearview mirror. He continues. "The door will be stuck because of the mud walls." He looks excited.

"My goodness," I manage to say. I'm on the fence. I want to understand where his mind is, but I also don't want him to think this is appropriate. "I hope that never happens. That would be terrible."

"OH! It will!" he confirms. "Let's go figure out where to bury you," he says. "Call me Spike! Yeah! Spike!"

I'm not keeping up with this conversation very well. I try to predict where we're going to go from here.

"You'll be dead before I'm a grown-up!" he says before I have time to respond.

I don't know if we will revisit these conversations or how seriously I should take him. But, I do know it freaks me out a little. He's only five years old. What on earth will he come up with when he's ten?

I wonder if the cats are safe as I walk around the corner, glancing up the stairs at my cat, Tigger, getting pulled by the tail, backwards, step by step, to the top. Jon sees me looking up at him, from the bottom of the stairs. Before I can say anything, he says, "Hey Mom! Can we get a dog if the cats are dead?"

"No. We can't," I say assertively. "Do not pull the cats up the stairs. That hurts. We are going to let the cats stay in Mommy and Daddy's room," I add, walking up the stairs, putting the cats in my room for the day.

His teacher writes a note home to tell us she has concerns. I meet with her after school the next day. She is clearly trying to be diplomatic, kind and thoughtful. She is holding back. I ask her to be honest with me, to tell me what is happening so that we can address it and make changes to help him. She lets go. She tells me he is manipulative, talks back, sets kids up to make bad choices on the playground and has a very sophisticated way of talking to authority, one that she has never experienced before in a five-year-old. She is concerned too, and her experience and redirection is not working. I can see she is frazzled, but composed. My heart breaks a little. I don't want him to be that kid in class, the kid that struggles, the kid that the teachers see coming and cringe. I don't want my kid to suffer that way. I also appreciate her candor. At the same time, I wonder how long she would have gone on trying to beat around the bush, trying to keep from labeling him as troubled, or challenging.

And Then There Were Two

By the start of the New Year, days have become long and hard. I want to believe love and patience is enough, that time will see us through this, that we can handle anything that comes our way. This has been such a bittersweet journey. I don't want to fail now. I'm ashamed to say that I wonder why we accepted him.

When we wake up in the morning, Vijay is happy to go to work. I look forward to dropping Jon at the bus stop for afternoon kindergarten. Like everything else these days, the bus stop is short-lived. Every afternoon, I load the boys into our plastic red wagon and head for the stop. As soon as we get there, Jon jumps out and runs around, waiting for the bus to arrive. No matter how much I try to get him to sit and wait like the other children, redirect, explain, and eventually bribe, it doesn't work.

On Monday we start our school routine over again. Carlito and Jon sit in the wagon and we review all the rules of the bus stop before setting off down the driveway. After arriving at the stop this particular morning, Jon runs around more frantically than usual, hunting the other kids with his finger gun. Another little boy joins in, much to the dismay of his mother. Jon cannot be calmed. I ask him to come talk with me and instead of coming to me, he turns and runs the opposite direction. All the other parents watch, as their children continue to stand in a row waiting for the bus. I yell down the street, "Stop!" "Wait!" but he won't. I have Carlito in the wagon and I begin a brisk walk in Jon's direction. He is sprinting now, all the way to the end of the street. I'm starting to panic. It's clear he isn't going to stop. He turns left and I don't see him anymore. I'm a good twenty-five houses away and begin to jog, pulling the wagon and its awkwardly low handle with Carlito buckled to it behind me. I get to the corner and look down the street he turned on, hoping to see him. I don't.

"Gotcha!" he says. I look down with relief in hearing his voice. Sitting on the dirt by the corner lot's fence line, he smiles and stands up triumphantly. Without a second thought, he sprints back to the bus stop before I have a chance to either catch my breath or sit him in the wagon. The bus arrives and he jumps on without a second glance at Carlito or me, as I try desperately to make it back to the bus stop before the bus pulls away.

I call his caseworker right away to let her know what happened. First of all, I want to document that he ran away from me, since I think this will become a problem now that he knows he won this round. Second, I want to know what the proper thing to do is, if I can't get to him.

"You may not restrain a child," I'm told. "You just have to let him run. If he goes farther than you can see, call the cops."

"Call the cops?!" I say, completely shocked. "He's five years old."

"Well, they will bring him back," the caseworker tells me, unfazed by this solution. I can't believe I may need to call the cops on a five-year-old. Am I that out of touch? Doesn't that seem extreme?

"What if he's going to run into the street?" I ask. Maybe I'm splitting hairs here, but I hardly feel like holding a kid's arm if he is going to run away is restraining.

"No. You may not restrain them. That is our policy," she reiterates.

"Oh my God!" I say. Now I have to refrain from holding his hand unless it's on his terms? Crossing the street just became even trickier. I try to step back from my personal situation. There are reasons these rules are in place. Somewhere along the line, someone got overzealous in restraining a child, so the line has been drawn. No tolerance. I can't help but feel desperate as I worry about future interactions.

When Vijay comes home from work each night, we tag-team. This provides even more stability for the boys and also gives me a break from managing both children. Because basically, that's what I've become: a manager. I can't do anything without second-guessing what the next best move is. We know Jon's behavior is not his fault and try to set up parameters, consistency and reasonable expectations, so that we are creating an appropriate parent-child relationship. We try to always give the benefit of the doubt first and keep in mind he hasn't had any chance at all.

We approach the bus stop again the next day, this time without incident. I get home feeling rather lucky and enjoy the afternoon with Carlito before going back for pickup. During drop-off, the bus driver has mentioned his behavior to me before: jumping over the seat, yelling on the bus and not listening. I'm not saying those things aren't problems, but they are all things any kid his age could do. This afternoon, however, I know something more serious than jumping over the seat or eating on the bus has occurred.

The driver pulls up, turns off the bus and gets off. All the children on the bus sit in their seats quietly, faces plastered to the windows, watching us. He asks for the parent of Jon as well as a little girl. My stomach drops.

I instantly feel what it's like to be that parent. You know

the one: the one other parents look at and judge. My child is broken and everyone is completely aware of it. I stand there feeling everyone's eyes stare at me, knowing everyone thinks I'm out of control, a bad parent, out to lunch. And, I know some of it's true. We are out of control!

A father approaches and begins a solemn conversation with the driver, all in Spanish. I know it is serious by the way the little girl hides between her dad's legs as they talk. I also can see the shock and horror in the father's eyes as the bus driver goes over the list of issues from the short ride from the school to the stop. I watch the little girl, a picture-perfect kindergartener, her perfectly braided hair with sweet little bows and big bright eyes looking up at me through her father's legs.

I look at Jon. He knows he is in trouble. I don't know why yet, but the look on his face suggests it is something serious. He isn't jumping around like he usually does. Today it's more of a stationary bounce.

It is my turn. The bus driver turns to me with a sympathetic frown.

"You are Jon's mother?" he asks.

"Yes," I reply, feeling a little embarrassed. Whether any of the parents at the bus stop are watching or not, I feel like all eyes are on me *and* my parenting.

"I'm afraid Jon pinned this girl down on the bus seat and repeatedly kissed her," he explains.

"Kissed?" I ask.

"Yes. She was screaming to get away and he was holding her down, kissing her," he continues. "I know they are just kids, but he cannot be doing this on the bus." He pauses a moment, then adds, "It isn't appropriate. He just wouldn't stop when I told him to. I had to stop the bus and move him."

"I see," I say, processing. I look up for the father, who by now has ushered his daughter to their car away from my little predator. I feel it: disappointment, misunderstanding, guilt, sadness. I don't want Jon to be that kid, the one parents avoid, the one no one will have over for a playdate, the one parents watch in disbelief. But they don't know our story. It sucks. All of it. It sucks for him and it sucks for me.

"I'm sorry, but we have had a lot of issues on the bus." The driver looks at me. "I'm afraid Jon will not be allowed to ride the bus any longer. I know they are just kids, but I am responsible for a lot of kids and this sort of behavior is unacceptable. He has to be able to listen to me when I ask him to do something. I really need to focus on driving."

"I understand," I tell him. I look at Jon. "Let's go home," I say to him. As we walk, he sings a little song and skips along. I'm sad for him. I let him know that once Carlito's speech therapist arrives at the house, I'll need to talk to him about his bus ride.

A few minutes later, I park the wagon in our garage and walk through the door into our kitchen. The boys sit at the table for a snack and Jon excuses himself to play in his room. I set Carlito up with his therapist and head up the stairs to the bedroom to speak with Jon.

"What happened?" I ask.

"What do you mean?" he says innocently, but looking at me with a smirk.

"I mean on the bus. Can you tell me what happened? I want to hear your side of the story." I try to sound calm and understanding so I can really get to the bottom of what he was thinking.

"I wanted to kiss her and she didn't like it," he says.

"How do you know?" I ask.

"She was yelling, 'STOP! STOP!'"

"Did you stop?" I ask.

"No," he says, looking down at his toy train.

"So, then what happened?" I ask.

"I held her down," he says.

"And then what?" I ask.

"She still was yelling, but then she started kicking my penis," he tells me.

"Well, you know, when someone asks you to stop doing something to them, you need to stop," I explain. "If someone is doing something to you that doesn't feel good, you have a right to tell them to stop. People should always listen to your feelings and respect you." I try to explain, but know I'm in over my head. I didn't expect this sort of situation and hadn't practiced this sort of talk before. I thought this would be a talk we'd have later . . . much, much, later.

"Yeah, well . . . the bus driver made me stop," he tells me.

"Well, that's a good thing. I think you really hurt the little girl you were sitting next to. You should not touch anyone's body," I explain sternly. "And, no one should ever touch your body. You aren't going to be able to ride the bus anymore because I can't trust that you have control over your body. I will drive you to school from now on," I tell him. Vijay is on his way back to the house, so I add, "You can stay in your room and play until Daddy gets home and then we'll talk about it."

Vijay pulls into the driveway a short while later. I talk to him first about what happened and then leave a message for Jon's caseworker, so that we can follow up and keep her informed. Vijay listens to extremely sad, traumatic, desperate stories all day. Then, he comes home to more. These troubles tug at his heart. He listens, keeps his cool and offers his thoughts on what our next steps with Jon could be. But, I can see he's tired, too.

The stories Jon tells are compelling, believable. They are also unsubstantiated. We report them all. No investigation is ever done. There is no money, no budget for investigation. At one point I'm told an investigator will go to the school to question him. They call the following day to say they don't have the resources to investigate. My journal is my safety net, the way I feel protected. He could say anything about anybody. He is smart. Knows the system, and is only five! He knows enough to manipulate the players but not enough to realize the consequences of those manipulations. He doesn't understand that accusations of abuse are serious, and that the attention you get from them is serious. It will alter the way he is cared for and who can do the caring.

Vijay's weekly calls to India continue. He doesn't share with his parents the challenges we face; we know what they would say. Instead, he rehashes the same conversation they've always had. "Yes, Mom. We're still trying." I know what they are asking. Our marriage is strained from all the ups and downs the Valley has brought. We signed up for this, but it isn't where we thought we would be. We aren't parenting together anymore. We are surviving individually, struggling separately, in our own ways.

Vijay suspects Jon has reactive attachment disorder (RAD). He suggests I buy books on RAD so I have a better understanding of what we are dealing with. As a psychiatrist, he gives me his medical text version, but recommends I read some mainstream books to help me grasp it on a more real level. I call Jon's caseworker. She agrees and suggests some titles. I order them and begin reading. I don't get very far before I realize the full gravity of what I am dealing with. Every list, every classification, every paragraph in these books has been written about Jon. It's as if the authors sat down with this child and wrote down exactly what is going on in his brain, life and daily interactions with me, with school and with his foster brother. There is nothing uplifting in these books, no silver lining or magic drug. They don't have a solution, hope or cure. They provide me with a reality check, the harsh facts, and an immediate need to get real.

Jon is five. He has passed the *three-year threshold*. The most formative years for *brain development, emotional awareness and conscience building* are gone. He will not get that time back. He can't *grow a conscience* if it was never developed to begin with. What is going to happen to this poor child? What is going to happen to us?

I thought choosing to be a stay-at-home mom would be enough, that being a considerate, reasonable person would get me far. I am not prepared for the battle I have just begun. Whoever said "all you need is love" forgot to mention psychotherapy, medication and RAD.

We explore therapy options. We read children's books to Jon about characters that need help identifying emotions. He relates to the *bad* characters, eager to emulate them. We try to align normal emotions with what he is doing so he understands that when you hurt someone, it is sad and when something is embarrassing, it's okay to feel embarrassed.

We make an appointment with a county behavioral health therapist and talk to Jon about going to a doctor to help us all make good choices. He enters the lobby and curls up in my lap. At first I don't understand. He has never cuddled before. He is so affectionate! Why would he do this?

"Mommy. Will you read me a story?" he asks as he cuddles. He burrows his head into my shoulder like a kitten and looks up at me and then to the rest of the *audience* in the lobby. I read the story, understanding exactly what he is doing. We are called back to the office. The psychiatrist takes one look at him and says, "Aww! He is so cute!" like she is looking at a puppy. "I want to adopt him," she adds.

Seriously?! I think. "I know. He is very cute," I sigh, thinking maybe this was a mistake. Jon is excused from the room to play in the courtyard, so we can talk openly. "You need to read my journal," I say with very little enthusiasm. "I don't know what to do. I don't know how to help him," I add. I hand her a copy of my journal and she begins to skim through my notes.

Reactive attachment disorder is confirmed. RAD is just what it sounds like. It is a failure to form normal attachment to someone. He has inappropriate ways of relating socially, and can't feel emotions like a normal person feels them.

Vijay begins to review charts at work and to rethink his relationship with the parents of children suffering with RAD. It's not textbook knowledge anymore. He feels what it's like to be a parent of a child with reactive attachment disorder. He feels an intimate connection to these parents now. He makes a point to connect with them even more strongly at subsequent appointments.

At home, Vijay tries to explain the extent of the disease to me. I don't believe him. I don't want to believe him. How can someone have an inability to emotionally attach to another? How can there be no cure or treatment other than maintenance?

"We can do this," he tells me. "We can care for him. If not us, who could do it?"

I look at him dumbfounded. "Are we willing to give everything up?"

"Yes," he tells me.

I think about what he's committed to. We are impulsive, but this life choice will affect everything so much more than we had anticipated a child would. We know every child is a gamble. No child comes without challenges. Jon's challenges are just so much bigger than average. We really need to keep this conversation open, revisit it often. I begin to think about how challenging and permanent this is going to be. I keep using *what if* scenarios in disbelief of what our future holds. What if he just gets worse? What if we aren't good enough? What if he hates us and kills us in our sleep? What if we want to have more children?

Vijay keeps restating that there is no cure and that his brain will probably never be able to develop emotions or feelings properly. He will most likely never be able to live in a family with other children safely. We could theoretically make small strides, but he is very broken.

So, now we begin a different kind of family-planning conversation. Do we want more children? I thought the answer was yes. How will we protect them? How will we protect ourselves? How will we protect other people? Am I strong enough to maintain this lifestyle? I doubt my prior optimism. I thought I could handle anything. I want to make a difference, but I can feel myself unravel. Am I so arrogant to think I can fix anyone? Am I so weak that I can't?

There is nothing redeeming in the end, no happy finale for this child, and no hope for a normal life. We need a new family plan, and we need it now. He's going to need so much more than a traditional family can offer. What are we going to do? We weigh the options daily. If not us, who? If we keep him, what will he do to us? How can we subject everyone we have relationships with to these challenges intentionally? Why didn't we have all the facts from the beginning? What will happen to him if he doesn't stay? How will I feel tossing him back? He isn't a fish. I am seeking all the help we can get, but it doesn't seem like enough. What are we going to do?

I tell myself repeatedly, he is only testing us. He just wants to see if we'll stick around for the long haul. I want to take this child in my arms and tell him: *No matter how you act, no matter what you do, you have a home here. We aren't going anywhere. You are loved unconditionally.* Of course I want to say these thing, of course I want to mean them. But, I can't say them if I'm unsure. I can't give him a promise that I can't keep. I don't know what will happen in his life. I am fearful that no matter who raises him, it won't be a happy one. He knows this. He's seen it before. Ten times to be exact. He knows the drill. He knows the signs. He knows how to test. And he knows how to sever.

CHAPTER 17

Who Needs a Time-Out?

In the following weeks, Vijay's parents start to catch on. "What do you mean you have two children now?" they ask. "Where are these children from? What are they?" They do not understand, and are worried, scared and disapproving of yet another cultural difference that they don't accept.

"We don't think we will get to keep Carlito. It looks like his mom is getting back on her feet," Vijay explains, but refrains from sharing any challenges we're having with Jon.

"But, you have added another child?" they ask. "What about getting checked? Has Liss been checked?" they want to know.

"We are focusing on this right now, Ma," Vijay explains.

A disappointed mother hangs up the phone. I know she thinks this is my fault, that this marriage is a problem. That

Who Needs a Time-Out?

Vijay would have been better off if he had just married a nice Indian girl. He'd at least have kids by now.

I thought we had the perfect combination of education, resources, patience and desire to raise any child. Now, I doubt our strength. Jon is a person, a human that needs unconditional love, a family, consistency, food and shelter. I am worn out. I have lost my cool. I am no longer patient. I'm disappointed in myself. Why did we agree to take this child? Why didn't they tell me everything I needed to know? I pass blame onto the system. I want him so badly. I want to cure him. But, in my heart I know we're just a stop in a long line of dysfunction. It makes me sick.

It becomes obvious that this little boy will become my life's work. A strong possibility exists that he won't get any better, and even more likely will become much worse as he grows older and more sophisticated. Should we dedicate our lives, our friends, our family, our resources to one life or four? We could work our entire lives for this child and nothing will change, and maybe things will even become far worse.

The miserable truth is clear.

But, in the end, the choice becomes his.

Our last night together begins like any other. Jon and I sit at the kitchen table working on his homework. He is testy, flip and unfocused. He is pretending he doesn't know the alphabet. I know he does. He squirms in his seat, restless.

"Let's do this tomorrow," I suggest. "You have afternoon kindergarten. We'll have all morning."

Jon doesn't like the suggestion. He dramatically rolls his eyes at me.

"Let's go read a book and take a bath instead," I say.

He slams the tip of his pencil into the tabletop and shouts at me.

"NO!" He kicks the leg of the table.

I can hear Vijay's feet at the top of the stairs. He's holding Carlito wrapped in a towel, uprooted from bath time. Vijay rounds the corner when he gets to the bottom and stands at the table, reminding Jon that yelling and kicking isn't how to behave. Carlito clings to Vijay, his big brown eyes watching the commotion.

"You need to go upstairs and cool down," he tells Jon.

Jon grunts, then runs up the stairs and immediately starts throwing his toys around the room. We can hear them colliding with the wall; he topples bins over and yells.

"I want to leave!"

"Call my caseworker."

"You guys have stupid rules!"

"I don't have to listen to YOU!"

He goes on and on, yelling and throwing, like a little tornado, demolishing his room. We can hear his verbal assault. "You're a wiener head! I don't have to listen to you guys! You are dumb, Mom! You are stupid! I hate you!"

I walk up the stairs as collected as possible, thinking about staying calm and focused. I need to help him work through this fit. I sit down on the floor next to his tantrum and explain the situation the way I see it.

"Your caseworker is at her home, Jon. If I call, it will be to the caseworker on duty." I can tell he's listening but he doesn't respond. He sits on his knees, forcefully pushing disheveled toys from one resting place to another. "I don't know what the rules are if you ask to leave. If you do leave, it will be permanently,"

Who Needs a Time-Out?

I continue. "Can we talk about this? I can't come get you from the receiving home if you choose to go there."

I watch him. He is pissed.

"Do you understand what I'm saying?" I ask.

"Yes. You have stupid rules. I don't want to live here anymore," he says more calmly. "You are stupid, Mom! No kid will ever love you! Call my judge! I want to talk to MY judge!" His voice rises with the last command.

There is a brief, awkward pause.

"Well . . . Call her! NOW!" he demands.

I just want to grab him and hug him. I want to make his pain go away. I want him to feel something other than rage all the time. But instead, I call, because I really don't know the policy if he's asking me to do this. He has rights too.

A woman picks up and I identify myself.

"Hello. Well, I don't know what to do in this situation," I begin. "We have two foster children. One is asking to leave our home and I don't know the policy for reporting it." Vijay goes across the hall to change Carlito into pj's as I tell the story. He's back before I finish.

After explaining our circumstances, she asks Jon's age.

"He's five," I say.

She laughs a little and asks, "Can't this really wait until morning? He may be traumatized if taken to the receiving home tonight."

She doesn't know any of us, and I understand her concern, but I'm also a little taken aback by her finding humor here. I'm trying to do the right thing, and I don't know what the right thing is. The system doesn't have assistance, support or even appropriate recognition for his challenges. I haven't been shown how to deal with him correctly or provided with any resources on how to address these issues. So, I answer her the best I can. "Well, under normal circumstances I'd agree," I retort. "I understand this could be a regular five-year-old tantrum." Maybe I do sound ridiculous, but I keep talking. "He is pretty sure he wants to leave. I agree a child should be traumatized in this situation, but this is his wish. He has absolutely no reason to listen to us, he has asked to leave, he is a runner, and we have another child in our home whom we are responsible for," I appeal. "We are worried about our other child's safety as well. Jon has not harmed Carlito, but we don't want to risk it, either."

Her humor fades once she realizes how seriously I'm taking this. "Let me talk to him."

I hand the phone to Jon. I have no idea how this conversation is going to go, but step out of his room into the hallway to give him a little space. I think about our situation some more. She probably thinks I'm pathetic, but I can tell this time is different. Something has snapped inside Jon. This isn't the first time he's yelled "Call my judge" or called me names, but this is the first time he looked like he had absolutely nothing left. He is so convincing this time, I have no idea how this evening is going to end up, but I do have actual concerns about what will happen when we all go to sleep. Will he run away? I don't trust him to stay. He certainly doesn't trust us anymore, if he ever did. I'm afraid, and my gut tells me something bad could happen. I stand in the hallway listening to him.

I hear his end of it.

"Yes."

"No."

"Yes."

Who Needs a Time-Out?

"They have stupid rules."

"No. I don't want to live here anymore. I want you to come get me."

"No."

"No! I'M NOT SLEEPING HERE! Come get me!"

He hands the phone to me. "Here, Mom. It's for you," he says, calmly holding the phone out for me, as if it's my mom on the other end. This is totally surreal.

"I'm a half hour away from the receiving home. In the morning you can call his caseworker and tell her about this. She'll recommend a solution," the caseworker says in a last-ditch effort to postpone the inevitable.

I repeat her sentence out loud so that Vijay can hear it. He shakes his head *no*. I'm kind of surprised, since he was the one with the "If not us, who?" stance on keeping Jon, but I stand firm without having a side conversation with Vijay.

Vijay continues to hold Carlito, watching me, as I continue speaking with the caseworker. "I really don't feel comfortable waiting until tomorrow," I continue. "We have another child here. Jon has absolutely no reason to listen to us. He's run from the house before," I remind her. I know Jon has made his mind up. He isn't going to back down. Nothing I can say will make a difference to Jon. I know kids test, play with limits, challenge you, but this is so far beyond that. I try to explain that no matter what, I feel this night is not going to end well.

She relents. "I'll meet you at the receiving home in thirty minutes."

I glance up from the phone toward Vijay as I listen to instructions. Vijay points to the living room and takes Carlito there. I nod okay and stay with Jon. Carlito doesn't need to witness any more of this; Vijay will keep him distracted in the other room.

A feeling of both defeat and relief are instant. I am sad that this is the way in which Jon's story in our lives is going to end. I am heartbroken that this is just another huge disappointment in what makes up his life. I wonder what will happen to him and feel like a failure for not being able to make a difference. But, I'm thankful that I have a safe place to take him. Also, I'm glad we can protect Carlito, whom we are also responsible for.

I hang up the phone and tell Jon the news. "Okay. She said I can take you. Are you sure this is what you want?" I ask him. "Do you want to talk about it?"

Without missing a beat, he gets into pj's and heads for the stairs, skipping, as if I just told him we are going to Disneyland.

"Would you like to take a toy with you?" I ask him, lamely.

"Oh. Yeah. Okay," he says like it's no big deal. He grabs a random toy lying at his feet and hops down the stairs with a spring in his step. He waves good-bye to Vijay and Carlito as if running an errand to the store to grab some ice cream. He's out the kitchen door and in the car before I have time to slip on my shoes. I get in after him and look in the rearview mirror. I back out of the driveway slowly, in case he has a change of heart. Nothing. I start driving. I'm still waiting for doubt. Some sign it's a bluff. Nothing.

He's happy, looking out the window, as if we're going somewhere fun. His mood has done an instant 180, so quickly, from tantrum to charm. He's in survival mode. He's turned off his anger and turned on the charm, because now there is even more damage.

Jon sits in the backseat talking away about his new home,

how his new parents are going to take him everywhere, how they already love him and he already loves them. He's back to his first two weeks in our house. He has it pictured. He doesn't care about leaving toys behind, nor does he ask about collecting them later. He has completely moved on. He is on a new adventure and extremely excited. I am merely a chauffeur. "Call me Raven, okay, Mom?" he says.

He tells me that I have to pick him up and take him out to eat once he's settled into a new home. He is so disconnected. I ask him if he understands what is happening. He explains that he wants to leave, that he doesn't want to live with us, or want us to be his parents. He understands that it is forever and outwardly, he doesn't care. He sounds . . . happy.

We arrive at the receiving home and enter the reception area. He jumps around exploring the nooks and crannies of desks, shelves and the intake room like a little squirrel, cataloging everything in his path to prepare for winter. He asks to be let into the locked unit three times to use the restroom. After each adventure he bounces back through the door to tell me and the caseworker about this new environment.

Once all the paperwork is complete, he gets up and hops over to the door to be let in, smiling and excited. He turns to look at me as he goes through the threshold, one last time. "'Bye, Mom. Have a nice life."

I stand, mouth open, and stare after him. I recover from the shock of his sentence in time to say, "'Bye, Jonathon . . . Make good choices." I put my arms out for a hug, just in case he wants one. He doesn't. Without a second glance, he skips into his new temporary home. My heart sinks in disbelief. He is gone. What is going to happen to this child?

The on-call caseworker walks me to my car. I'm a little

numb as we briefly stand in the parking lot together, talking. She says she is surprised. She's never seen a five-year-old this confident and independent. "He didn't act traumatized, like most kids do. I've never seen a five-year-old like this."

I reiterate that I believe this problem is much deeper, much worse. I drive the mile and a half back home reflecting on what just happened. Mostly, I'm sad, feeling defeated and guilty. I guess we aren't ready for everything that comes our way and I don't want to be a failure, but also, a weight has been lifted. Pulling into our driveway I have a nervous energy, a giddy reaction, the kind that makes you laugh at a funeral and feels much too inappropriate to share with others: relief.

In the weeks that pass, my focus turns to Carlito. We go back to quieter days, focusing solely on his needs. Carlito never looks for Jon. He doesn't go in his room, nor does he question his absence. He is more secure, happier. I continue morning walks with Sarah. I talk about everything with her. I tell her I'm both happy and traumatized. I'm all over the place, and she lets me grieve and celebrate my experience of letting Jon go.

Jon's caseworker calls to say she's going to pick up his belongings. With my renewed calm environment, I print all the pictures I have of him to make a scrapbook. No one seemed to have any pictures of him before he came to stay with us. I think he deserves to at least have some pictures of his childhood. The least I can do is put something together for when he's older.

She stops by a few days later to collect all the things he's accumulated. I hope these things stay with him, but honestly, I have my doubts.

"How's he doing?" I ask her.

"Oh. He's the same," she tells me.

Who Needs a Time-Out?

"Well, my heart hurts for him. Please let me know if there is some way I can advocate for him, even if he isn't here with us."

She just nods her head. We both know the system isn't that organized. It's going to be extremely difficult just to find him a home for him to live in, much less additional services.

Two months later, it is Carlito's turn. The day has come to say good-bye. He came to us a baby, with only the clothes he was wearing, pneumonia, anemia, sleep apnea and an extreme head-butting problem.

He will leave our home in speech therapy, healthy, sleeping well, friendly, happy and unconditionally loved. He can identify his eyes, nose and mouth and knows how to lick his lips, which he finds hilarious. He can say "Hi," "Moo," "Thank you," "Juice," and "Ut-oh."

Mom drives down from Los Angeles to watch him while I attend the final court hearing. We have all his toys, clothes and books packed up and ready to go, anticipating the verdict.

He awoke like any other day, and I awoke both happy for his mom and sad for us. We know he will be okay, but we also know that his life is going to be so different from the life we want him to have. Giving him back feels like he's going to die. We know we'll never get to see him again and I'm not yet sure how I will deal with that.

I drive to the courthouse and take my seat in the waiting room next to Kelly, his mother. We make small talk about how things are going while we wait for our case to be called. Both of us assume the verdict will be in her favor. After over an hour, we're called into the courtroom. Her attorney argues the reality of Kelly's life, that she has had a second child and is sober now. She tells the judge that should Carlito be returned to his mother, it may be an added stress for Kelly, but it is her reality. She needs to figure it out.

"Is his foster parent here?" the judge asks while flipping through Carlito's case folder.

"Yes," the caseworker says.

"So, what kind of boy is he?" He nods toward me without looking up, still reviewing the file.

I didn't know I'd get to talk, that I'd have a say. I feel like kicking myself for not knowing about this, or rehearsing some lines, for not coming up with something so moving, so powerful, everyone would *get it*. I don't actually have any real influence here. I know the judge has already decided what is going to happen. I'm a terrible in-the-moment responder. "He is such a sweet boy. We love him. We hope the best for him," I manage to squeak out meekly. I tried to emphasize the "him," but I don't really know if it was even audible.

The judge looks up at me.

"Oh, hi, Elizabeth." He recognizes me. I had recognized him as well. He had been to our house for a charity event, before we had any children. He doesn't know me well. I'm sure he didn't know we are foster parents. He looks back down for a moment and collects himself.

"I'm ready to issue my verdict. While you," he looks at Kelly, "have significant challenges in your life, you have been able to complete the required . . ." I heard all I need to hear. The rest is a blur. I know what's happening.

Carlito is to be returned to his mother. I walk out of the courthouse with Kelly. I congratulate her on everything she has accomplished. I remind her how wonderful Carlito is and what a gift he has been in my life. I tell her he is worth it. She nods her head in agreement. We walk together down the hall and into the parking lot. We stop before crossing the street to our cars. I look at her and pause, realizing no one gave us instructions. I haven't signed anything. We weren't told how or where to make the transfer of this little boy. The minute the verdict is ordered, Child Protective Services is done with their involvement. As far as the system is concerned, I just hand him over, like a piece of luggage.

"Where do you want to meet?" I ask.

"For what?" she replies.

"To get your son," I say and sigh, concerned, but not entirely surprised.

"Oh, right. How about around four o'clock?"

I look down at my watch. It's eleven a.m. I'm surprised she wants to wait that long, but also happy I'll get to have Carlito for a few more hours before I have to give him back. "Okay. I'll meet you at the Child Protective Services parking lot at four," I tell her. I drive home as quickly as possible to spend the last few hours I have with him.

It's sad. The child we want to keep we can't have and the child we want to have we can't keep. It takes a couple of weeks before I stop looking in the backseat when I pull into a parking spot or turn around wondering why I'm not hearing little voices. Life was so chaotic and stressful, the kind that fills your day and makes you complete. We know what we've lost and we've learned our limits. We purposefully signed up for this. Being a foster parent doesn't guarantee you a family forever. Knowing that doesn't make it any easier on our hearts, though. Jon and Carlito were and always will be a part of us.

It's quiet now. I sit on my couch in the morning sipping coffee and the house is completely still. Not a sound. No movement. It's strange. Chores became boring again. No toys to put away, no laundry filled with little socks or an occasional Matchbox car. I miss my daily kid routine of making food, reading books and bath time. I'm no longer redirecting behavior, resolving temper tantrums or protecting our plumbing from clogs or furniture from damage.

I try to get out of the house as much as possible, even if it means I've started spending a lot of time wandering around the mall looking at random home décor. I swear, more and more employees are starting to recognize me. Sometimes, aimless walking gives me inspiration, a quote I'll remember always. "If there ever comes a day when we cannot be together, keep me in your heart, I'll stay with you forever," printed on a canvas, seems fitting.

We know these children are so young they will probably forget us, and in Jon's case, may want to forget us. But hopefully some of the experiences they've had will stay in their hearts in a positive way. We hope we had an impact in establishing some of the services they desperately need and that the system will keep these resources going, even though it's so easy to get lost in the shuffle. I want to believe the days of "be nice to the kitty" could make them be kind toward animals or people, and the structure of our days together may be something that they hold onto in some little way.

Sometimes a broken heart and a burning desire to be a parent isn't enough. As it turns out, thinking you have a plan and actually executing a plan are two very different things. The last few years we've grown, loved and lost. We also forgot how much

Who Needs a Time-Out?

freedom we had when it was just us. Most people don't become parents and then take a break. We'll jump back in the game, but right now we need a time-out. We need to reconnect with each other and seriously talk about our family plan . . . again.

We'll be welcoming some more little ones in no time. Some may be temporary, others permanent, but they will all touch our hearts and be our children.

Vijay's three-year contract in the Valley has come to an end. I'm already counting the days until we move. I'm excited about leaving, starting over, but, my joy is short-lived. We find out, for immigration purposes, he'll need to renew his contract for one additional year. Turns out, we must have a transition year between visa types before I'll be able to sponsor him for a green card. I'm not sure I can do one more year in the Valley, though. I can't find myself again here. I've given the best of myself and there is nothing else left. I feel like my country's immigration process just pulled the rug out from under me.

I decide to leave. I need a time-out from this self-inflicted failure. A great, big, adult-size time-out, 150 miles away, before I have a tantrum. While Vijay wraps up his final year in the Valley, I say good-bye. Good-bye to the Valley. Good-bye to our house. And geographically, good-bye to Vijay. I decide to move to San Diego alone. I rationalize my move. It makes sense. My brother lives in San Diego and Vijay wants to do a fellowship at UCSD after his contract is up. I'm just going to get a head start. Reestablishing ourselves in a new city will be refreshing, hopeful. I'll reconnect with . . . myself.

"Oh good, son. You are going to be trying for a real baby now," his mother says after learning we are once again empty nesters.

"Yes, Ma. We will have babies. Some may be adopted and some may be biological," he explains. "That is what we want."

"Okay, son. When are you coming to visit? We are getting old, son," she reminds him. "It's been too long! Did you forget about us?"

CHAPTER 18

Recalculating Route

Mom has told me more than once, "Liz, you put it all out there. You invest your whole self and oftentimes, get hurt." I agree. I have an overinflated expectation of how things should be, optimistically wanting great outcomes. When the world comes crashing down around me, I do too. She tells me I need to protect myself more.

I hear what she's telling me and I know what she means. I just don't think I can do anything else. I am who I am. If wanting everyone to care as much as me, to invest in a better society for all, for everyone to be treated equally and fairly is an overinflated expectation, then my overzealous, optimistic self will have to suffer once in a while.

I think about my mom's advice mostly when I reflect on

the last three years. They were rough. We loved. We learned. We planned. We let go. We lost. We said good-bye. But, we didn't really heal or grow with each other. Vijay and I have disconnected somewhere along the way. I need a purpose other than being a wife. The first thing I need to do . . . is save myself.

The ink hasn't dried on Vijay's one-year contract renewal and I'm packing boxes in anticipation of a move. I can't stay another year. Not one more year.

When he joins me in San Diego, we'll be back to residency salary. The fellowship he's planning on completing is only a one-year program, but even so, I put more money in savings than usual in anticipation of the change in income and start searching job options and housing for myself.

Knowing our eventual destination will be San Diego, I spend most mornings on Zillow and Trulia. Dave, my brother, lives in La Jolla, but neither Vijay nor I are familiar with the city or neighborhoods. I contact a realtor, Linda, and start a preliminary search. Our first day out, she takes me to a few homes in central San Diego County, trying to get a feel for what I'm looking for.

We drive around neighborhoods. The houses are so expensive. I know we're talking about San Diego here, but I thought we'd find houses in better condition for under $400,000. I'm looking for something modest and affordable, with three bedrooms ideally, and a mortgage we can afford long term, no matter what jobs we end up with.

Vijay and I come to San Diego occasionally. Linda and I spend the day looking at house after house in disarray, while Vijay

RECALCULATING ROUTE

golfs. I'm discouraged. But Linda knows we'll find something.

"Let's drive by this one," she says, glancing down at her stack of printed MLS listings.

"Okay," I tell her.

"It was put on the market today. It's a little bit of a fixer, but very livable. It's still pretty close to the city and it is bank owned. The foreclosure process is complete," she continues.

"Okay." Feeling totally defeated, I agree to this final stop.

We round the corner and she parks in the driveway. I look around. The street is wide and quiet. With the exception of our neighbor's, the houses all look well cared for. Standing in the driveway, I look at our potential ranch-style home. I can see a chimney and an old skinny driveway leading to a garage in the backyard. It's charming. Linda pushes the code for the lockbox and opens the door. A small living room with wood floors and a fireplace are the first things I see. An adorable cabinet is built into the wall of the small dining nook and sun lights the room. It is bright and cheery. I start a mental list of all the work that needs to be done. It all seems pretty doable to me. The house has a funky little addition that leads from the second bedroom directly into the third, which probably explains the price, but I like it. I can already picture where I'd put our furniture. This one has potential.

Linda can sense my pleasure. She knows what I want and she's confident she's found it.

"If you want this house, you need to put an offer in today or tomorrow," she tells me. "It's below comps and will go fast. You have to put in a strong offer if you are serious."

It's a Friday. Vijay and I don't know the area at all, but we're both in town for the weekend. We're going to attend a charity fundraiser. So, I drive back to our hotel excited to share what I've found when he returns from golfing. I tell Linda I'll call her in the morning after I have a chance to talk to Vijay. If he is interested, he'll come walk through too.

Vijay opens the hotel door and can see my excitement.

"Babe! I found a house. I love it!" I waste no time telling him. I show him the MLS listing and talk to him about the house and my plans for it. He listens in his typically collected, unemotional way. He doesn't object or challenge me. He lets the excitement ooze.

"Does it need work?" he asks.

"Yes," I tell him.

"How much work, Liz?" he asks. "I don't want to relive Chicago!"

"Oh. I don't know. It's a range, right? A person could spend any amount of money fixing up a house. I know if we pick this one, I want to redo the kitchen and bathroom," I tell him. "I can do a lot of the work myself. It's mostly cosmetic stuff. The windows and roof have recently been redone. The third bedroom is a little funky. You have to go through the second bedroom to get to it."

He looks at me skeptically. "Liz! The kitchen and bathroom?" He looks worried.

It doesn't deter me. "I've been looking at houses, right? This one seems to be priced reasonably. It's in the range we want to spend."

"How much?" he asks.

"It's three seventy," I answer.

He thinks about this a while. It's more than the house in the Valley cost and less than half the size. I remind him the location is expensive.

"Three seventy and it needs work?" he asks.

"I know. But, it'll give me something to do," I tell him. "I could go back to work until we figure everything out. What if we foster again? What if I get pregnant? I could do a part-time job or something else temporary."

"Let's wait a little while before you search for a job. I think we both want you to stay home with kids. You can't begin a career and then have to quit again," he offers.

"I know I would want a real job, a profession. I mean, I'd probably start at the bottom trying to work my way back up . . . only to quit if we have kids." I've been out of work for three years. "How is a woman supposed to explain why she's been unemployed raising kids for three years in a job interview, if she doesn't actually still have any children?"

"I know." He understands my dilemma.

"If we don't buy something now, we could rent a while," I tell him. "But if we can find something we can afford, it just seems silly to be paying rent when we could be paying a mortgage."

We dress for the event and talk about our choices the whole time. After the auction is over, we drive to our potential neighborhood. It is eleven o'clock on a Friday night, perfect timing to see what the weekends are like. The teenage neighbors are sitting in the driveway listening to music. Aside from them, the street is quiet. We walk the block in our formal attire and peek in the living room window of our potential home. Vijay agrees to do a walk-through the next morning. I send Linda a message.

We open the door bright and early and Vijay looks at me. "Liz, it is a total fixer," he says, a little worried. "I thought we weren't going to get a house that needs a lot of work."

"Well, this is the top of our budget," I remind him. "We could spend more, but we'd have to go either east or north of the city or prioritize differently. We've moved so much. I know we want to buy something and stay this time. No more moving around. Really settle. It needs work, but we can take our time and do things we want to do to the house," I add. "Plus, it's close to the city. We want to be near the city, right?"

He is less than thrilled about the possibility of working on a house. I tell him I don't expect him to do any of the work and I promise to have it livable by the time his contract is up in the Valley, the following year. He squeezes my hand and gives me this project. He believes me when I say it will be done in a year.

I pack the remaining belongings gleefully into boxes and stack them in a U-Haul, Tetris style. Driving away from the desert and over the mountains feels refreshing and inspiring. I drive through the border checkpoint between the Valley and San Diego. A border patrolman stops me and signals for me to roll down my window. Usually I'm just waved through, but this time the patrolman asks, "Do you have any people back there, ma'am?" while looking at the truck.

"What?!" I say.

"People. Any people?" he repeats.

That's what I thought he said. I was just surprised he asked me such a blunt question. "No!" I say, still surprised. I get why a border patrolman would ask that, but, it's a weird question to be asked. The thought of putting people in a U-Haul is totally jarring to my feelings about basic human dignity. "Just stuff!" I say with a smile. He lets me pass without sending me to secondary to confirm.

Recalculating Route

A home, in a large city, with new opportunities makes me optimistic. I have a new beginning. I feel liberated. I selfishly view this as *my time* and start enjoying it immediately. I walk down the aisles of home improvement stores, looking at power tools the way I used to look at jewelry. I definitely will need a chop saw and a table saw. I note the prices and make sure to budget them into the remodel plans. A childhood friend moves to San Diego and helps me with the home improvement projects, which have become a full-time job. Little by little, the rooms get painted and cabinets are built. It feels great!

I join a local masters swim team and spend every afternoon in the pool. Lap after lap, my demeanor improves; I feel like myself. I'm happy, energetic and healthy. It's the best feeling in the world!

I agree to chair an event for the Alzheimer's Association. I've been volunteering for the Association for the past four years. I feel confident saying I have the time to invest in the cause. I am happy.

I've been having a hard time seeing when I swim, so I make an appointment for an eye exam with a new ophthalmologist I found on Yelp. I call to make an appointment.

"Yes, we are accepting new patients," the receptionist tells me.

"Okay, great! I'd like to make an appointment. We have VSP insurance," I tell her.

"Sure. What's your name?" she asks.

"Liz. I'm going to spell my last name, okay? It's C-h-e-n-n-a-m-c-h-e-t-t-y," I finish.

There is a pause on the line. Then the receptionist begins, "Um, can I ask you a personal question?" She sounds a little unsure about her question. "You don't have to answer it."

"Sure," I say, very curious about what she might want to know.

"Is your husband Dr. Chennamchetty?" She pauses a moment. "From the Valley?"

"Yes, he is," I say.

"Oh my gosh!" she exclaims. "I love him! He is such a nice man! I moved from the Valley to San Diego. I didn't get to work directly with him, but I knew him!" she offers enthusiastically.

What are the odds? I think to myself. I smile and thank her. I need to remember that. He is such a nice man. After everything we've been through, he is a nice man and we are nice people.

Now is the time to focus on the other half of me: my partner and our marriage.

Vijay begins his last year in the Valley. We consult a real estate attorney for advice on our Valley home. He tells us to leave it. We aren't able to rent it for the mortgage payment and it is significantly underwater—$150,000 underwater.

"It's not like the banks were being honest," the attorney tells us.

"We've never missed a payment or underpaid anything in our lives," I tell our new attorney. "We don't have the difference, and I don't think we could get a loan for that much," I continue.

"You need to think of this more like a business deal and less like your home," he explains.

I'm a bit shocked by this approach, but slowly change my view as I listen to him about the business side of things and our long-term financial security. The reality is, people are moving away from our neighborhood, and no one is moving in to take residence in the vacant properties. Even the real estate agent who helped us buy the house said he wouldn't be able to find a renter. We list our home as a short sale and cross our fingers it will sell eventually.

My itch for children never goes away. I go to our county's Child Protective Services office and begin the paperwork needed to reapply for a foster home license. Vijay still has eight months left on his contract and I am still working on the house. This is definitely premature. It's going to be a while before we are ready to get licensed or take a placement, but I collect the information anyway for when the time comes.

I know this break is smart and necessary. We need to be strong again, really strong. Vijay drives out every weekend, but we continue to struggle from the week apart. He spends his free time golfing. I spend my time working on the house. Our relationship becomes more and more neglected. We need to fix whatever is happening to us and make sure we are solid before we consider bringing children into our lives again.

Vijay has way too much free time now that he is on his own in the Valley. He begins to focus on *the meaning of life*, in a way that isn't conducive to having a family. He sees so much poverty and hopelessness from his patients every day. I don't know if it is guilt he feels, but on the weekends he questions the point of our possessions. He starts to show interest in Buddhism and discusses materialism obsessively. He questions our home and why we need three bedrooms. I wonder what's happening to him. Why did he purchase this home with me? Doesn't he want kids anymore? What is he talking about?

I want him to just focus on *the meaning of our marriage*. I remind him that golfing isn't exactly an unmaterialistic endeavor. I start to worry. Is this a normal marital strain? Is this expected? We had a rough three years. Should I let him have this crisis? Should I hold his hand through it? Should I ignore him?

I know we have things that some people in the world do not, but I don't feel guilty for wanting a home. He is voicing new goals that I don't share. I'm not going to move into a studio apartment somewhere and give up everything. But how do you get mad at someone who wants to be a better world citizen? How do you get angry at someone for wanting to give up everything he has for the supposed betterment of others? Yet how will it be better for others? I'm not exactly sure what he's proposing, and he seems serious about it.

I can't decide what to do. I consider going back to my therapist. She knows my story. I won't have to backtrack my parenting drama and explain my relationship. She's met Vijay. She's heard my challenges with his family. I decide to wait a bit. I focus more on myself and swimming.

By the time June comes around, I don't know if we can fix what's broken. We've started spending less and less time around each other. We talk about separating, but I'm not sure what that means or looks like. I'm confused and I know he is too.

The house is finally livable, Vijay's contract in the Valley is over and his fellowship is about to start. He moves into our home in San Diego and we create a new routine. I try to engage him more and he stops golfing on weekends. We start to talk about our issues and make changes in our relationship. It takes time and patience. We go slow, almost start over. It takes a while to sort it all out, but we stick with it. Gradually, we start doing things together again.

RECALCULATING ROUTE

Maybe that terrible marriage proposal eight years ago would have made things a lot easier. Getting married in graduate school would not have been romantic, maybe not even ethical, but it would have changed the trajectory of our lives. This is the first time I've looked back on my past and wondered how the simple act of *not* getting married changed us forever. The last eight years would have been drastically different. Who knows where we would be? His visa status added so many dynamics to our immigration struggle and our relationship. How would it have been different if he could have walked into any job after residency? In any state? With any agency?

It's been over two years since Vijay's parents have visited and even longer since we've been to India. I'm excited to plan a trip. I miss India. Reconnecting with Vijay's family may also help us reconnect somehow. It could be a step in the right direction.

"When are you coming, son?" his mom asks on a habitual phone call.

"January," he assures her. There is a pause and Vijay looks at me.

"My mom wants to talk to you, babe," he says, as I sit on the couch flipping channels.

I take the phone and say hello. We talk about our health, my parents, and then she asks what's on her mind. "Liss, are you going to go get checked soon?"

"I had my blood drawn during my last physical and everything is normal," I tell her, while thinking how annoyingly forward she is with discussing these things.

"Well, we have world-class hospitals here, Liss. When you come, we will get you checked. Don't worry. We will take you." I look at Vijay.

"I'm not sure about that." I stop at that.

"The hospitals are good here, Liss. We have nice facilities!"

What can I say to that? I pass the phone back to Vijay. I am never prepared with a good response. It's frustrating. I don't doubt the medical care in India. I'm sure there are good hospitals. I stare, exasperated, at Vijay talking away. I can think of a hundred responses now. I'm glad she came out with it over the phone, instead of waiting for our arrival to spring it on me. Vijay ends his conversation with his folks and looks at me.

"My brother's going to have a baby," he tells me. "They want us all to meet in India this trip."

"That's nice," I say, trying to decide how to voice my concern. I don't do it well. "I'm not going. I'm sure," I tell him. "Your mom told me to get checked out when I am in India!" I tell him, confident he'll be surprised and reassure me that we wouldn't do something like that.

He knows this already. I can tell by the look on his face. "It could be a good idea. It would make them happy," he tells me.

I can't believe my reproductive well-being has already been discussed, course of action decided and apparently agreed upon. There isn't anything medically wrong. Why doesn't he tell them there is no need? I'm incensed and decide instead of arguing, to bite my tongue. He follows up by claiming he understands both sides. I don't even bother looking at him. I just feel invaded. I don't *want* to be poked and prodded. I don't *need* to be poked and prodded. This is not a new conversation. He knows this. If I get pregnant, I get pregnant, but I don't want to take any extra steps. I certainly don't need to do it while trying to visit family in India. I'm irked, and he clearly doesn't share my outrage.

Before the we'll-take-you-to-get-checked-out-while-you-are-here conversation took place, I wanted to go back to visit. I want to move forward, try again, but now I've made a decision . . . I'll pass this time around. I'm not emotionally ready for a trip with his family. I know how they feel about me. I now know how intrusive the culture is. My body, my choice, thank you very much.

I know Vijay is disappointed. He understands where his parents are coming from; I get it. But, he understands where I'm coming from, too, and I don't exactly hear him defend me. I know I won't feel supported by anyone in India.

A month later, I fill a suitcase with gifts for his family and send Vijay on his way. Vijay's brother doesn't end up meeting him in India anyway. His parents keep the gifts for the new baby and promise to take them to Australia when they visit their first grandchild.

While he's gone, I think deeply about him, about us, about culture.

There is a reason Vijay doesn't live in India anymore, but I still can't figure it out. Vijay beats to his own drummer; he zigs when everyone else zags. He likes to play devil's advocate. I'm not sure what his cultural baggage really is. It's easy for me to do my thing, live my reality, in my culture.

When Vijay returns we have one last chance to reconnect. All or nothing, I decide. The distance and lack of contact and communication has drained us. We've grown apart. If this is going to work, we'll both need to try a little harder. I expect him to meet me halfway.

I let go of the baby pressure I feel from his parents. I'm not going to let their opinions affect me and I can't do anything about them anyway. I need to move forward and get over it. I reengage with the advice my therapist gave me after we lost our baby. I hear her words. "Just start dating again. You don't have to talk to each other, just go do things with each other. The rest will come in time." It has seen us through tough times before. I think it could work again.

He comes home from India and we start over. We reinvest in each other. We explore San Diego and our new neighborhood. It is pedestrian friendly, feels multicultural and has many new restaurants with farm-to-table foods and ethnic options. It reminds me of Oak Park, when we used to walk up and down the streets of our community after work in the evening. We don't need to talk about everything . . . we just need to start doing things together again. Spending time with each other.

This new environment, San Diego, begins to strengthen us again. Time starts to fly by. We're reminded of the big city we left when we first were married, our young married lives together, flirting at bars and eating at amazing Chicago restaurants.

"The rest will come in time."

One day, sitting in the waiting room of my new ophthalmologist, my cell rings. It's a number I don't recognize, but I pick it up anyway.

"Is this Elizabeth?" a woman asks.

"Yes," I respond.

"This is Jon's caseworker," I hear her say. "I was wondering if you would be willing to take another child?"

I'm pretty sure my heart skips a beat. "We don't live in the Valley anymore. I submitted all my paperwork to have our license closed?" I say as a question. "I live in San Diego now."

"Oh! Okay." There is a pause.

"Can I ask about Jon?" I ask.

"Oh yeah. Well, he's having a hard time. It's the same. We were able to find a place for him," she tells me. I know she can't tell me anything really. It's confidential and we aren't part of his case any longer.

"Okay. Well, if there ever comes a time when he needs some sort of advocacy, let me know," I remind her. I know, though, she won't ever call again. I'm sure as soon as she hangs up the phone, a line will be drawn right through my name on her list of potential placement homes. It's just a fact. What can I really do for him that would make any difference?

"Okay. Well, have a nice life," she tells me. The sentence lingers in my head. I know now where Jon got the good-bye quote he used on me at the receiving home. He repeated a lot of quotes he heard, and it makes sense now why this one would seem appropriate to him. It's what his caseworker says.

Vijay and I talk about Carlito, about Jon and about the baby we lost. We talk about what we want. We're clear about moving forward. We know we can make this work.

Christmas rolls around and Vijay's fellowship has six months left. I decorate our house the way adults with no children do. I put all the breakable ornaments on the bottom branches; I put framed pictures of Jon and Carlito on the top branches. I also place a spiny potted succulent ornament next to the framed pictures. I bought it on our horrific trip to Arizona post baby catastrophe. I love cacti for their beauty, their hardiness, their unique shapes. The thorns on cacti have a clever way of deterring prey from their carefully stored water supply. For many reasons, this is the perfect ornament to honor our baby.

These three ornaments are the first to be placed and the last to be packed, every year.

Along with my decoration overload, I put out the nice dishes we got for wedding gifts and spend more time sitting on the sofa admiring them than I should. I love how festive everything looks. I etch this moment in my memory and love the warmth the holiday decorations bring to our home.

Year after year, every time we set up our Christmas tree, I think about the sweet conversation I had with my mother-in-law about the American traditions of Christmas and the practicality of a Christmas tree. It makes me smile and appreciate the innocent moments when cultures collide.

Vijay and I have also been working our way through the foster care licensing process all over again. We have our home inspected, complete required classes and get a foster/adopt license. It's a much more complex process in San Diego and it is clear there are more resources here than there are in the Valley. I continue to work on the house, gardening, chicken rearing, and other odd projects.

The hurry-up-and-wait game is not my thing. I have to do something, keep busy, be productive. I begin to question being away from the workforce as long as I have. I'm not sure how marketable I'm going to be at this point. Should I go back to work after all this? Should I wait for some arbitrary scenario to transpire? If we get a placement this year, I'll stick it out and stay home, we decide. We still both believe a stay-at-home parent is a wise choice for us, especially if we have a child that needs a little extra attention.

We are careful this time. We want to make sure we understand our situation. So, we decide to work directly with the adoptions and concurrent planning unit this time around. With this program there is still a chance a child will be reunited with a biological family member, but the risk is lower than in the foster system.

Our adoptions worker sets up separate interviews. About ten minutes into a pretty general interview . . .

"So, what are your dreams for your kids?" the interviewer asks.

"I just want them to be self-sufficient, content members of society. People who won't hurt themselves or others," I respond. That is my dream. That is what I want.

"You don't have college in mind?" she asks.

"I'll support them, encourage them to go to college if they want to and are able to," I say.

"You know, so many people come in here with a list of stuff they want their kid to accomplish. Sometimes I have to tell them that college might not be in the cards."

I just look at her.

"Is everyone in your family on board with adoption?" she asks. I tell her yes with the exception of my in-laws, but that they live on the other side of the planet, so they most likely won't have a lot of input in our daily lives.

Vijay's interview is next. We both pass.

Vijay's fellowship has come to an end! His thirty-four years of schooling have finally paid off and with a green card now, he can work anywhere he wants. The freedom in those words! He can work ANYWHERE! We can live freely, without having to find a visa sponsor. He has taken his boards and is now dual-board-certified. He works for the county treating the uninsured, refugees and 5150s (involuntary confinement for being a danger to self or others). It's a good job. He doesn't have call and gets benefits that are great for raising a family. He is happy.

I'm impressed by his journey. Talk about stamina, determination and doing what you have to do! I'm proud of him. He didn't once complain. He didn't once whine. He accepted this as part of life, as part of the journey, as the line he needed to walk to get where he wanted to go, and I'm happy that this is the work he has decided to do.

With the New Year, our home is approved as safe for children and a foster care license is issued. We're told the wait could be close to a year. Vijay decides to take a quick trip to India before a potential placement, just a week this time. I pass for the second time in a row, because I don't want to miss a placement call.

This time, he comes home a completely different person and I'm ecstatic. He learned a lot about his own childhood and read a lot more research on early childhood development. He is enthusiastic, energized and self-reflective. This is the change I had hoped to see. I'm shocked that a trip to India was the catalyst. It helps strengthen our relationship further and makes me feel validated in my inklings about the way children are raised in India.

I keep busy by working on my everlasting list of home improvement projects. I watch job bulletins online, just in case the perfect job opens up and we don't have any children. Maybe I'll dabble while we wait.

Two years after moving to San Diego, our adoption worker calls.

Two children need a home.

And, they need it . . . today.

CHAPTER 19

Déjà Vu

It's Thursday morning, January 12. The weather is perfect, warm with a light breeze. Windows down, I drive my car through our local nursery, picking up plants and putting them in the back of my car. I love this drive-through nursery, for the convenience, the choices and the volume. It's inspirational. As I load a drought-tolerant shrub into the back of my SUV, I hear my cell ringing. I walk to the front seat and answer.

Our caseworker, Zoe, is on the other end. She presents a same-day placement. Two toddlers, a little boy and girl, one and two years respectively. My heart pounds. I immediately remember that first phone call I ever got, when a caseworker called to tell me about Carlito. I am excited!

I haven't said anything. I'm just listening. I can feel my heart beat in my neck.

"Are you in?" she asks. I jump back into reality. My head is spinning, running lists of possible next steps. The wait has seemed so long, but once the call comes everything moves so quickly. Hurry up and wait is here!

"I need to drive home and speak with Vijay," I explain, as I start unloading my car and placing the plants I'd just finished loading into the back of it on the dirt. I intended to buy them, but I'm certain I don't want to take the time to check out now. I hurriedly explain to the attendant, "I just got a call!" He looks at me a little confused. "I have to go! I might be back. I might not." The guy keeps staring. I unload my selection at his feet, waving good-bye. I'm fumbling excitedly. "I might be a mom!" I finally get out. He starts smiling and shakes his head *yes*, in confused agreement.

I call Vijay and tell him the news. He was on call the night before, so he happens to be home for the afternoon.

I walk in the house and share what I know so far. We call Zoe back, Vijay and I holding separate phones so we can both hear the information she's going to share. We hang up and very briefly consider the general description that was provided.

We call right back, and say . . . "Yes! Yes! We want these children."

"The children will be picked up and brought to your home this afternoon," Zoe instructs.

"What do they sleep in?" I ask.

"They are both in cribs," she says. Vijay and I look at each other. We need to run over to Babies"R"Us. We have only one crib and two twin beds. We also need some clothes and supplies, now that we know their ages and sex.

I call my folks and share the news with them. I tell them I'll call once we are all settled in. I am beyond excited. Who knows when we'll have another uninterrupted break? We lunch out and talk to each other with anxious anticipation.

"Here we go," I say, looking into Vijay's calm eyes.

We both sit, jittery.

Vijay calls in to work to tell the medical director our news. He requests the following day, Friday, off so we can spend it together.

As we eat warm crepes, we talk about how things may or may not be this time. We are both ready to do this! We are both going to be invested together. We are both going to parent these two little people. We don't know a lot about them yet, but agree that once we find out, we are not going to share any specific information we learn with anyone, including our parents—not because it could be a terrible story, or should be something to hide, but because it isn't our story to tell. They deserve to grow up like any other child. They deserve to tell their story to whomever they choose, when they understand it themselves.

When we had the boys, we made the mistake of being fairly open with family. We would share if the speech therapist was coming over, or if a visitation was cancelled and why. Inevitably a conversation would evolve about their past experiences and why they were in foster care. Then, usually a prediction of their possible future challenges would be offered. We talked about these situations because we were trying to make the best choices for them. We did it because we didn't have any other support. We did it because that's what families do.

We realize now, though, that sometimes people make judgments based on the information you tell them. The love you have for your child is endless and unconditional. After we shared our daily challenges with Carlito and Jon with family, they were no longer just Carlito and Jon. They became Carlito who had a drug-addicted mother, and Jon who had had ten placements. A curious family member, even with the best of intentions, can't keep from putting that rider on there, making assumptions about the children's past and trying to predict their future. It adds a dynamic that isn't fair to the child. It also isn't helpful.

We finish lunch and run our errands, picking up food and supplies. We know we've missed some things, but feel good about having the basics now. We head back to the house knowing the children are on their way home. We run around sticking all the breakable, decorative items hastily into boxes and throwing them in the garage. My backyard landscaping project will have to wait and décor seems completely unnecessary. We put toys in the living room so that the kids will see them as soon as they walk through the door. Are we ready? It doesn't matter. Here they come.

It starts to get dark. We sit, waiting on the sofa by the front door. I fidget, sit, pace and sit some more. Finally, after what seems like years, the doorbell rings and I'm right there to answer it. Vijay is by my side.

Two social workers walk in carrying two wide-eyed, precious children. "Hello!" says the first social worker, Lisa. "Sorry it took so long. It was a little more complicated than we thought it would be," she explains.

"That's okay!" I say.

"This is Malik," Lisa says. He isn't sure if he wants me to hold him. I back off and reach for Isabella, who is close behind.

I make eye contact with Malik. "Hello!" I say, smiling. I put out my arms for the baby boy, who happens to be the first through the door.

Isabella scans the room and looks at us skeptically. "It's okay," says Sally, the second worker, who is holding Isabella.

Their faces light up when they see the toys we've placed in the living room. Malik has four little teeth sticking out of what is otherwise a mouth full of gums and Isabella has dimples so deep you just want to kiss her. They nervously wiggle their way down from the comfort of Lisa and Sally's arms to play. Isabella takes charge and Malik holds onto furniture for support. The transition to our home is probably pretty confusing and stressful for their little psyches, but there is no sign of fear as they play.

I ask them if they want to see their bedroom. Isabella, who just turned two, says yes in a shy little voice, still uncertain of whom to hold onto. She is, however, sure she wants to see her room and heads there without pause. We have one for each child but put them together to start, for emotional support. We all round the corner and enter their room for the first time. They approach cautiously and play with the toys, looking up periodically to see if we're still watching. We want affection to be on their terms, but we also want them to know that they will be loved in this home. We watch and try to anticipate needs and reassure them. It's a delicate dance.

Malik, who just turned one, is still unsteady on his feet. He occasionally holds onto furniture for support and walks from one piece to another as he plays. Isabella looks after him and makes sure we know when she has a concern. The caseworkers sit with us as we play for about half an hour. Then Lisa says, "We need to do some paperwork. Sally will stay in here with Malik and Isabella while we go fill everything out."

"Okay." Vijay and I get up and let the kids know we'll be right back.

We sit at the dining table to read over their paperwork. It takes a fair amount of time. It's nice to have two caseworkers available for this transition. It makes it run much more smoothly. We sign our names on the final page and Lisa reminds us this isn't permanent. "There is still a family member being assessed that may or may not be approved."

We understand.

The caseworkers gather their things to leave. It's getting pretty late. Much later than we'd normally stay up with two children.

"The first night is always the toughest," Lisa says as she closes the front door behind her. I get a nervous twinge in my stomach and walk back to the bedroom to settle in with the kids.

It's late, but it doesn't seem like they are going to go to bed anytime soon. We decide to go ahead and bathe them before they sleep. A warm bath will be soothing. We put Isabella in the tub, followed by Malik. Their little bottoms slip and slide all over the bathtub as I write down *tub stickers* on my shopping list for the next day. Isabella watchfully checks on her brother, making sure she thinks he's cared for.

"Hair wet?" she asks.

"Yes. We're getting your hair wet," we explain.

"Okay," she says.

She watches the process and looks at her brother with concern as he is bathed. We take them out, dry them off and get them dressed. Judging from her agility earlier in the evening, we decide Isabella is much too grown-up for a crib and opt to try her in the big-girl bed. Her little body snuggles under the covers as I lie in bed next to her. We read a few stories that she doesn't follow. This, we can tell, is new for her. I talk to her until her eyes start to wander around, looking for a resting place. Her eyelids close slowly. I pull out the trundle under her bed and lie on the bottom mattress, just in case she wakes up and needs someone. Isabella is so brave. She sleeps through the night without a peep.

Unlike Isabella, Malik has no words to tell us what he wants. He fell asleep in my arms after bath time and I transferred him to Vijay so I could read to Isabella. We don't know what sort of comfort he's used to, but he doesn't want us to let him go. He can't settle alone. Vijay holds him all night, rubbing his back and snuggling.

Vijay's request for the day off was approved, so we wake up the next day, Friday, knowing we will spend it together. One of the big flaws with our previous approaches to making a family was not starting off as an equal team, something we've decided to make a priority with any new children in our lives. Be together as a family. Be present. Make time.

We realize Malik may not be able to sleep with Isabella in the same room. We wanted them to feel safe and comforted near one another; however, we also want Isabella to get good quality sleep. We tell Isabella we plan to move Malik's crib into our room and she doesn't show any signs she is worried about this change.

My list in hand, I need some supplies for the kids. We decide to divide and conquer. Vijay and Malik are playing nicely and neither child is acting insecure. I place Isabella into her car seat and head for Babies"R"Us. I put a kids' CD in the player. It's *Tarzan*. "You'll Be in My Heart" comes on. The entire song plays, without a sound from the backseat. Then, I hear a little voice say, "Again?" I press the repeat button and we listen to it over and over until we get to the store.

I have a pretty big list from the night before. We desperately need more clothes the children's size as they didn't come with anything except the clothes they were wearing. They are much smaller than the 12-month and 2T clothing we purchased the day before. It's like I'm shopping for a baby shower, but for myself, and my kids are already here.

Arriving at Babies"R"Us, I drag the crib box out of the back of the car to customer service, having decided Isabella will do just fine in her big-girl bed. I place her in the cart and ask her to sit on her bottom. She does so without a peep. I circle the clothing racks, looking for things her size. Each item I choose goes in the cart next to Isabella. She looks at me, then at the item, then back at me.

"Here you go," I say.

"For me?" she says in a small voice.

"Do you like them?" I ask.

She nods her head skeptically. "Thank you," she says in a whisper. She continues to stare and a small smile appears. She remains silent.

I look at her sweet little face. She stares at the clothes in disbelief.

"You can touch them. They are yours," I tell her.

Nothing can hold back that dimpled smile of hers. As she holds the clothes in her lap, I continue to load the cart with clothes, shoes and other supplies I overlooked buying the day before. Occasionally I glance down at her to see what she's doing.

Mostly, she just stares at the items in the cart, but then, gradually, items of clothing begin to come off their hangers and onto Isabella. We spend a significant amount of time going up and down the aisles looking for the items on our list. I know we'll be back a few more times in the days to come.

She rocks the layered look until we get to the register and I have to tell her we need to take them off to pay for them. We carefully remove the clothes. She helps me place each item on the conveyor belt to be scanned. Her dimples are deep and my eyes tear as I watch her.

We drive back to the house and unload the car to begin our first full day together, instantly realizing two toddlers are a lot more than one. Both of them run in different directions with their own independent agendas. We are already totally in love, but also in complete shock and beyond exhausted. We have a little fear we could lose them, but are also confident their circumstances are different from those of Carlito and Jon. We just have to give in and let the process take its course. Only time will tell. We live for today.

"You have two more children?" Vijay's parents ask, as he fills them in on his Saturday phone call home. They aren't surprised anymore. They just go with it. Vijay tells them about our new additions, but I don't ask for any details about the conversation. He doesn't share any with me. This relationship will take time to mend.

I don't know what it is about timing and child placement, but it's true what they say. When it rains, it pours. My brother David asks us to come to dinner. We meet him and his girlfriend, Lani, at a local restaurant, where they announce their upcoming marriage. In Vietnam! They want to have two weddings, just as Vijay and I did.

I love Lani and can't wait to see Vietnam. But, how are we going to travel internationally with two toddlers of whom we don't have legal guardianship? This is a whole new can of worms. This time, I'm not sure if the State of California will grant my request to leave the country.

I call the caseworker and ask what information she will need for a court order and how to obtain a passport for children who are guardians of the state. She's honest with me and says she has absolutely no idea. "I'll get back to you."

She calls back later in the week with a list of requirements. "This isn't exactly a trip to Mexico, you know. We are used to little weekend trips to Mexico. This is a little different."

We buy tickets, book an apartment and provide copies to the Department of Child Services, showing our contact information and itinerary, without having any guarantee the kids will accompany us. A hearing is set and I attend. The judge reads the request, asks where I am sitting, looks over the top of her glasses at me and grants the request.

We waste no time applying for passports and visas. Because the children are so young and we are going to be on the other side of the planet, where day will be night and night will be day, we also decide to bring along a dear friend and backup sitter. Credit cards charged, our debt $10,000 heftier, we are ready to see Vietnam and be there for my brother's wedding.

CHAPTER 20

Global Citizens

May rolls around quickly. We find ourselves on a twenty-four-hour travel itinerary with a one- and two-year-old. LA to Hong Kong to Ho Chi Minh City. Like India, the Vietnamese experience is similarly shocking, with new food choices, no car seats or seat belts, and chaotic traffic. Predicting needs for Malik and Isabella, whom we've had for only four months, adds all new challenges to our international travel experience. We are instantly grateful to have brought help with us.

The amenities are more convenient than those in India, but the city's cluster of cars, motorcycles and people everywhere are very stimulating for all of us. Malik and Isabella stare out the window of our car as we drive away from the airport. I mostly think about the logistics of walking around town with two energetic toddlers.

We check into the apartment complex we found online before our arrival. It has a pool and a playroom for the kids. It's a splurge, but worth it because of our new circumstances. Malik stares out the window at breakfast watching the motorcycles and cars drive by, honking and swerving in and out of traffic. He picks up some dragon fruit and chom chom. It's juicy and good, so Malik is happy. From Malik's view it probably looks like Dr. Seuss created our meal. It doesn't look like anything we're used to eating, but it sure does taste good.

We go out to eat and explore Ho Chi Minh City. One day Lan's family rents a small bus to take us to Mui Né beach in the South China Sea. Lani's family is all very kind and make sure we have everything we need for the kids. Malik and Isabella have fun playing in the sand and water and we eat chom chom fruit by the handfuls. The kids also think riding on the bus, on our laps, is awesome, as there are no seat belts. It's just something we safety-conscious American parents have to get over when traveling in a developing country. Car seats just aren't going to happen.

David and Lani's wedding takes place in a beautiful hall with many courses of food. We drink, dance and watch the newly married couple on the stage in front of all their guests. We sit and eat course after course with my parents, all of them, and I'm reminded of our wedding in India.

On days we don't plan outings, the kids play for hours in the pool and playroom. Vijay and I take turns staying up all night, as night is day and day is night. These kids cannot get their time zones straight. We don't even try to change their sleeping pattern since we are in town for only ten days.

It was a sleepless trip, but also an amazing one. These little guys are troopers. They did an amazing job adapting and meeting all our new family. There were a lot of people to meet, places to go and new challenges to face, but we did it. Our first trip as a family, and it was a big one! I am thankful to have been granted the opportunity to go and be a part of Dave and Lani's wedding.

The foster care judge has probably never had a request quite like this one before. I don't know if we got lucky or not, but I am truly grateful that our children were allowed to come with us. I am happy knowing if they do get to stay with us forever, they will have been part of this important family event. Our family is certainly turning into a global one, one I appreciate knowing, learning from and loving.

Back at home, the San Diego Child Protective Services office is much more thorough with their monthly inspections than the one in the Valley. The caseworkers come to the house without fail every month. In the Valley, the caseworker for Carlito used to just call and ask how things were going. Resources were scarce and she trusted me to report any concerns. The San Diego office follows the policy to a T, which I think is best for the children in the system. We are used to the inspections and questions. If anything comes up in between visits, I tend to overreport any perceived problems or challenges. I get used to the routine of having our caseworker come to the house, asking the kids how they are doing. It's always midweek, so Vijay misses these meetings, but they are uneventful. We gradually make our way through physical and developmental exams. I also begin to form a routine for our new days together. We have fun in swim lessons, go to story time regularly, and join the zoo near our house. We keep busy and active as we grow together. The months pass and we work our way through the system. I attend every court date, learning more and more about the children's case and the circumstances that have paralyzed their biological parents.

I walk into the courthouse for a hearing one morning. I notice a man in open seating outside of the courtroom. I walk up to him and sit.

"Hi," I say, glancing his way.

"Hi," he responds, nodding.

We make eye contact. I ask him how his day is going. He responds, "Fine." We continue the small talk until a court clerk comes out to register us.

"What case are you here for, sir?" she asks the gentleman. He sits up a little straighter to answer.

"Jones," he says.

"And you are?" she asks Mr. Jones.

"His father," he responds.

She checks a box on her clipboard. I look down at my lap, then to him. I think I'm sitting next to Malik's dad.

"What case are you here for, ma'am?" she asks me next.

I look up, startled. "Jones as well," I say. I can tell he's looking at me now.

"And you are?" she asks.

"I'm his foster mother," I respond.

I look at Mr. Jones. He looks at me. I venture a smile. "It's nice to meet you," I tell him.

"Yeah . . . hi," he says to me, eyes shifting. The woman walks away and I go for it. I tell him all about Malik. What he is doing, what he can say now. I tell him I wasn't expecting him to show up, but if he is going to come to all the court dates that I would bring pictures for him. I ask him if he has any pictures of Malik from when he was a baby. He shows me a picture on his phone that he took when he was born. I ask him to print it for me the next time we have a court date, so that Malik will have a baby picture. He tells me he will. A few minutes into the conversation his phone rings.

"Yeah, uh-huh . . . No, I'm sittin' right next to her. Uh-huh." He sits listening for a minute. "No, not her . . . Are you crazy!? I wouldn't sit next to her . . . Yeah, the foster mom." He pauses a little while longer this time. "No! No! I'm cool with her. Yeah . . . She's cool." He finishes his conversation and hangs up. He turns to me and continues to talk, telling me stories about Malik's bio mom, about him, stories he probably shouldn't be sharing, but I'm glad to have the information.

He's cool with me, I keep thinking to myself as I listen to his stories. I can't contain my smile. I couldn't be happier. That's a great place to start.

Court cases continue for months but I never see Mr. Jones again. Eventually his parental rights are terminated. I bring a packet of pictures to the termination hearing, but Mr. Jones doesn't come. I give the packet to his public defender and ask that he get them. His attorney looks at me surprised and says, "Well, that's nice of you," and assures me he will forward them along.

Visits with Malik and Isabella's mom continued through all the hearings, but eventually she, too, has her rights terminated. She is granted one last good-bye visit. Vijay, Mom and I bring Malik and Isabella to the Child Protective Services office for her last visit. We bring our camera so that we can get pictures with her for Malik and Isabella. The environment is artificial at the CPS office. There is a playground, but also people with clipboards staring at you. It's uncomfortable to say the least, and I feel awkward and sorry for their mother.

Malik and Isabella recognize her but are uncertain about how to interact with her. They cling to us as we walk around, looking for toys to play with. We encourage them to slide down the slide, backing away and cheering to encourage play with their mom. They cry and reach for us. We hold them and sitting in a circle, give the snacks to their mom so she can hand them their treat. They take it, but keep themselves planted firmly in our laps. Vijay and I try to remain upbeat and inclusive of the children and her.

We tell her we are open to communication and she says, "Okay, I'd like that." She adds, "I'm planning on getting a job, so maybe I'll get them a toy."

"That would be very nice," I agree.

We leave the visit an hour later with a heavy heart. We are sad for her and her situation. I don't know how likely it is we will ever see her again.

The case is now officially turned over to the adoptions unit. This is the bittersweet part of any foster system situation. On one hand, Vijay and I are overjoyed and ecstatic that it is only a matter of time before these children will be our forever family. We love them more than anything else. They give us purpose beyond belief. On the other hand, we are extremely saddened that the biological parents of these amazing children are not able to do what they need to do to care for another person reasonably. It's a complicated story.

Summer is here before we know it, and Dave and Lani are getting married again in Mom and Papi's backyard for the American folks who couldn't travel overseas. They ask Isabella to be the flower girl. She has a beautiful ruffled white flower-girl dress and sprinkles the flowers from her basket down the grass aisle, weaving back and forth between the tables. She waits for guidance for her next step before eventually making her way down to Dave and Lani, staring at them like they are her idols. The ceremony is short and sweet, the reception quirky and fun. Malik and Isabella dance and play all evening as we all enjoy the festivities.

The rest of the year flies by—Halloween, Thanksgiving, birthdays, Christmas. A new year begins. We've been a family for an entire year. We've hit our stride now; we just need to make it official! Throughout the year, as we anxiously await adoption dates to be scheduled for Isabella and Malik, we attend adult adoption panels and open adoption discussions to try to better understand the sentiments of an adoptee. We want to be as open as possible with our children, in a way that is age appropriate.

Child Protective Services has a funny way of taking away parental rights and then recommending you engage in a relationship with the parent whose rights have just been taken away. Ideally, we would have an open relationship. The reality is, we need to be careful and wise about our boundaries, while being open and honest with our children.

We want our kids to know their story, the facts that surround their situation, and, if possible and safe, know the people who brought them into this world. We request a referral to speak with an adoption therapist. Nothing has been more helpful. She's worked with people whose parental rights have been terminated by the state, people who have adopted children and the children who find themselves caught in the middle. Her perspective is priceless.

A family therapist should be a required step in the adoption process, not an afterthought or something that needs to be requested. The therapist we meet with helps us sift through how to set up realistic boundaries, reviews the reality of our situation and suggests how to move forward. She role-plays possible scenarios with me so that we can be strong and use language that is both clear and direct about this potential future relationship. She has me practice statements like "I'm sorry, I can't give you money right now" and "No, I'm not going to be able to give you a ride." Not because I should be cold, but because the more I give at the beginning, the trickier it is to set limits in the future. If and when we form a relationship, it needs to start off with clear boundaries until our relationship grows. The ball is 100 percent in our court right now. Should we move forward in knowing Isabella and Malik's biological family, we feel confident and educated about how this may work in the future. Ideally, we are prepared to march forward, but only time will tell how well we manage these potential relationships.

We know our kids. We can tell what makes them happy, sad, frustrated and excited. They are their own individuals, so different from each other, and they love each other fiercely.

Isabella is headstrong, smart, funny, determined and fearless. She knows she is a princess and dresses in her fancy clothes every chance she gets, wearing them to shreds. She'll try anything and isn't afraid to take chances. She is a loving little girl and an all-around fun kid. I'm so excited to see where life takes her.

Malik is sweet, strong, funny and fast. I mean really fast! That kid can run. He is starting to put words together and they are the funniest little sentences I've ever heard. He is in love with Nemo, airplanes, dinosaurs and trash trucks. He is all boy and my little cuddle love.

Isabella is assigned an adoption court date first. We make our way to the courthouse on what she refers to as "the day I get to go out and get an ice-cream cone" day. Grandma and Grandpa come and bring her princess balloons. She wears her crown and her fancy dress. After the order is signed, we all meet at our neighborhood ice-cream parlor to celebrate this little Chennamchetty.

We still have a few months before Malik will get his adoption date. We settle in just the same, confident his will be scheduled soon.

Our neighborhood is growing fast, and there are many fun, family-friendly restaurants in our area. One evening we decide to try a place we'd just heard about. It has a play area, is a microbrewery and allows dogs in the restaurant. What could be more fun? We go, order the kids grilled cheese and tater tots, get ourselves some food and sit outside the fenced play yard, watching the kids play as we eat. It's a great setup!

"Hey look, Mom!" Malik says. "A dog."

"Yeah!" I say.

"Can I pet it?" he asks.

"Let's ask," I say.

He bounces over to the family. I ask the couple at the table if it's all right to pet their dog. "Sure," they say.

We bend down to pet the dog and it lunges forward, biting Malik in the face, quickly and without warning. I look at Malik. He is screaming, blood is dripping off his face and I can't tell where it's coming from. I pick him up and rush to the bathroom to get some paper towels. I find the teeth holes and hold the paper towel on them. Luckily, it doesn't look like there is serious damage at first glance. I leave the bathroom, making a beeline for Vijay. "I think we need to go to the ER," I tell him. My heart is pounding. Seeing my baby so scared and vulnerable is one of the worst feelings I've ever had.

I look over at the table where it all happened. The people are gone.

We take Malik to the ER, get him a course of antibiotics and get his face cleaned up. The bite is not severe and luckily is in his hairline and under his chin. We fill out the dog bite report and call our caseworker right away. This is definitely a reportable incident—an incident, I am worried, that could jeopardize his placement with us.

On Monday, our caseworker calls us back and asks for an explanation. I tell her everything that happened. She says she knows the restaurant; she's been there. "Well, this just doesn't look good," she tells me.

My heart sinks. My eyes tear. I know she isn't saying she is going to come pick him up, but she is going to investigate. She tells me to keep her up to date on the restaurant's response. I tell her I will. Her comment makes me nervous. I am scared about the consequences of our family outing. How fast something so simple and fun can change!

In the weeks that follow, Malik's face is healing nicely, without infection. Our luck is overwhelming. This could have been worse. Much, much worse. The restaurant reviews their tape but says they don't have a view of that table and don't know who the people are. Animal control does not find the dog. Zoe, our caseworker, has accepted our explanation and the investigation team has agreed that it was not negligence on our part.

A few months later, Malik's court date finally comes. We meet Grandma and Grandpa at the courthouse and wait our turn. Malik does not understand what is going on as he shakes the judge's hand, but is happy to get the stuffed animal from the court officer once his adoption is finalized. We go out for brunch, ordering his go-to special treats: french fries and apple juice, in honor of our son.

2013 has turned out to be quite a year! Isabella and Malik are officially and forever our children. We can rest easy knowing our family is complete and no one can change that. Our life has picked up speed. There is never a dull moment. Parenting is a nonstop job that I am so lucky to have. Vijay and I are the strongest and happiest we've ever been. I'm so lucky to be able to stay home with our kids after all these years of waiting.

Officially adding these two to our family, the United States Chennamchetty population has doubled in size. Vijay and I watch as our children learn, grow and discover new things in their world, a world that includes us as their parents. My dreams for my kids are never ending. I want them to be happy and content. I want them to try new things, test their comfort zone and find joy and peace. The adventures of Malik and Isabella have begun. Hopefully our little global citizens will have many opportunities to see new places and understand new cultures. My wish is that they will be able to do a better job bridging the culture gap than I have done so far. They might be my guides. We know we aren't perfect, but we are happy, healthy and so very lucky!

"It's been a long haul, honey!" I tell Vijay, watching the kids run around our yard.

"Yes, it has!" Vijay agrees. We sit on our chairs, holding hands, watching them play.

"Come on, Mommy! Come on, Daddy!" they say. "Come play in the sandbox."

The sitting never lasts long.

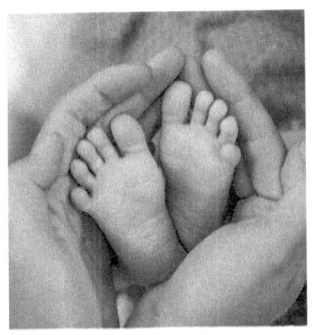

CHAPTER 21

One-Hit Wonder

Occasionally I think back to the first year we lived in our San Diego home. We started a tradition of having an annual Halloween party. We were empty nesters just trying to connect with each other again. We hired a psychic to give readings to our friends. When it was my turn to have my telling, she said, "I see a pool, right here." She pointed to the backyard.

To which I said, "Yeah. Okay."

Then she added, "And I see four grandchildren for your parents. And, a trip across water. A lot of water. A long journey."

Reminded of those words, I smile thinking about how it almost all came true. We frequently use a kiddy pool in the yard, and we did all fly to Vietnam for my brother's wedding.

The only thing she got wrong was the four grandchildren. Maybe my brother will have another. His daughter isn't that old; there's time for that.

Our second year as a family feels a lot more secure than our first. Isabella and Malik could not be any more adorable. We've spent so many years unsure of our position and status with all the children we've cared for, living in the shadow of policies, rules, inspections, requests, approvals and court orders; now we can live our lives, completely free, in peace. It's a beautiful thing.

Vijay and I also make sure to remember the importance of connecting with each other, making time in our relationship. We make Thursday night date night. Usually it's just a quick bite out, but it gives us an opportunity to reconnect and touch base. We don't want to revisit the mistakes of the past, taking each other for granted. Our weekly reconnect is a perfect way to stay in the present.

"We should take a trip for our ten-year anniversary," Vijay says to me as we scan the menu of our favorite Thai takeout. "It'll be ten years next November." He looks up at me. "What do you think?"

"What?" I ask, looking over the top of my menu. "That's a year and a half away."

"I know! But, we could put some money aside. Plan for it. We should go somewhere. Just us! Do you think your mom would watch the kids?" he continues. "We never went on a honeymoon. We're settled in now, with the kids. Do you think you'd feel comfortable leaving them?"

"Maybe!" I'm getting excited. I love the idea and I'm a planner. This is right up my alley. I have a year to figure out the perfect anniversary escape. This trip would be great for our relationship. "The honeymoon we never had! Yes! I think it's a great idea! I'll ask Mom what she thinks."

Mom agrees to take care of the kids, so we brainstorm destinations. We don't want to go too far away in case anything comes up. We've never left the kids for longer than a night and even though this break would be welcome, I'm apprehensive about leaving them for long. We'll make it a long weekend.

Two weeks later, on a Thursday afternoon, I return home from story time at the park with the kids. Our sitter arrives to watch them for our regularly scheduled Thursday night date. I have an hour before Vijay gets home but I'm beat. I can't shake how tired I feel. Naps are not my thing, but today I just have to lie down.

"I'm just going to go rest for a bit," I tell our sitter.

"Okay," she responds.

Neither one of us thinks anything of it, but I can't even get up for our Thursday date night. By Friday afternoon my head is pounding and I feel really off. Three hours later, I'm admitted at UCSD with meningitis. I've never left the kids for long and certainly never because of an illness. I lie on the gurney feeling a new type of anxiety—vulnerability.

I'm in crisis. My head hurts; I'm stiff and in pain. I just want drugs to make it stop hurting. The nurse complies and takes the edge off. I ask for more. "You know, just to stay on top of the headache!" I explain. She fulfills my request.

I feel much better as the medication kicks in. It feels so great, in fact, now I decide I should call Vijay's old boss, the psychiatry director for the department Vijay did his fellowship with at UCSD. I'm in the same hospital; why not say hi?

"Hi!" I say happily to his secretary over the phone. "This is Vijay's wife. I was wondering if I could talk to Dr. Lewis." She asks me to hold. Dr. Lewis immediately picks up the phone in his calm, kind voice. Vijay has always respected his soft-spoken demeanor. He is kind and gentle. It's no different on the phone with me.

"Guess where I am?" I've never called him before, or had a conversation with him outside of professional gatherings. He came to the kids' adoption celebration party, because Vijay invited him. I wrote him a thank-you note for the gift he brought to the party, but never mailed it because I don't have his address. I don't have his address because we are really not that close. Nevertheless, in my extremely drugged state, I felt the need to call him and explain all of this . . . while he is at work.

"I don't know. Elizabeth? Are you okay?" Dr. Lewis sounds concerned.

"I'm at UCSD! I have meningitis!" I explain happily.

"Meningitis? That's pretty serious!" he says. "You have meningitis and you felt the need to call me to apologize for not sending a thank-you note?" he asks.

"Yep. My cat is sitting on my shoulder right now," I tell him. "He's purring."

"I'm going to stop by and visit you," he tells me. "I'll be down in a little while, after my rounds," he adds.

I hang up the phone knowing that didn't sound right, but I can feel my dead cat Tigger cuddled up purring on my shoulder. I decide I'd better call Vijay, just to make sure that's possible. I get as far as the cat comment and he says, "Oh my God, babe, I'm on my way," and hangs up the phone. I know by the tone of his voice that he is worried and that maybe I shouldn't tell anyone else about my dead cat.

Next thing I know, I wake up with Vijay and his old boss in my hospital room checking on me. Mom, who's on vacation, takes the next flight home to take care of the kids. They decide not to give me quite so many painkillers and Vijay brings me home. I have viral meningitis, so it just needs to run its course and it's better done at home; there's less risk of getting another infection there than at the hospital. Mom takes care of the kids and manages the house while I sleep for the next week at home.

A few weeks later, the illness has indeed run its course and I'm starting to feel back to myself, and slightly embarrassed. Dr. Lewis did end up leaving his address for me, so in turn I send the thank-you note.

"That was rough, babe!" Vijay tells me. "I think we're good where we're at, with two kids. I'm really happy. I think I should get a vasectomy."

"I'm happy too," I say. "Are you sure you don't have the energy for just one more?" I ask him, teasing just a little.

"We have until I'm forty. Once I turn forty, I'm getting a vasectomy," he says. "One year. If it happens, it happens."

A month after my meningitis episode, Vijay and I ask Mom to watch the kids so we can go on a date to a Padres game with our friends from Los Angeles. She agrees and says we can have the whole night off.

"Get a hotel! Have a fun night and sleep in," she says.

I book a room and know sleeping in will be just as much fun as the rest of the night. Vijay and I meet our friends at a bar near the ballpark. We don't get to see Elbatmanuel and Blu very often. We haven't seen them since their wedding, the year before. They look happy. I have to admit I'm a little jealous of their rested demeanor and seemingly relaxed lifestyle.

We finish our drinks and leave the bar.

"So, anything new with you guys?" I ask.

"Well…" She looks up at me with a sly little grin. "I'm pregnant!!" Blu smiles.

Blu is a friend from high school. I have known her for over fifteen years. I could not be more excited. Elbatmanuel is over the moon. Beer is free flowing and eventually Elbatmanuel starts hugging family, naming his future potential boy after his father-in-law and talking about how being a father is going to be the best thing that ever happened to him. It's so adorable, sweet and intoxicating.

This date was a wonderful idea. Vijay doesn't have any family in the States and I don't have much extended family in California. These lifelong friends feel like family. We're excited Malik and Isabella will eventually have a pseudo-cousin to grow up around.

We head back from the date relaxed and rested. It's funny how some days feel long; I hope for a little break or a nap. But then, as soon as I leave the house, I miss Malik and Isabella so much I just want to be with them again. I am well rested, but eager to be home with them. We eat a quick brunch and head back, happy to see the kids again and hear if they behaved for Grandma.

Although I am completely involved in child rearing, I still enjoy working on the house. Construction projects are my main hobby. I'm always finding things to work on. I have decided to finish that backyard landscaping project I was in the middle of when we got the call for Malik and Isabella over a year ago. I know I don't have a ton of time to dedicate to it, but eventually it'll get done. I'm at the point now that I need a more substantial delivery of supplies and a chunk of time for uninterrupted work. I take the kids to the landscaping center and order pavers, rock and decomposed granite. I schedule the delivery for Friday so that the kids can watch the forklift deliver the supplies while Vijay is at work. Then, once he gets home, he can play with them over the weekend, while I work on my project: a flagstone patio and fire pit.

I work through the entire weekend, creating a new outdoor space. I spread thousands of pounds of rock and decomposed granite all over the yard. Sweating, making progress and transforming it is exhilarating. I start to cramp and bleed a little, concluding it's a combination of dehydration and the beginning of a period. I drink a lot of coconut water and I make a mental note to stay more hydrated. It feels good to get my hands dirty and create something new that we'll be able to use.

Monday rolls around quickly and I'm back to my usual routine. My cramping has stopped but also, I'm no longer bleeding. I call my gynecology office and ask to make an appointment.

"Hi. I would like to make an appointment to see someone. I think something is off. I thought I started my period, but there is no blood now. It's kind of strange," I tell the receptionist. "I'm not sure if I need to see someone?"

"Well, have you taken a pregnancy test?" the receptionist asks.

"Ahhh. Ha-ha. No." I laugh out loud and roll my eyes.

"Okay," she says, unfazed. "Well, our next regular

appointment is in four weeks," she continues. "I can put in a message for the triage nurse and she can call you back if you'd like? Just in case you want to go over your symptoms with her."

"Wait! You think I should take a pregnancy test?" I ask, thinking this through a little more. "But I was bleeding this weekend. It can't be that. Can it?"

"No. I'm not saying that. I just want to know what to tell the triage nurse so that she has all the information when she calls you back," she responds.

"Okay," I say, but in my head I'm thinking, *Oh crap! I'd better buy a test!*

I hang up the phone. Maybe I really should go get a test so I don't sound like a complete idiot when the nurse calls back. I load the kids in the car and drive to our local Target super center. I put the kids in the cart, push it to the pharmacy area and purchase a pregnancy test.

Test in hand, I make a beeline for the restroom, just in case the nurse calls back quickly. "Come on, kids," I say, ushering them into a toilet stall. "Face the door, guys," I encourage, as I always do when I'm out and have to use the restroom.

I pee on the pregnancy stick, convinced I'm going to get a negative result. I hold it upside down and look up at Malik's little face, eyebrows scrunched. They know the routine.

"Turn back around, Malik," I say.

"Wat are oooh doing, Mama?" he says.

"I have to go pee-pee," I tell him.

He turns back around and starts to hum. Isabella is busy trying to figure out how to unlatch the lock on the swinging stall door.

I look back down at the pregnancy stick.

It's positive!

Really!? Pregnant?! How did that even happen? Literally, the only night Vijay and I had for each other in a long time was our date night with Elbatmanuel and Blu. I sit for a minute looking at the plus sign on the test stick. ONE NIGHT! ONE NIGHT! Really? What are the odds?

Okay! Pregnant. That freakin' psychic was right. There will be four grandkids! I stare at the test as Malik and Isabella stand between me and the stall door. I throw the test in the little metal trash can on the wall, tell Isabella she can unlatch the door and leave the restroom. I put my kids back in the shopping cart and head straight for the stationery section. I look at the wall of pregnancy, baby shower and new arrival congratulatory cards, finding the one I want. It's a card with nine identical faces of a crying baby. Under each crying baby head is a word that describes what expression the reader is looking at: *cold, sad, needs a diaper, hungry, tired, excited.* Then, I head to the liquor aisle for a case of beer.

I drive home in our Honda CRV, thinking about how a third baby will change our lives completely. I didn't actually believe the *until-I'm-forty* conversation. I didn't actually think we'd really get pregnant. Rapid-fire thoughts just start flowing uncontrollably. *No more one-on-one. We are going straight defense now. Are we going to fit in our house? How will we fit in our car with three giant car seats? Our kids are two and three. By the time this baby is born, we will have three children four and under! I hope Malik is potty-trained by then! We are never going to sleep again! How is Vijay going to feel when I tell him this news? We've been talking about how complete we feel! He's been wanting to get a vasectomy! Oh man!*

I get home and fill out the card. *Hey babe! Guess what I learned today?* I write inside. I place it in the envelope, write his name on the front and put it on top of the case of beer, on the dresser, in our room.

A few hours later, Vijay walks in the door from work. Our kids run up to greet him like they always do, running around in excitement that he's home.

"Hey, babe. There's something in the bedroom for you," I tell him.

"What?" he asks as he walks through Malik's room to get to ours. A few seconds later, I hear, "Why did you put beer in the bedroom, babe?"

"Read the card, hon'," I say.

He opens the envelope and looks at the crying baby faces. His eyebrows scrunch in confusion. He opens it and reads silently. The message is short, so I'm pretty sure he should have a response by now, but he doesn't. He looks at the front of the card again and rereads what I've written. He puts the card down, thinking about what he read.

"I don't get it. Who is having a baby?" he asks. "And why are we celebrating with beer?"

I look at him for a moment. "Really?" I say. "It's addressed to *you* and it's from *me*."

"OH . . . Wait!" he looks at me. "You mean . . .WE are having a baby?" His shocked face is a fantastic expression I'm not soon to forget, followed by joy.

"Yes! We are going to have a baby!" I say. "I thought you might need a beer!"

"Oh my God!" he says. "Three kids, Liz! We are going to be busy!" The initial shocked look on his face changes to a slightly stressed expression, followed by a smile and ultimately a kiss. "How did that even happen?"

I smile. " Oh my God' is right!" I say. I can tell he's processing; it's the way I was on the car ride back from Target. I give him a minute.

"No more construction projects, babe!" Vijay realizes what I spent the weekend working on. "I'm serious!" he adds when he sees my face.

"I only have a little bit left," I tell him.

"Well, hire someone," he concludes. "No more manual labor, Liz!" He looks at me and I agree. "Let's go tell your parents!" he adds with a smile.

I decide I don't want to go back to the same ob-gyn office I used the last time. I want a fresh start and a different experience. I find a new doctor and schedule an appointment. I also send an e-mail to the psychotherapist who helped me when we lost our baby. She is still working at UCSD, and I tell her I'd like to touch base while I'm pregnant just in case there are any hiccups. Vijay tells me he will take time off to come with me to every appointment. "I'm going to be present for everything. We are going to do it right this time," he tells me. We've learned from our mistakes.

I have a reoccurring dream each night for a week leading up to our first appointment. Two eggs are traveling down my fallopian tube. Two of them. When they get to my uterus, they are both fertilized and one of them splits, resulting in three fertile eggs. Certain this very graphic dream must be accurate, I'm terrified of our first appointment and focus exclusively on needing to see one heart flutter at the first ultrasound.

The day has come to see our little jelly bean for the first time. I lie on the gurney and Vijay sits next to me.

"Just one!" my new obstetrician says.

"Oh good!" I sigh. "Three children four and under will keep me plenty busy!"

"Yes, it will!" she agrees.

We have eight months left to plan for this little arrival. We have every reason to assume everything will be okay this time around. Our ob-gyn tells us since our son's defect was random, she has no concerns that something may go wrong this time.

We start talking about how a baby will fit in our house. When we bought it, we knew it was a little awkward. There are three bedrooms, but to get to ours you have to walk through Malik's room. There is no independent hallway. Depending on whether this baby is a boy or a girl, either Isabella or Malik is going to have to share a room and the other will eventually want and deserve some privacy without us walking through his or her room all the time.

We look into real estate in our area, and in a few communities north of us. We're priced out of anything that's four bedrooms in our zip code. Besides, we love our neighborhood and want to stay. It's as diverse as San Diego gets. We want our kids to grow up in a melting pot. We don't want them to be 1 percent of the population at their school or in the neighborhood they grow up in. Instead of moving, we decide to complete one final construction project, adding a room onto the kitchen to create independent access to our master bedroom. That will give us three independent bedrooms, and give everyone some privacy.

We call a contractor, get quotes, secure a loan and start the permitting process. We spend December waiting for permits to come back and begin packing the house. Construction begins in January; they have until the beginning of June to finish adding onto the back of the house and knocking down a wall that goes through the center of our home. We move everything we'll need into Isabella's room and set up camp. Good thing the kids are ours. Licensing would not have been a fan of this.

I leave the house with the kids one morning to buy more boxes. I ask them to head for the car, then set the alarm and lock the door. As we walk toward the car, Isabella turns to me and asks, "Are we going to Home Depot to get boxes for the new baby?" Her little eyes look up at me so sweetly.

I look down at her and say, "No, we need them to pack some stuff up . . . because of the construction."

Then, Malik turns to me and says, "Is the baby going to be a T. rex?"

Isabella starts shaking her head. "No, Malik, she's going to be a baby," she says.

Malik dramatically raises his arms and suggests, "How about a BIG, HUGE alligator?"

"No, Malik." She lets a big, dramatic sigh out. "She is going to be so tiny!" Then she makes a fist with her little hand. "SEE! Like this big." I look at her little fist. It's maybe the size of a tangerine.

"Oh! She is?" Malik considers this for a minute. "Really, Isabella?"

"Yep!" she continues confidently. Then adds in a little squeaky voice, "She is going to be soooo tiny and really adorable!"

Malik accepts this. "Oh! Okay."

We continue with all the screenings and extra prenatal care. We get genetic counseling, even though we have no genetic risk of having an issue. "Yep. You are right—there isn't a genetic risk," we are told. "We just like to go over everything just in case." Overkill maybe, but we understand why. Vijay doesn't miss an appointment. He is there for every one.

Malik has taken to sleeping cuddled up against my stomach at night. When he wakes up he's usually right in my face, staring into my eyes.

"Good morning, Malik," I say to him. He is always the first one awake.

"I want to talk to the baby," he tells me.

He lifts up my shirt and looks at my stomach. He has decided that my belly button is the hole the baby can hear through. He presses his lips up to my belly and starts. "Hello, baby. I'm your big brother." I watch him talking. He rubs my stomach gently. "I have dinosaurs. Do you want to see them?" he grabs a T. rex from his toy bin and holds it to my navel.

"Malik?" I say. He looks up at me. "Are you going to help me with the baby? Big brothers have a big job!" I tell him. "She is going to cry all the time and we'll have to try to figure out what she needs."

His sweet, innocent eyes look up at me. "She's going to cry all the time, Mommy?" he asks.

"Yes. That's how babies tell you they need something," I say, thinking we are going to start listing things babies might need. I'm also trying to prepare him a little. He's my baby and I know he'll feel left out when the baby comes and demands attention too.

"No, Mommy!" He sits up. "She is going to be a good baby!" He looks at me with those sweet brown eyes and grins. I grab him and give him kisses.

The construction continues and I keep reminding our contractor we're soon approaching our due date.

"How many days do I have left?" he asks.

"Three weeks," I tell him.

"It's going to be close! But, we'll make it!" he assures me.

A week before our due date, we move our furniture back into the house. I sit on the sofa, cross-legged, with Isabella on one leg and Malik on the other. This is the last time just the three of us cuddle together because my contractions begin to get stronger and I think my water broke.

By two a.m., and after a few complications, our baby girl is born via emergency C-section and taken to the NICU. I'm less than pleased that I have to wait for my legs to start working again before I can see her. I practice bending my knees and pointing my toes until a nurse tells me they are actually moving.

"Okay," I say. "If they are moving, take me down."

She complies with my request and wheels me down to the NICU. Our baby girl is one mad little peanut and I can't do anything to help her yet. I can't hold her until we've both been more thoroughly assessed. I have to be able to sit up and stand to enter the NICU.

After a few tedious days in the NICU, she's finally released and brought to our room. Mom, who has been caring for Malik and Isabella, brings them to the hospital to see their baby sister for the first time. They are precious. Little baby Blu, named for the friend whose pregnancy rubbed off on us, bought Malik and Isabella big-brother and big-sister presents. They are a hit. They play with them and hold their new baby sister in their laps for the first time. But most of all, they love the hospital bed, which they quickly kick me out of to make it go up and down.

We are finally told we can go home. We are so excited! The nurse cuts the LoJack off of baby Blu's ankle and we're off. Mom tells us she'll help as we learn to navigate this new normal. It's a welcome offer. I don't know what I'd do without her support, and I'm not sure how she raised us on her own, without much money and with absolutely no family around to assist. I am beyond impressed with her strength and grateful to have her now.

About a week after we're home, I wake in the middle of the night, wet. The first thing I think is how wise my neighbor, who just had a baby, was to suggest I put a mattress pad on my bed, "because no one tells you the weird stuff that comes out of you after your baby is born." The second thing I think is *Really, Liz!? You just peed the bed?* I make my way to the bathroom, trying not to wake anyone. I sit on the toilet and pee. There is a lot of pee. Too much to have just wet the bed. I close the door and turn on the light. Blood drops make a path on my floor from our bed to the toilet. I stand up to investigate. I see a little drip, like a leaky faucet dripping blood, collect into a small puddle by my feet. It's not coming from anything that should be bleeding. I can't figure it out.

"Vijay?" I whisper.

He doesn't stir.

"Vijay!" I say a little more assertively.

"Huh?" he murmurs.

"I think I need help here," I insist.

He gets up groggily and makes his way to our bathroom. He looks at the blood and then at me.

"Oh babe!" he says with a sigh. "Your C-section is split open. There is a hole in your stomach."

"A *what*?!" I say, imagining the worst. I picture myself bleeding out on the floor of my bathroom and mentally jump forward to a life without me, Vijay totally stressed out taking care of three kids all alone. "What do you mean 'a hole'?"

"You need to go to the hospital."

"It's two in the morning! I can't drive there myself, can I?" I ask. "We can't all go to the hospital right now! Everyone is asleep! When is everyone ever asleep?"

"Okay. I'll call your mom," Vijay says. She doesn't pick up. Like I said, it's two in the morning. Who should we call? We finally decide our neighbor might pick up.

Vijay, who is much more collected about this whole thing, calls the neighbor. He is abnormally chipper for two in the morning, as he loads me into his car and drives me to the hospital. I hold my wadded-up, bloody pajamas over the hole in my stomach as he drives. Like everything else in my life, this might as well be dramatic too.

He pulls into the roundabout and tells me he'll go park the car. I tell him not to wait; I'll figure out a ride back later. Who knows how long this will take. I walk up to triage. The nurse is sitting on the other side of a glass wall. She opens the slider, looks through the window and says nicely, "How can I help you this morning?"

"I had a baby last week and I think my incision opened up," I tell her.

She looks up more alertly and stands when she sees my

bloody pajamas.

"Come to the door." She points to the door, meets me there with a wheelchair and ushers me into a room quickly. "Sit down. I'll page the doctor," she says.

Another nurse enters and starts taking vitals. "I don't normally get to see the moms after they have their babies," she tells me. "I only see you guys before you go to the delivery room. Do you have a picture of your baby?" she asks.

"Yes! On my phone," I respond. I find one and hand the phone to her.

"Oh!" she exclaims, sounding surprised. I look at her, kind of confused. She sees my reaction and explains, "Oh, I was expecting a white baby!"

"Oh?" I say in response, surprised by her comment.

The doctor walks in at that moment and starts examining me. She pokes around inside the hole in my stomach, trying to gauge how big it is. Then, she gets a long piece of gauze and starts stuffing my stomach with it.

"This is going to be uncomfortable," she says, as she packs the gauze into the hole. "We'll need to admit you until Monday. Your doctor can follow up with you then," she says.

"What?! No!" I say. "I have a baby and two children at home. I can't be admitted."

"Okay then, you will have to come back twice a day until Monday," she tells me. "They can look at it and maybe stitch it up then," she adds.

I'm annoyed that this is happening. My heart starts pounding in frustration. After she is done packing me, the nurse gets me a cab voucher.

"It's on us," she tells me. "Our gift to you. We'll see you back here at two o'clock to repack it. Okay?"

"I'll be here," I tell her. *Some gift*, I think as I walk out of the lobby and get in the cab.

Monday rolls around and I'm excited to have my wound stitched. Vijay drives me. My regular ob-gyn is out delivering a baby, so I get one of her partners.

"So, I'm going to order home health for you. You'll need a wound care nurse to pack this for you twice a day. Probably twice a day for two weeks," she tells me. "It's a nice-size hole."

That's it. I can't take any more. Aside from this baby, I have a three-year-old and a four-year-old at home. I don't have time for this. "Are you fucking kidding me?" I yell at her.

"I'll be right back," she says curtly, and leaves the room.

"Babe!" Vijay says with a shocked look on his face. "I can't believe you just said that!"

"What did I say?" I really don't know. I just know I'm frustrated.

"You just said, 'Are you fucking kidding me?'" he tells me. "You didn't just say it. You yelled it at her!" He goes on to explain what she wants to do. "It's called healing by secondary intention." He explains why it has to be that way.

"No I didn't... Seriously? Did I?" I just know I am angry. I was mentally prepared to have this thing stitched up and move on. Now I have to have a hole in my stomach for two weeks?

The doctor comes back into the room and directs all further communication through Vijay. We decide instead of getting a home health nurse we'll just have Vijay pack the wound for me. I'll check in once a week with the doctor to make sure everything is going well.

Two weeks later is Vijay's citizenship day. I'm grateful this randomly assigned date didn't occur while I was in labor or while my stomach was a gaping hole. Also, I love the fact that all the children will be there for his citizenship ceremony. His thirteen-year journey has come to an end. He is officially a U.S. citizen now. The kids hold American flags, try to listen and play on their tablets.

After the ceremony, friends and neighbors come celebrate with us. We had a food truck come to serve hamburgers, macaroni and cheese, fries and fried Twinkies. The only things you could possibly serve at such a celebration.

Vijay's family leave soon runs out and he goes back to work. I am on my own during the day. Mom drives the forty-five-minute trip several times a week to give me support, which is a total blessing. Isabella will start transitional kindergarten this fall and we're going to look for a part-time preschool for Malik.

After the first few weeks of school, Isabella has it down. She loves her school and her friends. She's an enthusiastic little learner. We've gotten to the point where I can drop her off for school in the morning. She knows how to get to her classroom and runs there excited for her day to begin.

I get to the gate in front of her school and open the sliding door of our van. Isabella climbs out, says good-bye to Malik and Blu, picks up a sippy cup that fell when the door opened, hands the water to Blu and looks up at me. "Have a great day, Mom! I love you!"

She's picked up our morning routine. "Okay, Isabella. I love you too!" I tell her.

She pauses for a minute, finger on the "close" button of the car door. "Oh Mom! I almost forgot! Be a good girl today, okay?"

I can't help but laugh. "Okay!" I smile. "You too, Isabella!"

She giggles as she presses the button and the sliding door closes. I watch her as she gleefully skips away to her classroom. I'm not sure anything else is this precious.

Blu gets bigger and bigger, and my daily routine starts to become easier. I venture out with all three kids on my own more frequently. We go to the park, the zoo and museums, and do our regular shopping. I'm a pro at loading my squirrelly kids and various items into the cart as if playing a sorting game. The kids run to greet Vijay when he gets home from work, excited to see him after their long day of school and playing. It melts my heart.

The thing I will probably never get better at predicting or responding to, though, is people who stop to ask me questions. I will always be shocked by the way some people insert themselves into my life. I brought it up before, what it's like to be the wife of an immigrant in America, but it's different now. These are my children. I'm still certain the reason white people approach me is because I'm white too. I also know we don't look like a traditional family, so it's natural for people to be curious. But it throws me off when complete strangers ask personal questions. I never had random people ask me questions about Jon's heritage.

"Are you a day-care provider?" I'm asked while shopping at Vons, kids in the cart.

"Oh, I just figured you sleep around," someone says to me at one of Isabella's schoolmates' birthday party.

"You know, I'm so proud of my daughter because she just doesn't see color!" I'm enthusiastically educated by a white friend. I don't respond to this, but *I'm pretty sure everyone can see skin color.*

"What nationality are your kids?" Everyone seems to want to know this. For some reason this question has become the one that most frustrates me. My response varies, but I'm definitely thinking whoever is asking needs to look up the definition of *nationality*. Usually I just say, "American. Yours?"

"What are they?" someone says, sitting next to me on the playground bench. *Children. These are children.*

"It's nice that you finally have your own baby!" I'm congratulated. *I understand what you are trying to say, but they are all my babies. And yes, it is nice to have them. Thank you.*

"Do your kids tell you, 'I don't have to listen to you because you aren't my real mom'?" I'm asked on a playdate.

"Do you worry their real mom will come and take them back?" I'm asked with concern.

"I need to know their story," I'm told by a friend who also has a kid. "I need to know if I need to protect my kid." *No, you don't. It isn't your business and it isn't my story to tell.*

"Your kids are really brown," a white lady says while playing with her children at a park.

"Isabella could pass as Indian," Vijay's parents tell me. *That's not really how identity works.*

"Isabella looks like her dad and Malik looks like you." I don't have a response for that.

"Do you feel differently toward your biological child than you do your adopted children?"

The need for people to put everyone on a team of like individuals, make everybody part of a mold, is so strong. People feel differences so deeply that they are completely crippled by them. I don't walk up to families and ask the parents personal questions about their children. I don't ask because it's none of my business. I get the curiosity. I get the perceived comfort in asking me and knowing our story. I get the intrigue in wanting to know why we all look different.

To say something like, "Oh, you finally have your own," in front of my children is hurtful at the very least. The assumption that one is somehow different from the other, maybe somehow better, is terrible. I can put this issue to rest, though. I can let you all in on my little secret. There is absolutely no difference. How I became their mother doesn't leave my heart any more or less whole for any of my children. My heart cheers for their successes and weeps for their failures equally.

A few more months roll by and Vijay and I celebrate ten years together. Climbing into bed one night, we lie down exhausted. Our feet touch and rub against one another. Vijay doesn't recoil anymore. In our ten years together, he's learned to cuddle feet. "So much for that anniversary trip!" Vijay says with a smile, looking at me.

"I'm pretty sure these guys are the best anniversary we could have." I'm exhausted, but mean it.

"Good night, babe," he says.

We have entered a land of firsts with our children. Our first day of school. Our first report card. Our first lost tooth. Our first cartwheel. Our first bike ride. Our first license. Our first date. Our first kiss. Our first broken heart. And everything in between. I'm so excited for all of our firsts!

And for the first time in my life, I am in absolutely no hurry at all.

CHAPTER 22

Om

I assume most people living in the States are used to hearing *Om* in yoga class. In India, it happens for a lot more reasons and can mean many things to many people. It is said to represent all of consciousness: what was, what will be, what can be. It is used as a tool for meditation.

The first couple of months after having Blu threw us for a loop. I wasn't sure how we'd bounce back as a family. That *oh shit* moment when I realized my abdomen ripped open, dripping blood—that was my last straw. I doubted if I'd be able to pull it all off. Three kids, all so young and energetic, is a full-time, nonstop carnival ride. There's puke, diarrhea, germs, colds, dirty toys, grime, sand, mud, overstimulation and overload.

A tickle fit that turns into projectile vomit on Christmas day, that's funny stuff! Happy holidays! When I'm out alone with all three kids and I've just got to go? I've learned how to hold Blu on my lap in an oversized restroom stall, asking Malik and Isabella to stand facing the door, all while changing a tampon. It's a fine hygienic balance, making sure your two older children don't touch the wet toilet paper on the floor, holding your squirmy baby on your lap, all four limbs moving in different directions. Oh yeah! Totally doable. Forget the petition-signing for changing tables for the dads; this shit is real now!

Don't get me wrong. We also have snuggles, kisses, hugs, hilarious conversations and a tremendous amount of love. We've settled in once again. We've ventured out camping, we've gone to Disneyland and we handle the grocery store, bedtime and meals. You know: life. I am commander of this ship.

"We want to meet our granddaughter," Vijay's parents tell him. "We aren't sure about coming to the States again, son," his mom adds. "We won't stay long, since the last time was so hard."

"It's different now," he assures them. "We really want you to visit. Liz and I both want you to come," he urges. He is in the dining room talking on the phone just outside our bedroom door. I am lying in bed. I can hear him promise "things will be different," that "Liz is not the same person," the "mistakes of the past will not be repeated" and that they are welcome. I can hear the pause in the conversation. I'd like to sleep. But I'm listening to him trying to convince his mother that she will have a good trip this time. That things really are different.

Om

What a terrible thing for a son to have to do, convince his mother to visit. No one should have to beg that of a parent. I also know for a fact that things *will* be different. For one thing, I don't have an abundance of time to devote my energy to how I do or don't respond to my in-laws. Also, I am not as sensitive toward other people's perception of me. This time I won't hold on quite so tight. I'm confident any challenges that may arise will not take as much energy as they once would have. I will suck it up. I will do whatever it takes. I will let go. I will go with the flow. If I misstep, I won't take it personally, I'll shrug it off. I will meditate. I will *Om!*

The next day is Saturday. I'm weeding in the yard and the kids are running around playing. Vijay is in the house while Blu naps. He comes out to see how we're doing. I tell him, "Babe, these are your parents. I'll do whatever you want me to do to make their visit a pleasant one, but, you have to communicate with me if I'm missing something." I add, "If there is some sort of ritual sofa-burning tradition that has to happen in our driveway, so be it. You just have to let me know!"

His smile is big; he gives me a hug and lets out a huge sigh. I think he is confident now that this trip really will be better. I am confident I meant what I said.

Om! I say to myself. Yes, *Om* is how I'll handle this visit.

After being reminded repeatedly of their horrible, terrible, no-good, very bad visit with us the last time they came to the States, I send an e-mail assuring Atha Garu that their accommodations will be nice, that they will find San Diego pleasant and that I am aware of the troubles of their last visit. Also, Vijay asks me to look up the rules for bringing cigarettes into the country. I look online and forward what I learn.

Hi, Atha Garu and Mama Garu,

Vijay said you had a question regarding cigarettes. I was able to find a site about bringing in cigarettes to the US. It looks like each person traveling can bring 200 cigarettes into the country. You need to each declare 200 on the immigration form (so 400 total).
We are happy to buy you as many additional cigarettes as you may need when you are here. We have a store that sells cases of them close to the house.
I am very hopeful that you have a good visit this time. We are thrilled you are coming to see your grandchildren! We will have a very good time. I know that your last visit was a little stressful. Please believe me when I say that I am looking forward to this trip and much was learned from the past. I do hope you find comfort and joy during your stay with us.
Love,
Liz

dear liz,
hope you all are fine. thanks for the information about cigerrets. we are keen to see all of you. may god bless you all see you soon

love atha.

"We will stay one week, son," Vijay is told. His mother has agreed to come, but needs some stroking. "One week is enough, son."

Om

Everyone who has Indian parents who come to visit relatives in the States, from India, knows that one week is not enough. They know a one-week visit is an insult and that it truly does take twenty-four hours to get here. They are on the other side of the planet. There isn't exactly a direct flight. "One week is not long, Ma," Vijay responds. "You are getting older. By the time you come you will have to leave. It takes so long to get here!" he continues to urge. There is a fine balance in bartering. Enough time to compliment the visitor. Not so much that the stay lasts a year. They reluctantly agree to stay for three weeks to see their new granddaughter and the rest of the collateral damage that is Vijay's family.

"What airline will we be flying, son?" Vijay is asked. "Will it be Singapore Air?" We all remember my previous experience in Hyderabad, when I was transferred to Singapore Airlines. It made a strong impression.

"No, we found you a flight with Qatar Airways this time," Vijay says and waits for the questions. He listens for a while and then says, "Yes, it is a very nice airline. It is very comfortable, nice food service. You will like it as much as Singapore Air," he promises. "And, you'll get to fly through Dubai this time."

Two weeks before Vijay's parents arrive, he gets that vasectomy he's been wanting. "What's the recovery like?" I ask him.

"I think it depends on how I feel, maybe one-day rest," he says. "When you're out today, could you pick up two bags of frozen peas?"

"Of course," I say. "Do whatever is recommended." I ask him to bring all the paperwork home with him in case he's too medicated to remember the guidelines. I drop him off at the hospital and pick him up a few hours later. He says he's not in any pain. I walk him into the house and tuck him into bed, propping his balls on a bag of frozen peas, atop a pillow, and set the timer. I'll have to stay on top of the frozen pea exchange: twenty minutes on, twenty minutes off.

He looks up at me in the sweet drug-induced state people are in when feeling no pain. "Thanks, babe. I think I'd like to spend my time in bed reading your story," he says. "There's no excuse. You've asked me to read it before. Life is just so chaotic; I have plenty of time right now."

My stomach sinks a little. His parents are literally coming in two weeks. This is probably the absolute worst time for him to read such a thing. We are in the beginning stages of starting over with his folks, making a fresh start for our relationship. I'm determined this visit is going to be a success. How will he feel reliving the worst parts of our marriage? He may not want to revisit the dreaded trip his parents had the last time they were here and my interpretation of all the events. I'm apprehensive, but want his feedback. He's never read this.

"Okay! But, I'm a little worried you might not like all of it," I tell him.

"I want to read it," he tells me. "Is it printed out?"

"It might be bad timing. Do you really want to revisit all that drama right before your parents come to town?" I ask. I really want the feedback, though . . . so I'm on the fence about how hard to push back.

He says he's sure he wants to read it and begins. I nervously wait for a comment, something, as he rests his frozen-pea-draped balls, perched high on a pillow, in our bed, reading what I've written for the very first time. I hear an occasional chuckle come from the room. I enter for water refills and frozen pea swaps, but otherwise leave him alone.

At lunchtime, I bring him a plate. Looking at the pile of facedown pages he's read so far, I'm anxious. "Babe. This is quite good," he says, carefully removing the peas and handing them to me. "Can you set the timer for me? I'm on twenty off . . . time for a rest," he says with a smile.

"Sure." I hand him lunch and set up a tray next to the bed with silverware and water.

"I'm so glad I'm reading this. I never realized how bad our time in the Valley really was. I never stopped to really think about it. I was so detached," he adds. "That's how I dealt with everything. I am sorry. I was in my own little world." Looking at me he smiles, then removes his sheets and stands to give me a hug.

I'm surprised. This is going much better than I thought it would. With his new appreciation of my view and my new motto on how to handle all life's challenges, what can go wrong?

We tell the kids Daddy's parents are coming from India. I ask Isabella and Malik if they have any ideas about where their grandparents could sleep. Isabella chimes in right away. "I want to move into Malik's room while they are here. We can have a slepover together!"

Perfect plan. I know it will become a round of musical beds, with the most likely scenario being all three children sleeping in our room with us. But, Vijay's parents will need a little privacy and Isabella's room is the best option, as it has a trundle. We spend the week before they arrive packing toys and moving furniture into Malik's room. We put flowers in a vase on a table in Atha Garu and Mama Garu's room and make a poster that all the kids write on, with welcoming words, handprints and pictures of them glued all over it.

Our Indian friend Rahul, who we new from our Amherst days, lives down the street from us now. His mother is also planning to visit from India. He decides to buy her ticket at the same time, so that his mother will have a little company while she's here. He wants her to have other Indian parents to talk to.

Vijay and Rahul met at UMass before I joined the program. They remained friends through the years. A few years after Vijay and I got married, he, too, married a white girl. They moved to San Diego and had a son. Eventually, they went their separate ways and ended up getting a divorce. During his divorce we became quite close. The kids started playing together and our friendship became even stronger as time went on. He has become a great ally for me. It'll be nice to have him this time around—someone else who understands both sides of the coin. I can't imagine a major event without him in it. He's part of the family now.

Rahul's mom, Meena, arrives one week before Atha Garu and Mama Garu arrive. She's the real-life preview I need to remind myself about Indian culture. A precursor to the many qualities Indian parents have and how they respond to America.

We have a very relaxed friendship with Rahul. Usually we just walk into each other's homes, opening the fridge and taking what we want if we get hungry. But when Indian parents are involved, it becomes a whole event, with protocol.

Rahul officially calls to invite us over for a visit. "Mom would like to have you over for chai," he tells me on the phone. "Would you like to come over this evening to visit?"

"Of course," I respond, knowing we need to bring a small gift with us. I go to the store and buy pistachios and a canister of mixed nuts, her favorite thing. I get home, grab a gift bag and pack the family into the car. A few minutes later we are standing at Rahul's front door, ready to greet our auntie.

The door opens, Meena is smiling and the kids run into the house. As they squeeze past the legs of the lady they have never met to play with toys, I think to myself, *Who is training these children, anyway?* I make eye contact and greet her. "Namaste, Auntie," I say, palms pressed together, head bent down toward the ground. I can tell when I look up that I've already scored points. So far, so good.

"*Awe bita*," she says, making a pucker with her fingers in the air toward my cheek, twisting her hand as she grazes my skin. "You are a good Indian wife," she continues, pointing at my bangles, toe rings and other Indian jewelry. This, a sure sign she accepts me and has protected me from the evil eye. She has stolen it away for my longevity and happiness. Within five minutes she is telling me what she likes about me and what she doesn't like about me, what she likes about Vijay and what she doesn't like about Vijay. We are discussing Indian culture, about how white I am, and how Rahul also married a white girl but tragically, it did not work out. She cries a little; we listen a lot. It's an Indian thing. *Om!*

Back in the car, on the way home, I turn to Vijay. "This was perfect timing!" I tell him. "Just the reminder I needed before your parents come to town." I'm excited. I can handle this. Nothing is going to be too much this time. It's all just cultural. I got this.

"Yeah," Vijay sighs. He doesn't say anything else.

There was probably a lot more to the conversation that

I didn't get. Meena speaks broken English and a lot of the conversation was in Tamil, which Vijay speaks fairly well. I don't need to know and I don't want to know. *Om!* It's all good.

"Your Thatha and Ava are arriving today," Vijay tells the kids.

Vijay and I decided Isabella will be our child ambassador. She is the most well behaved, the oldest, and is excited to go to the airport to pick up the grandparents she has never met. "Mom! I want to get fancy!" Isabella says, putting on her fanciest princess dress, Princess Tiana. I braid and curl her long Rapunzel hair, adding sparkles and fancy jewelry. She grabs the poster board they made earlier in the week and jumps into the car. Our little child ambassador will do her job well. They leave for LAX and I stay home with Malik and Blu.

When they arrive with the grandparents late in the afternoon, everyone's exhausted. I show Atha Garu and Mama Garu around the house and make sure they are comfortable. I know they're tired; the journey was a long one, twenty-four hours. They'll want to rest. But, I also know there is a strong possibility they won't sleep through the night, since day is night and night is day for them. "There are frozen curry meals in the fridge if you wake up and are hungry," I tell them. "The kids have a bedtime routine we try to follow. I'll take you to the market tomorrow so that you can pick food you will enjoy while you are here." I see the agreement head swivel, which means *it's all good*. I retreat to my room to get ready for bed myself.

The first morning in the house is a Monday, also a work and school day. I'll try to keep our schedule as consistent as possible.

The kids respond well to schedules, and there are too many of us in the house to mix it up too much without total chaos. Vijay has taken vacation time during his parents' visit, so he will be working only twenty hours per week, going in late and coming home early. This will help tremendously with getting the kids to school and open up the afternoon to spend time with his parents.

Isabella sits next to her grandmother at the dining room table. "Ava?"

"Yes, Isabella." She looks at her.

"You are Daddy's mommy?" she asks.

"Yes!" Atha Garu answers. "But, you can call me Nanamma?" she asks.

Vijay begins his defense of the name Ava. "We taught her Ava, Ma," he tells her.

"But, Sanjay's family says Nanamma. It is how I am called," she adds.

"Let your mother be called what she wants," I offer. "She is the grandma. She should be able to come up with her own name." Vijay shakes his head yes and doesn't say anything else.

"We are going to call her Nanamma, Isabella." I look at our daughter's sweet little confused face. "Can you say Nanamma?" I urge her to try it. She tries her best and we remind her day after day, since we have spent her childhood practicing Ava.

I make the kids their favorite breakfasts, which they sit and eat. I also prepare breakfast for all the adults, something I don't typically do on a weekday. It's usually a cup-of-coffee situation for me. We haven't been to the Asian market yet, but will go when it opens mid-morning. For the first morning in our home I make an American breakfast.

I make a scramble. There's a little bit of everything in there. It's spicy and is loaded with veggies. I cook some parathas, Indian tortilla-type things, to go with it and put it on the table.

"Oh no, Liss! I'm a vegetarian today. No eggs." I look at Vijay and then at his mother. I don't say anything. *Om, Liz. Om.* I wish I had known before I cooked it or during preparation, while everyone was sitting at the table watching me cook. I could have separated out everything else! *Om, Liz.* This is just the beginning.

"You can have cereal this morning, Ma," Vijay offers his mom. I'm grateful he gets it. We still have to get two kids out the door for school. I don't know what else I would make; I'd have a hard time coming up with something before having to leave.

I get out a bowl, spoon and our cereal assortment, place it on the table with a smile and sit in my seat lovingly. I'm proud of myself. I do not feel perturbed. A light bulb has gone off somewhere inside me and I'm totally cool with it! *Om!*

I didn't pre-purchase Indian groceries or anticipate what their needs would be. I know if I had done it, it wouldn't have been right, so I just waited. Why set myself up for failure like I did before? We can pick up whatever they want from the store as soon as it opens. We live close to an Asian market. It isn't quite the trek it was when we lived in the Valley the last time they visited. I tell Atha Garu that I will take her to the store to purchase any food items she wishes after I drop the kids at school.

"Oh no, Liss—we are here such a short time, we do not require such things," she tells me.

The cultural bargaining begins. "Oh no, Atha Garu,

I will take you and we will purchase whatever you require while you are here. I know you will be happy with your own food preparations," I encourage forcefully. I do this because I remember learning that "No" is really a polite response for "Yes, please," and that for some reason you have to demand that they accept an offer. She smiles and swivels her head from side to side.

Atha Garu, Blu and I get in the car and drive to the store. Mama Garu stays home to shower, smoke and rest. We load up the cart with all the spices, vegetables and fruits we need. We check out and then drive to the local grocery store for some meat. It's a completely uneventful and pleasant experience. I think my mother-in-law has everything she wants and I make sure she understands if something is missing, we can come back and get it at any time; she just needs to let me know.

As soon as we are home she begins prepping for lunch. All Indian food is made from scratch. It's time-consuming, tedious and tremendously tasty! I can already smell India as she begins prepping the garlic, ginger and vegetables. We unpack all the spices, easily twenty of them. Together we add them to my spice container, and other canisters, ready for daily use. She begins looking in cabinets, familiarizing herself with everything.

"Where is your rice cooker? And the pressure cooker, Liss, where is that?" she asks.

I forgot all about them. I have no idea where the pressure cooker Vijay brought with him from India is. We've moved since their last visit. I will have to look for it. It isn't something I use or unpacked. His pressure cooker freaks me out, with all the whistling and steaming and banging. I have a feeling I packed it in a *things Daddy brought with him when he came to America for the first time* box when we moved from the Valley.

I bet I'll find it in there. I know the rice cooker broke some time ago.

"Liss. Where have you kept your rice cooker?" Atha Garu asks me again.

"Oh. It broke," I respond. "The toggle stopped working a few years ago. It isn't something we use on a regular basis and I never replaced it." I know this might be a problem, as I see her mouth droop, but rebound when our eyes meet looking strong with acceptance.

"How do you cook your rice?" she asks, confused by my response.

"I just use a pot if I make rice," I tell her, realizing quickly that is not a solution that will work for us, as India has a serious rice habit. At least two of our three daily meals will include rice.

"Oh! It's okay, Liss, I will try. But, it would be so much easier with a rice cooker. Cooking with a rice cooker and a pressure cooker is so much better, Liss," she says.

"I'll go to Target right now to get them right away," I tell her.

She shakes her head. "Oh no, Liss. I don't require. It's just food will take so much longer to cook this way. It will take time, Liss," she tells me. I watch her facial expressions. She, too, is trying so hard to accommodate this most inconvenient hiccup.

"I'll go to the pressure cooker store and buy one," I tell her.

"I told Vijju that I can bring a mixy. Our mixy is really good. It crushes the lentils well. We could have brought a pressure cooker and all," she adds. "He said you don't require." I watch her explain. "It's no problem to bring such things. We took to Australia for Sanjay," she says. "It would not have been any trouble. We can get them readily in India."

Om

"I'll be right back." She's in the middle of cooking, so I need to get it now. I put Blu in the car and say I'll return in a few minutes.

I walk straight to the kitchen section of the super-sized Target near our house. I choose a mid-range rice cooker from the selection and place it in the cart. I can't find a pressure cooker anywhere. I see an associate walk past the end of the aisle I'm standing in.

"Oh! Excuse me?" I say to the gentleman in a red shirt. "Do you know where the pressure cookers are?"

He looks at me confused and says, "Oh no! We don't sell pressure cookers here!" as if it were common knowledge.

"Oh, bummer!" I say. "Man! I just really need a pressure cooker, like right now."

He gives me a confused look like I'm crazy, or maybe a little scary, and walks away. As soon as I see his face and think about my intense need, my first reaction is to say, *Oh no! It's for cooking with!* as if the terror alert level is so high on pressure cookers, Target won't even sell them anymore.

I call Vijay from the parking lot, explaining that I couldn't purchase a pressure cooker. "You don't need to buy a pressure cooker, Liz," he tells me.

"Well, maybe explain the situation to your mother," I tell him. "She seems like she's stressed out about it. She told me it will take a lot longer to cook everything, which is probably true. I think I can find it in the garage if you give me some time to hunt for it."

I pull into the driveway, unload Blu and our new rice cooker and carry them into the kitchen. I set Blu down and unpack the rice cooker, reading the directions, and instruct Atha Garu how to use it. Within ten minutes, basmati rice is steaming away and the strong smell of fresh curry wafts through the house. My mouth starts watering as the familiar smells encourage my appetite. This is going to be a great visit!

We revisit the "we could have brought one from India, Liss" conversation again and again as she watches over her curry simmering on the stove. She looks at me to make sure I'm listening and I shake my head in agreement, reminding her we have a pressure cooker somewhere. I just have to find it.

An hour later I pick up Malik from preschool and bring him home. I leave Blu with my in-laws. It's nice to leave her home when I go to pick up Malik. I don't have to lug her in and out of the car during their visit, a bonus I'm sure I'll be sad to give up when they leave. I'm used to our routine, but without her I feel like I'm on a mini-vacation. I have no interruptions when I pick up Malik from preschool, and I get to hear how his day went at school without trying to multitask needs.

I remind Malik we have company and that our afternoon routine might be a little different as I load him into the car. I've decided to be more laid back about television and tablet use during their visit. He doesn't know that yet, but I know it will help me wrangle the troops and keep them busy if I'm sidetracked. We pull in the driveway and Malik runs through the front door. Mama Garu is sitting in the living room watching Netflix. A ninja movie is on. The ninjas are fighting in a slow-motion battle scene. This isn't something that I'd normally let a four-year-old watch, but Malik stands still, staring at the television, eyes wide, and whispers, "Oh wow!" I look up too, trying to decide what to do with him, since the living room is the only common room in the house besides the kitchen. I'm about to suggest we go outside to play, but before I have time to

OM

come up with a plan, the screen changes to a village filled with de-limbed ninja victims. "OH MY GOD!!!" Malik exclaims. I look up and see the bloody scene. "MOM!" Malik yells. "Look, Mom!" he continues. "What happened to all their pieces?" Mama Garu looks up. It slowly sinks in that I'm not exactly excited about the situation. I'm not sure if it's my horrified face or Malik's, but he gets up off the couch, hands the remote to me and walks out of the room, without saying a word.

Vijay comes home early. I like this new schedule! I wish he always worked a twenty-hour week. I tell him briefly about our ninja experience, in case Malik needs to process it later and I'm not around. Vijay gets out his tablet and gives it to his father to use when the kids are home, saying, "Here, Daddy, you can watch anything you want on this."

The evening rolls around quickly. The kids eat their typical picky-eater dinner of carbs and dairy. Vijay and I join Atha Garu and Mama Garu for some great curry and conversation. We scoop the food onto our hands, and the tastes all linger in my mouth the same way they have so many times before. It's nice to have someone else cook a meal for a change and it's a break from the usual kid fare that we've been eating the last few years. After dinner, Atha Garu brings out gifts for the kids and us. Jewelry and Indian clothing are a traditional gift parents give when visiting from India, I'm told. The little bangles for the girls are adorable. She brought clothing for all the children and jewelry. Sanjay also sent a gift for Blu.

A week before Blu's first birthday, Atha Garu and Vijay sit at the dining room table casually talking over breakfast. I'm standing at the sink rinsing blueberries for the kids. I catch part of the conversation. Atha Garu says, "We need to shave Blu's head for her first birthday."

I hear her and look at Vijay sitting next to his mom. "No. We aren't going to shave her head, Ma," he responds. I'm glad he said that, but still curious where this is going. I glance at Blu, sitting in her high chair grinning with a mouth full of blueberries and a head full of curly hair. *Om, babe*, I whisper to Vijay in my head.

Atha Garu says, "No, son! Her hair will grow in so nice. It will be thick if shaved, son. You need to shave her head."

Vijay responds, "We aren't going to shave her head." My eyes ping-pong back and forth between the two.

Atha Garu continues, "Even in Australia they do it, Vijju. You must shave it."

"Who, Ma? Who does it in Australia? Indian people, Ma?" he responds.

She can tell he is digging in his heels. Her face becomes discouraged. "Everyone, son. That is why Isabella's hair is not so thick, son! She has thin hair because it was not shaved."

Isabella looks up from her plate, but doesn't seem to really understand the conversation. She glances at me and I smile back at her, giving her a scoop of blueberries. She smiles and eats. I look at her waist-length hair and think about all the princess updos this child has worn. It may be thin, but she can rock any style and it holds a curl like nothing else.

"Indian people, Ma. Lots of people don't shave heads." He sounds a bit frustrated now and they both stop talking for a little while. *Om?*

I stay completely out of the conversation and am glad I don't have to say a thing. I guess if the shaving happens, it won't be the end of the world. It's just hair. But, she has a lot of it, and it's finally long enough to put in a ponytail, so I'm glad Vijay holds his stance. I look over at Atha Garu sitting at the table, lips pursed . . . silent.

She looks over at Isabella. "Do you want to come home with us to India, dear?" Isabella looks at her.

"HUH?" Isabella looks toward me for direction.

"You can pass as Indian," Nanama says. "You come. Stay for a year. You will learn Telugu. Learn to be Indian," she encourages.

"UM? Is Mommy coming with me?" she asks, nervously.

"Oh no, dear, we'll keep a lady to watch over you," she says, swiveling her head from side to side. "You and your cousin can come," she offers.

"Um? No?" Isabella answers timidly.

"It's okay, Isabella. We'll all go together as a family sometime," I offer.

"Ah, Riya is also not keen for this idea," Atha Garu says in understanding.

I am grateful for my sister-in-law.

Each morning the kids say good-bye to Vijay, in varying degrees, depending on what stage of getting ready for school we're in. This morning Isabella and Malik are running around half naked watching *Wild Kratts*. It's usually just me and the kids in the morning. So, when my daughter runs through the house naked to throw her pj's in the hamper, or gets dressed in the living room while dancing around, I usually don't think anything of it.

The look on Atha Garu and Mama Garu's faces when she does this gives me pause for the first time. Mama Garu averts his eyes as Isabella giggles, twirling her pj's over her head like she's a helicopter, skipping to the hamper naked as can be. Running back, she jumps on the easy chair in the living room, butt in the air, ready to put her clothes on for the day. A joyful ignorance, she's completely uninhibited, and doesn't think anything is wrong with it.

I guess five is getting a little old to be running around without any clothes on. I can remember my grandmother yelling, "Have you no modesty?" when I ran out of the house naked to get my bathing suit off the clothesline. Maybe it's time I start teaching my kids some.

"Let's get dressed in our bedrooms," I suggest. I can hear her thinking, *Why would we do that, Mom?* but she just looks at me skeptically and hops to her room.

A few seconds later, Vijay grabs his cup of coffee and heads for the door. I'm holding Blu, standing with Atha Garu and Mama Garu on the porch, waving good-bye to him.

"'Bye, Daddy! Have a good day!" I wave, Blu watches.

As soon as the car door closes, Atha Garu looks at me. "Liss?" she begins.

Uh-oh, I think to myself. "Yes?" I look at her as the car pulls off the curb.

"Vijay should get a hair transplant," she says.

I try not to laugh at the suggestion and say, "What?"

"Yes. He should. He has gone bald. You people should fly to India. It is cheaper there." She looks up at me. "They give nice transplants!"

"Oh! That's okay." I don't think Vijay wants to get a hair transplant. I shake my head as I look at her to reinforce my stance.

"Oh no! They have nice facilities. They do a very good

job, Liss. You are his wife; you should encourage him to get it done."

"I don't know about that," I say. I have no idea what else I *can* say. *Om?* The idea will have to sit out there; I'm not touching this one.

"Curly-haired people aren't supposed to go bald," Mama Garu says. "I don't know what happened to him . . ."

Atha Garu adds, "Yes . . . I don't know why he's bald. He had curly hair. Those chaps don't lose their hair."

I just smile and think about Vijay with a hair transplant, silently. We aren't very vain people. I can't imagine him actually wanting to get one, but I'm not going to speak for him.

"Riya is keen to have Sanjay do it when they go to India the next time," Atha Garu says. "But Sanjay doesn't want to do it either." I'm glad my brother-in-law doesn't want to do it. I fear if he had, it would add pressure on us to follow suit.

I can't wait to have this conversation with Vijay when he gets home! It'll go like this: "Hey, babe! Your parents want you to get a hair transplant. So, if we are going to spend thousands of dollars on a trip to India for you to get one, it needs to be some serious blond Rapunzel shit. Or, no! Red flowing Ariel hair! Go big or go home! Am I right?" I practice my delivery.

A short time later, he comes home for the day and doesn't think it's funny.

"Yeah. Okay, babe. Thanks a lot," he says.

"Oh, come on," I say. "It's funny! Seriously? A hair transplant?"

He doesn't respond.

"Oh, come on! It's cultural! *Om!*" I encourage. Now I know who's handling the trip well! This girl! I hope Vijay can jump on the funny farm wagon too.

A few days later, Rahul is bringing his mom, Meena, over for a visit. Atha Garu talks about how worried she is about his divorce. "Whatever you do, don't mention the divorce," she says to us as we sit at the dining room table before they arrive.

"It's okay. He doesn't mind," I respond. "He knows that we know he is divorced. We were all friends when they were married. He came over with his son every other weekend for two years before he got a place in San Diego."

"We should not talk about it," she says, looking rather stricken.

"Well, they talk about it," I say. "Really, it isn't a big deal."

"*They* can talk!" She looks at me seriously. "*We* cannot talk. It is not ours to talk about," she explains.

"Okay," I say. "I won't mention the divorce." *Om, lady. Om.*

They arrive shortly thereafter and before anyone has a chance to talk about anything else, Rahul follows Atha Garu into the kitchen where she is preparing chai.

"Ah yes, you are divorced," I hear Atha Garu say to him in the kitchen.

"Yes, Auntie," he responds. "I am divorced."

"That's okay. You made a mistake the first time, with the American girl. Marry a nice Indian girl now! You won't have problems with an Indian girl," she says confidently to him over the pot of boiling chai. "You won't make the same mistake again with an American girl."

As I watch the exchange, I think, *Really?! I'm standing right here!*

After the parents sit down with their chai in the living room and start talking, Vijay and Rahul go into the kitchen to drink whiskey. I walk through the room and Rahul asks, "Liz, do you need a drink?"

OM

"Ah, not whiskey!" I say. "Maybe a beer."

"It gets better, Liz." Rahul continues, "Not only do I need to marry an Indian girl, your father-in-law told me to marry a nice Mali girl. He says they are loyal, won't talk back and give you no trouble." He smiles at me.

"Thanks!" I say. "Well, Vijay sure didn't get a Mali girl," I tease.

Vijay interjects, "Mom was so flattered my dad complimented her heritage. She has never had a compliment about making a good wife before. She is happy he is acknowledging her."

"Where's my beer?" I ask. *Ommmmm.*

A few days later, I am sitting in the backyard watching the kids play before Vijay arrives home from work. Atha Garu asks me, "Why did Vijay have a vasectomy?"

"We have three kids," I say, thinking that's a good reason.

"But don't you want to try for another child?" she asks.

She looks disappointed. "Four kids?" I say. "That's a lot!" I don't add what I'm really thinking . . . *We still could end up with four kids if Malik and Isabella's bio mom has another one.* I know that isn't what she means, though, and I'm not going to go there. *Om!*

A little while later, Vijay arrives home. I walk in from the backyard to greet him, noticing the mess on the floor. The kids had a snack earlier and I hadn't cleaned it up. I sweep the floor and bend down to wipe up some food that's stuck on the wood.

"Oh, son? Do you have Indian broom?" Atha Garu asks Vijay.

"Huh?" Vijay looks at me cleaning the floor.

"Oh. I just used a broom," I say, thinking maybe she didn't see me do that part.

"Well, in India when you use a broom *all* the stuff comes up the first time," she says, watching me wipe the floor with a wet paper towel.

"Well, we have an American broom right over there, Ma," Vijay says.

"OH! Hmm," she says before retreating to her room for a rest. I stay where I am until I'm finished. *Om.*

My new perspective and realization that most of the time it really is just cultural, allows me to enjoy our relationship and love my Indian family even more. I repeatedly find charm in our cultural confusion that I wasn't always equipped to handle before.

And in the end . . .

Vijay didn't schedule a hair transplant and Blu is not bald! Although I suppose we could have just shaved the hair off Blu's head and glued it to Vijay's.

Om!

Om

Acknowledgements

Vijay, thank you for one hell of an adventure. And to **my little ones** who make my heart sing.

Mom, because of you I grew up knowing I could become anybody and love everyone. Thank you for raising me to be strong, independent, and willing to try anything. You are my hero. **Papi**, I admire your lovable humor and outgoing nature. Thank you for the encouragement and support, reading and editing my story. **Dave**, I could not have a better brother. I love you.

Atha Garu and **Mama Garu**, knowing and loving you has changed my life and world perspective. I am so glad to be a part of this family. **Thatha**, I wish you were still here for more Telegu lessons and yoga sessions. And to **Bava Garu**, thank you for being my tour guide and taking such care in showing me your India.

Dad, you stoked my belief that I can build anything I set my mind to, which my power tool collection can attest to. I love our project time. **Elida**, as long as I've known you, you've been an example of endless strength, courage and optimism in the face of uncertainty. You inspire me to truly live every day. **Ana** and **Grandfather**, your dedication to the English language and love of books rubbed off on me—finally. Thank you for encouraging me to write this in the first place.

To my writing group. **Ghislain Labonte**, you motivate me with your writing, your incredible story and your love. You're next! **Carol Schnaubelt**, I will be forever grateful for the heartfelt consideration you gave my story. Thank you for sharing your loving family with mine. **Mary Scanlon**, without our writing group I wouldn't be here! Thank you for creating us.

To our friends who have been instrumental in our journey. **Emily Abrams**, thank you for reading, re-reading and listening—always. I can always count on you dear friend! **Arun Gajendran**, I don't know what I'd do without you. Thank you for your friendship, reading, editing, brainstorming, and of course your unbelievable ability to include *data points* in practically every conversation. **Christine and Alper Bozlak**, sometimes simply being present at the right moment makes all the difference. Thank you for being there—literally. **Iccha Basnyat**, there aren't many people who travel around the world for me. I love you. Also, I'm really super duper sorry my kid bit your kid that one time in Australia. **Bertha Rascon**, you are true blue! Life doesn't give a lot of friends like you. I still have the plant—and it's alive! **Sabrina Butler**, you helped heal a broken heart all those years ago. **Mackenzie Brew,** thank you for loving my babies like they are your own and for going with the flow—no matter how wacky. **Kate Bello**, thank you for some great graphics and years of friendship and support. **Tara Alton and Manny Sandoval**, we wouldn't have her if it wasn't for your Dodger obsession. **Cynthia Gomes**, I could never thank you enough. You pulled me out of the worst heartache I'll ever face and helped me learn how to move forward again.

Monkey C Media, for the cover of a lifetime, an amazing website and a team of kind and thoughtful talent. You met me and got me! Thank you for guiding this clueless author through the publishing process!

Lisa Wolff, my editor. Thank you for making me appear literate. Seriously, my, use, of, commas, is, out, of, control.

Promises2Kids, for the gift of motherhood! Thank you for protecting those who can not care for themselves. And to the families who are struggling or separated for so many reasons, don't ever give up on your dreams. Keep fighting to get better, stay safer and become whole.

To the countless people in my life that I have failed to mention, you keep me grounded, enthusiastic and optimistic.

Bangles, Bindis and Babies

Acknowledgements

www.ingramcontent.com/pod-product-compliance
Lightning Source LLC
Chambersburg PA
CBHW021114300426
44113CB00006B/150